SEDONA HIKES

SEVENTH EDITION

By
Richard K. Mangum
and Sherry G. Mangum

Look for Our Other Publications

NONLIABILITY STATEMENT

While we have expended considerable effort to guarantee accuracy and have personally taken every one of these hikes, errors in field notes, transcription and typesetting can occur. Changes also occur on the land and some descriptions that were accurate when written may be inaccurate when you read this book. One storm, for example, can block a road, or the Forest Service can change a trail. In addition to the problems of accuracy, there is the problem of injury. It is always possible that hikers may sustain harm while on a hike. The authors, publishers and all those associated with this book, directly or indirectly, disclaim any liability for accidents, injuries, damages or losses whatsoever that may occur to anyone using this book. The responsibility for good health and safety while hiking is that of the user.

Produced by GraphTech Digital & Printing, Flagstaff, Arizona
Cover Design by Joan Carstensen, Sullivan-Santamaria Design, Inc.
Cover Photo by Sherry G. Mangum:
Sunset at Cathedral Rock, Sedona, Arizona

Publishing History

First Edition, 1992
Second Edition, 1994
Third Edition, 1997
Fourth Edition, 1998

Fifth Edition, 2000
Sixth Edition, 2001
Seventh Edition, 2003

Table of Contents

About The Authors

Dick was born in Flagstaff and has lived there all his life. When his family acquired a second home in Back O' Beyond, south of Sedona, in 1951, he began his love affair with the redrock area. He learned that by driving 25 miles (the distance between Flagstaff and Sedona) the hiking enthusiast can hike year around: in cool Flagstaff in the summer and warm Sedona in the winter—and in either place in between.

After graduating from Flagstaff High School in 1954, he became a lawyer. He practiced law in Flagstaff for 15 years, then became a Superior Court Judge for Coconino County in 1976, retiring in 1993 to devote full time to hiking and writing.

Sherry has lived in Flagstaff since she was seven years old. The daughter of hiking parents, she has enjoyed getting into the outdoors from the time she was a toddler. She loves the scenic beauties of Sedona.

She also inherited a love of photography from her parents, both professional photographers. She has refined her skills to produce the photographs you will see in this book. Adept at all aspects of photography, she prefers landscapes. Her work has been published in books and periodicals locally, nationally, and internationally, since 1978. Sherry likes to work with a Nikon F5.

Tips On Sedona Hiking

Access
Many of these hikes can be reached on paved roads. For hikes reached on unpaved roads, you need to pay attention to conditions. Some of the roads become slippery and impassable when they are wet. Some, such as the upper part of Schnebly Hill Road, are closed during the winter by locked gates. The table on page 11 shows which hikes require driving unpaved roads.

Rock Climbing
We do not provide any rock climbing information in this book. If you want to go rock climbing, you are on your own. Much of the rock around Sedona is sandstone, a notoriously unstable substance.

Thorns
It seems sometimes that every plant along the hiking paths in the Sedona area has thorns, spines or sharp-edged leaves. Pay attention. Learn to identify the fanged plants and avoid them.

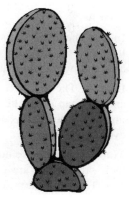

Varmints
Sedona is in a life zone favorable to rattlesnakes. Even so, we have only seen one on all our hikes and he was just warning us from several feet away. There are also some scorpions and black widow spiders in the area, though we have never seen either. Pests like mosquitoes are scarce. There are no chiggers nor swarming insects like black flies. Our advice about varmints is: be watchful but not paranoid.

Water
Do not count on finding water anywhere. Take your water with you. In Sedona's hot dry climate you will need plenty of it.

Weather
Sedona is in a high desert location, at an elevation of about 4,000 feet. Its finest weather is from October to May. During the summer it can be quite hot, with many days over 100 degrees F. Some of the strenuous hikes can be exhausting in this kind of heat, so be forewarned.

6

How To Use This Book

Alphabetical arrangement. The 134 hikes in this book are arranged from A-Z.

Index. The index starts at page 252. It groups the hikes by geographical area and by special features.

Layout. The text describing a hike and the map of the hike are on facing pages so that you can take in everything at once.

Maps. The maps are not to scale but their proportions are generally correct. The main purpose of the maps is to get you to the trailhead. The maps show mileage point-to-point. The text gives cumulative mileage.

Larger scale maps. For the big picture, buy a Forest Service map or *Experience Sedona.*

Bold type. When you see a trail name in bold type it means that the hike is described in this book.

Ratings. We show hikes rated as easy, moderate and hard. We are middle-aged hikers in normal condition, not highly conditioned athletes who never tire. Hikers should adjust our ratings for their own fitness level. The hike-in-a-box on each map may best show how hard a hike is.

Mileage. Driving distance was measured from the Sedona Y, located at the junction of Highways 89A and 179. All hikes start from this point. Milepost locations are also shown on the maps (as MP) on highways that have them.

Access roads. To reach many of these hikes, you will have to travel unpaved roads, some of them rough. Our vehicles have 4-wheel drive but not much clearance. Our access ratings were based on how well our cars handled the roads. Some drives require a high clearance vehicle.

Safety. We avoid taking risks on hikes. None of these hikes requires technical climbing.

Wilderness Areas. The Sedona area is blessed by having many of its hiking places included within federally designated Wilderness Areas. This is great for the hiker. Please read *Leave No Trace* on page 256.

Cairns. These are stacks of rocks used as trail markers. Some are officially placed, while others are made by hikers.

Mileposts. Major Arizona highways are marked every mile by a sign about three feet high on the right side of the road.

Crowds. We show how crowded a trail is likely to be with a symbol.

Handy Charts and Data

Hours of Daylight

☀☾	JAN	FEB	MAR	APR	MAY	JUN	JUL	AUG	SEP	OCT	NOV	DEC
SUNRISE	7:35	7:26	6:57	6:14	5:36	5:14	5:16	5:35	5:59	6:21	6:48	7:16
SUNSET	5:26	5:55	6:22	6:48	7:12	7:35	7:45	7:30	6:54	6:11	5:33	5:15

Normal Precipitation—Inches

JAN	FEB	MAR	APR	MAY	JUN	JUL	AUG	SEP	OCT	NOV	DEC
1.70	1.54	1.67	1.17	0.56	0.49	1.89	2.42	1.51	1.16	1.32	1.73

Normal Temperatures F°—High and Low

JAN	FEB	MAR	APR	MAY	JUN	JUL	AUG	SEP	OCT	NOV	DEC
55	59	63	72	81	90	95	92	88	78	65	56
30	32	35	42	49	57	65	64	58	48	37	30

Converting Feet to Meters

Meters	910	1212	1515	1818	2121	2424	2727	3030	3333	3636
Feet	3000	4000	5000	6000	7000	8000	9000	10000	11000	12000

Average Walking Rates

Time	1 Hour	30 Min.	15 Min.	7.5 Min.
Miles	2.0	1.0	0.5	0.25
KM	3.2	1.6	0.8	0.4

FOREST SERVICE ROAD CODE (What the shapes of the signs mean)	Primary route, well maintained. For passenger cars.	Maintained, but not as smooth. Usually OK for passenger cars.	Road for high clearance vehicles, such as 4x4s and pickups.

Hike Locator—Text

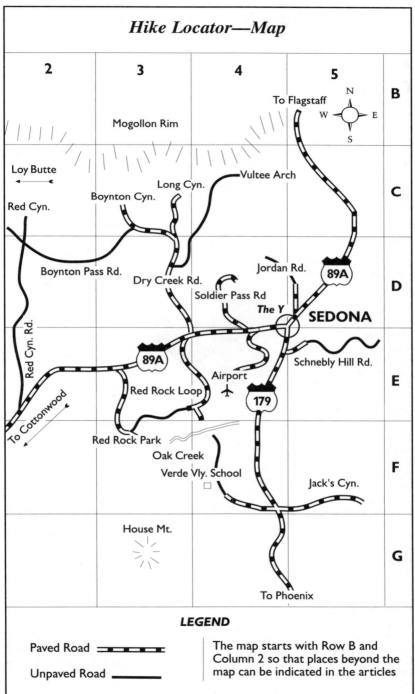

Hike Locator—Map

LEGEND

Paved Road ▬▬▬▬

Unpaved Road ▬▬▬

The map starts with Row B and Column 2 so that places beyond the map can be indicated in the articles

Hikes Rated by Difficulty

Trail Length in Miles, One Way, Unless Shown as a *Loop*

Easy

Allen's Bend—0.5
Carruth— 0.9 *Loop*
Cibola Pass—1.0
Coffee Pot—1.0
Cow Pies—1.5
Crescent Moon—1.0
Honanki—0.25
H. T. Trail—1.25
Jail Trail—0.5
Low Chimney Rock—1.5
Mystic—1.0
Oak Creek-Verde—0.25
Overlook—0.7
Page Springs—0.75
Palatki—0.6/0.3
Rachel's Knoll—0.5
Red Rock State Park *Mixed*
Robbers' Roost—1.5
Slide Rock—*Mixed*
Submarine Rock—1.0
Sunrise—1.2
Thunder Mtn.—2.0
Two Fences—2.1
Van Deren Cabin—0.3
V-Bar-V—0.5
West Clear Creek—1.0

Moderate

Airport Loop—3.6
Arizona Cypress—2.7
Baldwin—1.75
Bandit—0.9
Bear Sign—3.25
Beaverhead—1.1
Bell Rock—1.0
Bell Rock Pathway—3.7
Bell Trail—3.25
Big Park Loop—2.6
Boynton Canyon—3.25
Boynton Vista—0.33
Brewer—1.0
Brins Mesa—4.5
Broken Arrow—1.5
Carroll Canyon—4.3 *Loop*
Chapel—2.4
Chimney Rock Pass—2.25
Cockscomb Butte—0.75
Cockscomb Trail—2.5
Courthouse Butte—4.3 *Loop*
Dawa—2.9 *Loop*

Dead Horse Ranch—*mix*
Deadman Pass—1.4
Devil's Bridge—1.0
Doe Mountain—1.8
Dogie—4.0
Dry Creek—2.0
Fay Canyon—1.2
Goosenecks—1.8
Herkenham—2.0
Hidden Cabin—2.5
HS Canyon—2.0
Jim Thompson—3.0
Jordan—1.5
Kel Fox—2.0
Lime Kiln—2.8
Little Horse—2.2
Long Canyon #122—3.0

Loy Canyon—4.0
Margs Draw—1.4/2.0
Mescal Mtn.—2.5
Mitten Ridge—2.5
Old Post—3.0
Parsons—4.0
Rabbit Ears—2.75
Raptor Hill—2.8
Rattlesnake Cyn.—0.75
Red Rock Loop—1.8
Rupp Trail—2.0
Sacred Mt.—0.35
Schuerman Mtn.—1.1
Soldier Pass Arches—1.5
Soldier Pass Trail—2.2
Sugarloaf Loop—1.0
Summit Route—0.66
Table Top—1.9
Tavasci Marsh—1.0
Teacup—1.6
Templeton—3.5
Verde River Greenway—2.0
Twin Pillars—1.0
Vultee Arch—1.6

Weir Trail—2.5
West Fork—3.0
Wilson Canyon—1.5
Woods Canyon—3.25

Hard

A. B. Young—1.6
Apache Maid—3.75
Bear Mountain—2.2
Casner Canyon—2.0
Casner Mtn. South—2.0
Cathedral Rock—0.7
Cookstove—0.75
David Miller—7.3 *Loop*
Girdner—5.0
Harding Spring—0.8
Hot Loop—3.0
Huckaby—3.0
Jack's Canyon—5.0
Long Canyon #63—2.5
Mooney—3.75
Munds Mtn.—2.9
Munds Wagon—4.5
Purtymun—1.0
Ridge—2.3
Schnebly Hill—2.4
Secret Canyon—5.5
Sterling Pass—1.65
Telephone—1.25
Thomas Point—1.0
Turkey Creek—3.5
White Mesa—2.2
Wilson Mtn. North—4.3
Wilson Mtn. South—5.3

Rating Notes

We rate our hikes as
Easy, **Moderate** or **Hard**
based on length, steep-
ness, footing, exposure to
sun, and other factors.
This table shows you
how we have classified
them and also gives the
mileage and is not meant
to imply that the length
alone gives the rating.

Driving Distance to Trailhead

Italics = unpaved road, all or part. **HC**=High Clearance

5 Miles or Less

Airport Loop—1.5
Allens Bend—2.3
Bandit—2.6
Brewer—1.5
Brins Mesa—1.7
Broken Arrow—2.1
Carroll Cyn.—2.6
Carruth—2.1
Casner Cyn.—2.6
Cathedral Rock—4.1
Chapel—3.6
Chimney Rock—4.3
Cibola Pass—1.7
Coffee Pot—2.85
Cow Pies—3.8—**HC**
Girdner—4.4
H. T. Trail—3.6
Huckaby—1.3
Jim Thompson—1.7
Jordan—1.7
Little Horse—3.6
Lower Chimney Rock—4.3
Marg's Draw—0.9
Mitten Ridge—3.8—**HC**
Munds Wagon—1.3
Mystic—3.15
Overlook Point—1.5
Ridge Trail—2.6
Schuerman Mtn.—4.5
Soldier Pass Arches—3.0
Soldier Pass Tr.—3.0
Submarine Rock—2.1
Sugarloaf Loop—2.85
Summit Route—4.3
Sunrise—1.5
Table Top—2.6
Teacup—3.0
Templeton—4.7
Thunder Mtn.—4.3
Wilson Cyn.—1.1
Wilson Mtn. South—1.1

5-10 Miles

A. B. Young—8.8
Arizona Cypress—5.2
Bear Mtn.—8.9
Bear Sign—9.6—**HC**
Bell Rock—5.2
Bell Rock Pathway—6.2
Big Park Loop—6.2
Boynton Cyn.—8.0
Boynton Cyn. Vista—8.0
Cockscomb Trail—8.7
Courthouse Butte—6.2
Crescent Moon—7.0
David Miller—8.6—**HC**
Dawa—6.7
DeadmanPass—7.9
Devil's Bridge—6.5—**HC**
Doe Mtn.—8.9
Dry Creek—9.6—**HC**
Fay Cyn.—8.2
Goosenecks—7.3
Herkenham—6.2
Hidden Cabin—7.3
Hot Loop—9.55
H. S. Cyn.—8.6—**HC**
Jacks Cyn.—9.4
Long Cyn.#122—6.7
Mescal Mtn.—6.7
Munds Mtn.—6.6—**HC**
Old Post—6.2
Purtymun—8.4
Rabbit Ears—9.4
Rachel's Knoll—7.7
Red Rock Loop—5.9
Red Rock State Park—8.8
Schnebly Hill—5.5—**HC**
Secret Cyn.—8.6—**HC**
Slide Rock—6.9
Sterling Pass—6.2
Two Fences—5.2
Van Deren Cabin—7.6—**HC**
Vultee Arch—9.6—**HC**
Wilson Mtn. North—5.3
Woods Cyn.—8.6

10-20 Miles

Apache Maid—17.2
Baldwin—11.3
Beaverhead—11.2
Bell Trail—17.2
Casner Mtn. South—19.6
Cockscomb Butte—10.7
Cookstove—12.7
Harding Spring—11.4
Honanki—16.2
Kel Fox—12.6—**HC**
Long Cyn.#63—18.0
Loy Cyn.—15.5
Mooney—18.1
Page Springs—14.0
Palatki—13.5
Robbers Roost—19.2
Rupp Trail—10.7
Sacred Mtn.—18.1
Telephone—10.9
Thomas Point—10.5
Turkey Creek—11.9
Twin Pillars—11.9
V-Bar-V—17.4
Weir Trail—17.2
West Fork—10.5
White Mesa—17.2

More Than 20 Miles

Dead Horse—21.5
Dogie—20.7
Jail Trail—20.1
Lime Kiln—22.4
Oak Creek-Verde—22.4
Parsons—34.3
Raptor Hill—21.5
Rattlesnake Cyn.—23.0
West Clear Creek—29.5

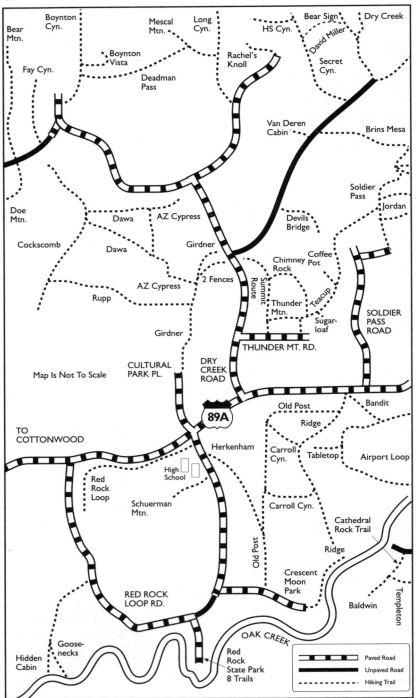

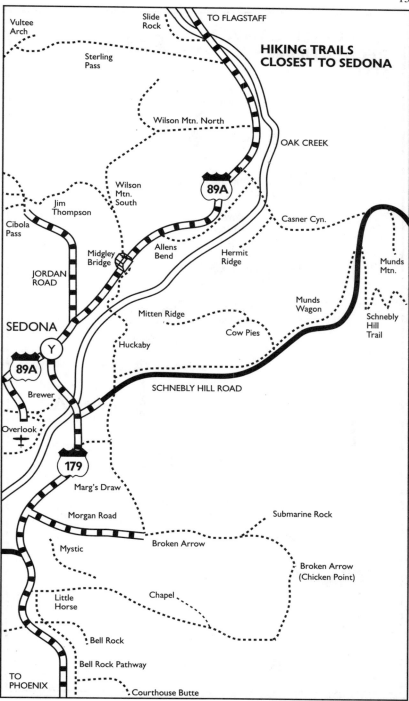

HIKING TRAILS CLOSEST TO SEDONA

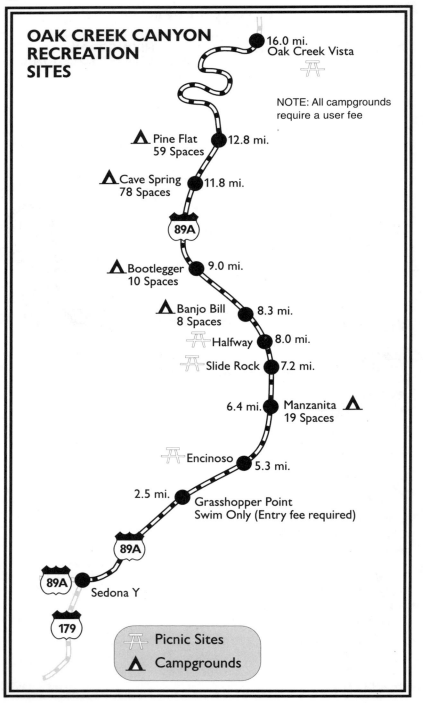

OAK CREEK CANYON RECREATION SITES

16.0 mi.
Oak Creek Vista

NOTE: All campgrounds require a user fee

Pine Flat
59 Spaces — 12.8 mi.

Cave Spring
78 Spaces — 11.8 mi.

89A

Bootlegger
10 Spaces — 9.0 mi.

Banjo Bill
8 Spaces — 8.3 mi.

Halfway — 8.0 mi.

Slide Rock — 7.2 mi.

6.4 mi. — Manzanita
19 Spaces

Encinoso — 5.3 mi.

2.5 mi. — Grasshopper Point
Swim Only (Entry fee required)

89A

89A
Sedona Y

179

Picnic Sites
Campgrounds

Changes For This Edition

New hikes for this edition

1. Airport Loop Trail
2. Arizona Cypress Trail
3. Baldwin Trail
4. Bandit Trail
5. Big Park Loop
6. Brewer Trail
7. Carroll Canyon Trail
8. Cockscomb Trail
9. Dawa Trail
10. Herkenham Trail
11. H. T. Trail
12. Jail Trail
13. Kel Fox Trail
14. Munds Wagon Trail
15. Old Post Trail
16. Raptor Hill Trail
17. Ridge Trail
18. Rupp Trail
19. Summit Route
20. Table Top Trail
21. Templeton Trail
22. Two Fences Trail

Revisions to trails in the previous edition

1. Brins Mesa Trail
2. Carroll Canyon Trail
3. Dead Horse State Park
4. Girdner Trail
5. Huckaby Trail
6. Lime Kiln Trail
7. Lower Chimney Rock
8. Soldier Pass Trail

Deletions

1. Blodgett Basin Trail
2. Buddha Beach Trail
3. Cathedral Loop Trail
4. Cathedral to Oak Creek
5. Chasm Creek Trail
6. Deer Pass
7. Flume Road Trail
8. Gaddes Canyon Trail
9. General Crook P 5-7
10. General Crook V 13-14
11. Grief Hill Trail
12. Hermit Ridge
13. Little Sugarloaf
14. Lost Canyon
15. Merry-Go-Round
16. North Mingus Trail
17. Packard Mesa Trail
18. Pumphouse Wash
19. Towel Creek Trail
20. Verde Hot Springs
21. Walker Basin Trail
22. Woodchute Trail

Comments

Sedona has truly become one of the nation's hiking headquarters and the Forest Service and other entities involved in trail construction have responded magnificently with a surge of building activity.

The fruits of this trail building boom are to be enjoyed in this book, with 22 new system trails just waiting for you to sample them. One of the benefits of having these trails is that they are close to Sedona, and we are able to delete some of the more distant trails that used to be in this book. Only nine trails require driving farther than twenty miles from downtown Sedona, a boon to hikers, especially those who are here for a short stay.

We have added two new pages, showing the hikes rated by difficulty and driving distance, in our effort to make this book useful and user-friendly.

Sedona is a great place to hike. Scan the book, pick out a couple of likely sounding hikes, and hit the trails! We hope to see you there.

Dick and Sherry

A. B. Young Trail #100

General Information
Location Map B5
Munds Park and Wilson Mt. USGS Maps
Coconino Forest Service Map

Driving Distance One Way: 8.8 miles *14.0 km* (Time 20 minutes)
Access Road: All cars, Paved all the way
Hiking Distance One Way: 1.6 miles *2.6 km* (Time 80 minutes)
How Strenuous: Hard
Features: Views

NUTSHELL: This is a steep trail up the west wall of Upper Oak Creek Canyon near Bootlegger Campground, 8.8 miles *14.0 km* north of Sedona.

DIRECTIONS:
From the Sedona Y Go:
   North on Highway 89A for 8.8 miles *14.0 km* (MP 383). Parking is scarce, with no official parking area for the trail. Sometimes you can park in the Bootlegger campground, but you must pay a day use fee. There is a shoulder on the righthand side of Highway 89A with space for two cars at the Bootlegger driveway.

TRAILHEAD: Walk through Bootlegger Campground, where you will see a set of steps going down to the creek. Go to the creek, which you must wade or try to hop across on boulders. There is a marked trailhead on the other shore, for this is a maintained trail; its sign reads, "A B Young #100."

DESCRIPTION: Once you get across the creek you will see an old road running parallel to the creek. This old road was formerly the main road through Oak Creek Canyon and it is not the hiking trail. Your trail goes uphill and the way is marked with a rusty iron sign.
   The trail is broad at the beginning. It started its life as a cattle trail, but was improved during the 1930s with CCC labor; so it is better engineered than many of the former cattle trails that are now hiking trails. It was widened and the grades were moderated so it is not as vertical as it was originally, although it is still very steep.
   An interesting thing about the hike is that you pass through three life zones. Down at the creek, there is the lush riparian life zone. As you begin to climb, you get into a high desert life zone. At the top, you are in a pine forest. Once you rise above the trees at creekside, you are on an exposed face with no shade. This can be a very hot hike in the summer though it is

in the cool upper canyon.

The hike is steep, so although the trail is a good one, it is a hard climb. You get some fine views as you go. At the top, you will notice that the trail continues. For the purposes of this book, we have ended the trail at the top, but you can continue southwest about 1.25 miles *2.0 km* to the East Pocket fire lookout tower. If this tower is occupied, the ranger may be willing to have you come up and share the tremendous views. This part of the rim is called East Pocket.

From many vantage points both above and below the A. B. Young Trail you can see it zigzagging up the face of the west canyon wall. It makes sharp diagonal turns at the end of each zag and is so obviously a route cut into the face of the canyon wall that some people mistake it for Highway 89A when they see it from a distance.

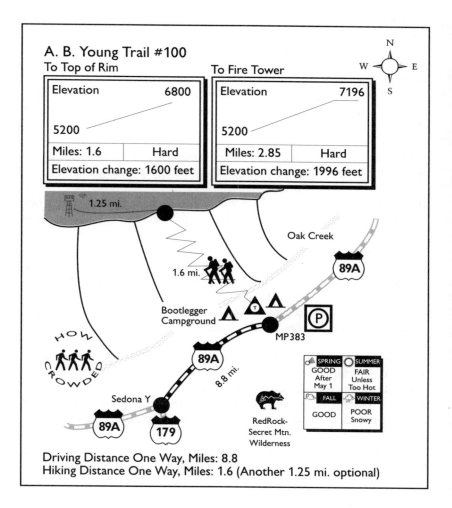

A. B. Young Trail #100

To Top of Rim

Elevation	6800
5200	
Miles: 1.6	Hard
Elevation change: 1600 feet	

To Fire Tower

Elevation	7196
5200	
Miles: 2.85	Hard
Elevation change: 1996 feet	

1.25 mi.

Oak Creek

89A

1.6 mi.

Bootlegger Campground

MP383

P

HOW CROWDED

89A

8.8 mi.

Sedona Y

89A   179

RedRock-Secret Mtn. Wilderness

SPRING	SUMMER
GOOD After May 1	FAIR Unless Too Hot
FALL	WINTER
GOOD	POOR Snowy

Driving Distance One Way, Miles: 8.8
Hiking Distance One Way, Miles: 1.6 (Another 1.25 mi. optional)

Airport Loop Trail

General Information
Location Map E4
Sedona USGS Map
Coconino Forest Service Map

Driving Distance One Way: 1.5 miles *2.4 km* (Time 10 minutes)
Access Road: All cars, Paved all the way
Hiking Distance, Complete Loop: 3.6 miles *5.76 km* (Time 2 hours)
How Strenuous: Moderate
Features: 360-degree views

NUTSHELL: This trail takes you around the circumference of Airport Mesa, so that you see all of Sedona.

DIRECTIONS:
From the Sedona Y Go:
   Southwest on Highway 89A for 1.0 mile *1.6 km,* to Airport Road. Turn left onto Airport Road and drive uphill half a mile, to the 1.5 mile *2.4 km* point. Here you will see a parking lot to the left big enough for 12 cars.

TRAILHEAD: Through the gap in the cable fence on the east side of the parking lot. You will see a 3-panel trailhead sign with maps there.

DESCRIPTION: Walk uphill on the main **Overlook Point Trail**. When you reach the crest, turn to your right, and you will see the Airport Loop Trail running along the side of the mesa. The trailhead signs did not show this trail on our most recent hike, but it is easy to locate.
   The trail hugs the 4600-foot contour on Airport Mesa. It circles the mesa and there is no encumbering timber or shrubbery to block your views, so this is a great scenic hike. On the first part of the trail one hikes along the southeast face of the mesa, looking down on Oak Creek and the Bell Rock area. At about 1.5 miles *2.4 km* you reach the end of this face of the mesa on a toe.
   You then curve around to the north and at 1.8 miles *2.9 km* reach the **Table Top Trail** junction. Here the airport fence is to your right and you will walk along very near the end of the runway. If you are an airplane buff, as one of our friends is, you may enjoy watching the planes take off and land. As you pass this point and come to the next face of the mesa, the trail dips.
   At 2.3 miles *3.7 km* you will see Bandit's grave on the right side of the trail, where there is a metal cross and a mound of stones. The size of the

grave and its presence suggest that Bandit was a well-beloved dog. A short distance farther you will reach the intersection with the **Bandit Trail**, coming in to your left. Pass this and keep going around the mesa. The trail will rise again.

At 3.5 miles *5.6 km* you will curve back to the road going to the airport at a point directly across from the parking lot where you began. The endpoint seems unfinished, as the trail abruptly ends where it bangs into a guardrail. There are no signs or any indications about the trail here. You have to hop over the guardrail and walk across the road to the parking lot.

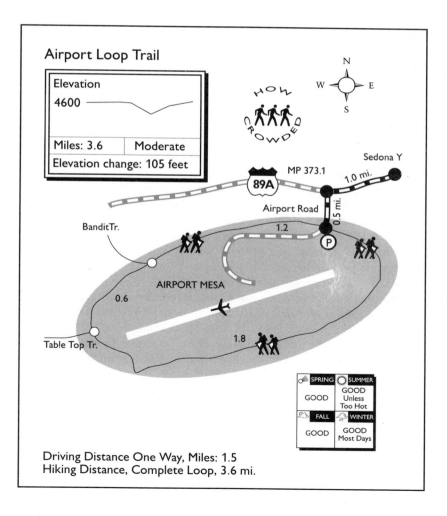

Airport Loop Trail

Elevation
4600

Miles: 3.6	Moderate
Elevation change: 105 feet	

MP 373.1
89A
Sedona Y
1.0 mi.
Airport Road
0.5 mi.
1.2
P
BanditTr.
AIRPORT MESA
0.6
Table Top Tr.
1.8

🍴 SPRING	☀ SUMMER
GOOD	GOOD Unless Too Hot
☁ FALL	❄ WINTER
GOOD	GOOD Most Days

Driving Distance One Way, Miles: 1.5
Hiking Distance, Complete Loop, 3.6 mi.

Allens Bend Trail #111

General Information
Location Map D5
Munds Park USGS Map
Coconino Forest Service Map

Driving Distance One Way: 2.3 miles *3.7 km* (Time 10 minutes)
Access Road: All cars, Paved all the way
Hiking Distance One Way: 0.5 miles *0.8 km* (Time 30 minutes)
How Strenuous: Easy
Features: Creekside walk, Small Indian ruin

NUTSHELL: This trail, located 2.3 miles *3.7 km* north of Sedona, provides an easy, yet delightful creekside ramble.

DIRECTIONS:
From the Sedona Y Go:
    North on Highway 89A 2.3 miles *3.7 km* (MP 376.5) to the Grasshopper Point Recreation Area. There is fee parking at the lot. The parking formerly available on the shoulders has been blocked.

TRAILHEAD: Rusty sign at north end of creek-level parking lot.

DESCRIPTION: The parking lot is open only during the summer season, roughly May 1-November 1. If it is open, you can drive down a paved road to a loop parking lot that has capacity for a couple of dozen cars. It also has a toilet. If the gate is closed, you will have to try to find parking off the shoulder of the road as near to the driveway as you can get. There is no longer an upper parking area. It's about 0.33 miles *0.5 km* to walk to the trailhead from the beginning of the driveway.
    The trail does not go down toward Oak Creek. Instead, it hugs the west wall of the canyon. The trail is easy. For about the first 0.15 miles *0.25 km*, it moves along a redrock ledge. In some spots stones have been mortared into place to pave the trail and to make steps. You walk along the base of a 100 foot tall red cliff, which is undercut and is very interesting. The cliff is not nearly so towering as many in the Sedona area, but it has its own charm and is more human sized and intimate. The creek is to your right (E) at all times, anywhere from 20 to 100 yards away.
    At 0.19 miles *0.3 km* you reach a fork. The main trail is the left fork. The right one goes to the creek, to a scenic spot that is well worth a short detour. The trail is shaded all the way and the creek—if by nothing other than its sound—offers refreshment.

Just beyond this fork take a look to your left and you will see what appears to be a small Indian ruin in a shallow cave.

The vegetation along the trail is agreeable, a forest of sycamores, cypress, juniper and shrubbery.

At 0.41 miles *0.66 km* you reach another fork. You are almost at the end of the trail here. To your left you will see an abandoned stone building and some rock walls and a flat area. This is an old campground. The building was a public toilet. If you take the left fork, you will go uphill and join Highway 89A at the **Casner Canyon** trailhead. If you go right, you will end at a nice scenic place on the creek.

We prefer the back country but every trail has its charm and its contribution to make. This is a pretty trail that is accessible any time of year, and is one of the few that goes right along the creek bank.

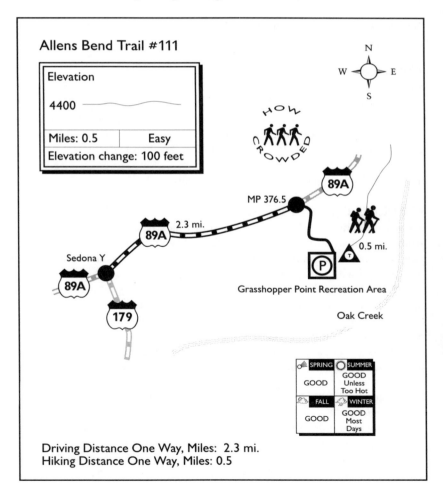

Apache Maid Trail #15

General Information
Location Map G6
Casner Butte and Apache Maid USGS Maps
Coconino Forest Service Map

Driving Distance One Way: 17.2 miles *27.6 km* (Time 30 minutes)
Access Road: All cars, Last 0.3 miles *0.5 km* gravel, in good condition
Hiking Distance One Way: 3.75 miles *6.0 km* (Time 2 hours)
How Strenuous: Hard
Features: Views of Wet Beaver Creek country, Rock Art

NUTSHELL: You hike the Bell Trail for two miles, then branch off to climb Casner Butte, 17 miles south of Sedona.

DIRECTIONS:
From the Sedona Y Go:
    South on Highway 179 (toward Phoenix) for 14.7 miles *23.5 km* (MP 298.9), to the I-17 intersection. Go straight here rather than getting on I-17. Follow paved road FR 618 until you see a sign for the trailheads at 16.9 miles *27.1 km*. Turn left. Parking is at 17.2 miles *27.6 km*.

TRAILHEAD: Signed and marked at the parking lot.

DESCRIPTION: From the trailhead, you take the Bell Trail. It goes upcanyon along Wet Beaver Creek, sometimes near it, sometimes away from it, but always following its path. Even when you are not near the creek, you can hear water running, a pleasant sound in desert country. The water-way is lined with tall sycamores and cottonwoods.
    As you look up the canyon, you see a flank of the Mogollon Rim, a giant uplift running across Arizona and New Mexico. The rim marks the southern boundary of the Colorado Plateau. Its base is the northern boundary of the Sonoran Desert; so it is a highly significant land feature.
    The trail is an old jeep road, broad and easy to walk. As you go along the trail, note the canyon walls: they contain the same redrock as in Sedona in the lower layers but the top is covered with a thick cap of lava. If it weren't for that top layer of hard rock, this country would be just as eroded and colorful as Sedona.
    At about 0.6 miles *1.0 km*, look for a large boulder on the left side of the trail. On the side facing away from you is some rock art.
    At the 2.0 mile *3.2 km* point you will hit a fork where the Apache Maid Trail, #15, branches to the left and climbs Casner Butte. This is a steep

climb, rising about 1000 feet in 1.75 miles *2.8 km*. You will be rewarded by good views at the top, but the trail itself is uninteresting. We suggest stopping at the top.

The trail goes on to the head of Wet Beaver Creek, and is the point of departure for the rugged types who hike Wet Beaver Creek from top to bottom, a multi-day trip, definitely not an undertaking for day hikers.

The Apache Maid Trail was built as a cattle trail, not as a scenic path. Sedona ranchers would graze their animals in the lower warm country in winter and then take them to the high county on top of the rim for summer. Apache Maid is the name of a mountain on top of the rim where one of the largest ranches of its day was located. There is a lookout tower on top of Apache Maid that you can drive to by taking the Stoneman Lake Exit off I-17, then FRs 213, 229 and 602.

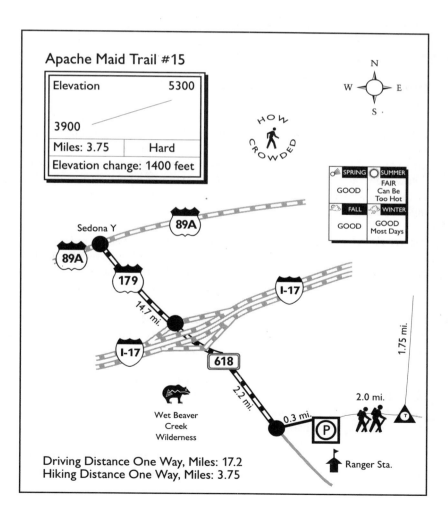

Arizona Cypress Trail

General Information
Location Map D3
Loy Butte and Wilson Mt. USGS Maps
Coconino Forest Service Map

Driving Distance One Way: 5.2 miles *8.3 km* (Time 15 minutes)
Access Road: All paved
Hiking Distance One Way: 2.7 miles *4.3 km* (Time 1.25 hours)
How Strenuous: Moderate
Features: Interesting ramble through the Dry Creek Canyon area.

NUTSHELL: Located 5.2 miles *8.3 km* west of Sedona on good paved roads, this trail winds around an interesting area. It passes through stands of Arizona Cypress trees, hence its name. It connects to other trails.

DIRECTIONS:
From the Sedona Y Go:
Southwest on Highway 89A (toward Cottonwood) for 3.2 miles *5.1 km* (MP 371) to Dry Creek Road. Turn right on Dry Creek Road and proceed to the 5.2 mile *8.3 km* point, where FR 152, the Vultee Arch Road, branches off to the right. Don't take the Vultee Arch Road. Instead, look to your left, below the road, and you will see a small trail sign on a post. Park at the side of the road as near to this sign as you can get. There is no designated parking.

TRAILHEAD: Orphan. Access via the **Girdner Trail**. Start at the trail sign mentioned above, marking the Girdner Trail. This trail has no outlet to any parking area or even to a road. You must hike to its beginning on another trail. We have chosen the Girdner Trail access from Dry Creek Road.

DESCRIPTION: Start by hiking the Girdner Trail. At 1.1 miles *1.8 km* you will pass the trailhead for the **Two Fences** trail, reaching the start of the Arizona Cypress trail at the 1.25 mile *2.0 km* point.
You turn right (NW), hugging the base of a large hill. Soon you cross over a small wash and after that will reach Dry Creek. From this point the trail follows the course of Dry Creek until the end is reached. You cross Dry Creek four times. You walk through an Arizona Cypress forest here, the trees marked by their bark, which scales off in curly shreds. There is another nice stand of the trees ahead of you.
At 1.75 miles *2.8 km* you reach a marker for the **Dawa Trail**, to your left. At 2.1 miles *3.4 km* you will find the marker for the **OK Trail**. Soon after

this you will see that you are walking along an old jeep road.

The end of the trail, where there is a barbed wire fence with a stepover gate and a trail sign, is reached at 2.7 miles *4.3 km*. It seems a funny place to end because it is nowhere, just a point on the road. There is no designated parking area or any directional signs. If you walk the road for 0.5 miles *0.8 km* you will come out on the Dry Creek Road a few feet south of the stop sign at the Long Canyon Road junction.

The Arizona Cypress *cupressus arizonica* is found in many locations around Sedona. It seems to favor sheltered, shady areas where there is more than the usual amount of water. We like the cypress forests, which seem quiet and restful; there is something about them that is very friendly.

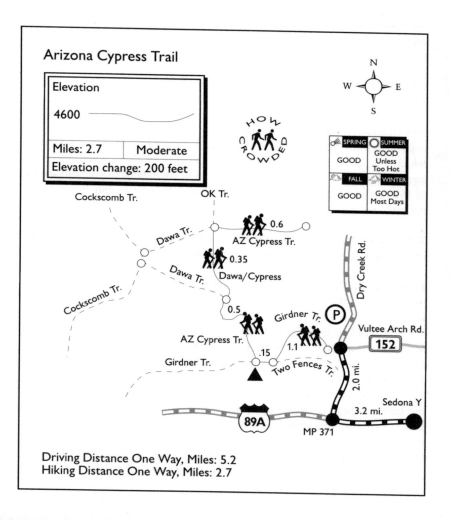

Arizona Cypress Trail

Elevation

4600

Miles: 2.7 — Moderate

Elevation change: 200 feet

HOW CROWDED

SPRING	SUMMER
GOOD	GOOD Unless Too Hot
FALL	WINTER
GOOD	GOOD Most Days

Cockscomb Tr.
OK Tr.
Dawa Tr.
0.6
AZ Cypress Tr.
Dry Creek Rd.
0.35
Dawa Tr.
Dawa/Cypress
Cockscomb Tr.
0.5
Girdner Tr.
P
Vultee Arch Rd.
152
AZ Cypress Tr.
1.1
Girdner Tr.
.15
Two Fences Tr.
2.0 mi.
Sedona Y
3.2 mi.
89A
MP 371

Driving Distance One Way, Miles: 5.2
Hiking Distance One Way, Miles: 2.7

Baldwin Trail

General Information
Location Map F3
Sedona USGS Map
Coconino Forest Service Map

Driving Distance One Way: 11.3 miles *18.1 km* (Time 30 minutes)
Access Road: All cars, Last 1.0 miles *1.6 km* good dirt road
Hiking Distance One Way: 1.75 miles *2.8 km* (Time 1 hour)
How Strenuous: Moderate
Features: Rock formations, Views, Oak Creek

NUTSHELL: You hike along the southwest face of Cathedral Rock, and then emerge onto the banks of Oak Creek; then you curve around the face of a redrock butte, away from the creek, to join the Verde Valley School Road.

DIRECTIONS:
From the Sedona Y Go:
    South on Highway 179 (toward Phoenix) for 7.2 miles *11.5 km* (MP 306.1), to the Verde Valley School Road, where there is a stoplight. Turn right (W) onto Verde Valley School Road, the first 3.0 miles *4.8 km* of which are paved. Follow it to the 11.3 mile *18.1 km* point where there is a sign marking the **Turkey Creek Trail**. Just beyond the sign you will see FR 9216B, a dirt road to your left. Take FR 9216B, turning left into the first parking area you see.

TRAILHEAD: Walk back to the main road, cross it, and turn to your right (SE). Walk the road for 250 paces until you see the trail marker to your left.

DESCRIPTION: The first part of the trail was formerly unofficial, known as the Buddha Beach Trail, (see Sedona Hikes #6). It has been expanded and is now a system trail.
    You will see massive Cathedral Rock, one of the favorite, most-photographed of all Sedona landmarks, to the northeast. To your left is a smaller, round-topped red butte. The trail goes through a pass between these two formations.
    The approach to the pass is fairly level until you get to the area between the buttes, where it moves up and down a bit, but nothing very difficult. Bikers love this area and there are social trails all over the place, so be sure to follow the markers. You will reach a place where you can see through a U-shaped notch, framing tall trees that grow along the banks of Oak Creek.
    At 1.25 miles *2.0 km*, where you emerge through the pass, you will go

through a fence and meet the **Templeton Trail** at the point where the Templeton ends. Here you turn left. You will hear the sound of nearby Oak Creek, but will never go to the water. At 1.4 miles *2.2 km* be sure to take the left fork, marked with an arrow, rather than going down to the right, toward the water. The correct trail hugs the base of the redrock butte and goes up.

At 1.75 miles *2.8 km* you will come out onto the Verde Valley School Road. There is a 2-panel trail sign here and a big parking lot across the road. You can now backtrack, in which case you will have a total hike of 3.5 miles *5.6 km*, or you can turn to the left and walk back down the road to your car, in which case you will make an entire loop of 2.5 miles *4.0 km*. If you walk on the road, be careful because there are some blind spots where drivers can't see you.

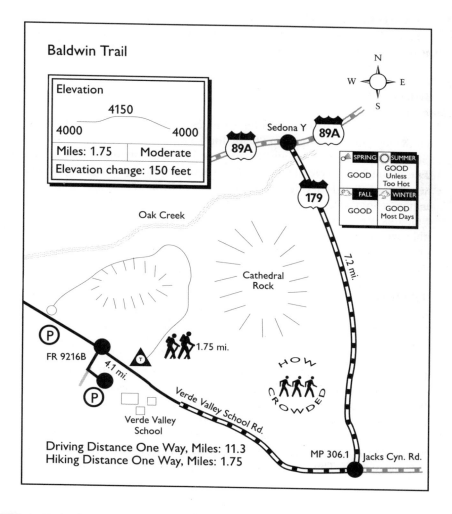

Baldwin Trail

Elevation	
4150	
4000	4000
Miles: 1.75	Moderate
Elevation change: 150 feet	

N
W — E
S

Sedona Y 89A
89A
179

SPRING	SUMMER
GOOD	GOOD Unless Too Hot
FALL	WINTER
GOOD	GOOD Most Days

Oak Creek

7.2 mi.

Cathedral Rock

1.75 mi.

HOW CROWDED

P
FR 9216B
4.1 mi.
P
Verde Valley School

Verde Valley School Rd.

MP 306.1 Jacks Cyn. Rd.

Driving Distance One Way, Miles: 11.3
Hiking Distance One Way, Miles: 1.75

Bandit Trail

General Information
Location Map E4
Sedona USGS Map
Coconino Forest Service Map

Driving Distance One Way: 2.6 miles *4.2 km* (Time 10 minutes)
Access Road: All cars, Paved all the way
Hiking Distance One Way: 0.9 miles *1.4 km* (Time 35 minutes)
How Strenuous: Moderate
Features: Views, Near town

NUTSHELL: This short trail takes you up onto the hip of Airport Mesa, where it connects with the **Airport Loop Trail**, giving you access to a very widespread trail system. The Bandit Trail itself seems designed to give access to the trail system to the neighborhood.

DIRECTIONS:
From the Sedona Y Go:
Southwest on Highway 89A for 2.1 miles *3.4 km,* to a stoplight. Turn left on Shelby Drive. Continue on Shelby for 0.5 miles *0.8 km* (just past Stanley Steamer) and turn right into the parking lot of a building known as La Entrada, at 2155 Shelby Drive. At the back of the paved parking lot you will see three trailhead parking signs. Park at one of them. (Note: the parking situation is somewhat fragile and the parking spaces may not endure. At the time this was written, in the summer of 2002, the parking places are available and open to the public, but the Forest Service is trying to create a larger parking area located on public land, which may replace the parking area described above).

TRAILHEAD: Aside from the parking signs there are no trailhead signs or markers at the starting place. Look for a small footpath going into the trees to the south. This is the path to take, and foot traffic has made the path recognizable.

DESCRIPTION: Start walking on the trail. Almost immediately you will come to the junction with the **Old Post Trail**, which goes off to your right. Pass by this junction. Soon after this you will reach the junction where the Bandit Trail starts, marked with a trail sign, where you turn to the left.
The Bandit Trail then skirts the boundary of private properties, bringing you up very close to the fence that surrounds a storage yard, where you cross a drainage ditch. This is an ugly, industrial part of the trail. Then you begin

to climb, making a steep ascent on to the shoulder of Airport Mesa, and moving away from the buildings. At 0.6 miles *1.0 km* you will intersect the **Airport Loop Trail**.

This is the official end of the Bandit Trail, but it isn't much of a hike to this point. From the trail junction you do have some nice views of West Sedona, but otherwise the trail has only been a leg-stretcher. We recommend that instead of stopping at the trail junction, you continue for a while longer, making the brief climb to Bandit's grave, so that you can see how the trail got its name.

Turn to the right, still climbing, on the joint Airport Loop trail. At 0.9 miles *1.4 km* to your left at the side of the trail you will find a metal cross with a nameplate reading "Bandit" and a small mound of stones. There is nothing more to explain the site, but it would seem that Bandit was a well-loved pet. This is where we recommend that hikers end the Bandit Trail.

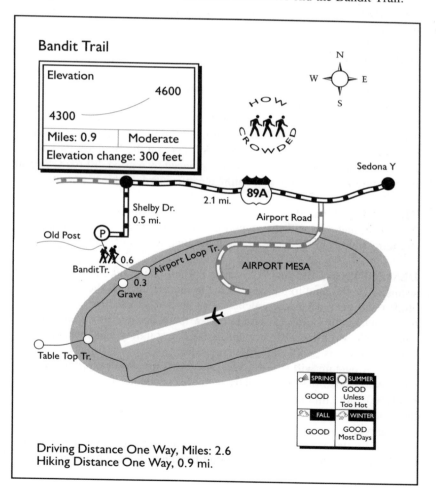

Bandit Trail

Elevation
4600
4300
Miles: 0.9 | Moderate
Elevation change: 300 feet

HOW CROWDED

N
W ⊕ E
S

Sedona Y

Shelby Dr.
0.5 mi.

2.1 mi. 89A

Airport Road

Old Post Ⓟ

Bandit Tr. 0.6 Airport Loop Tr. AIRPORT MESA

0.3
Grave

Table Top Tr.

SPRING	SUMMER
GOOD	GOOD Unless Too Hot
FALL	WINTER
GOOD	GOOD Most Days

Driving Distance One Way, Miles: 2.6
Hiking Distance One Way, 0.9 mi.

Bear Mountain Trail #54

General Information
Location Map C2
Wilson Mountain USGS Map
Coconino Forest Service Map

Driving Distance One Way: 8.9 miles *14.3 km* (Time 20 minutes)
Access Road: All cars, Last 1.2 miles *2.0 km* dirt, in good condition
Hiking Distance One Way: 2.2 miles *3.5 km* (Time 90 minutes)
How Strenuous: Hard, Very steep
Features: View

NUTSHELL: Climbing this prominent mountain 8.9 miles *14.3 km* north-west of Sedona is a challenge, but the views from the top are superb.

DIRECTIONS:
From the Sedona Y Go:
   SW on Highway 89A (toward Cottonwood) for 3.2 miles *5.1 km* (MP 371) to Dry Creek Road. Go right on Dry Creek Road to the 6.1 mile *9.8 km* point, where Dry Creek Road joins the Long Canyon Road, both paved. Turn left here, on FR 152C, and go to the 7.7 mile *12.3 km point*, where it joins the Boynton Canyon Road. Turn left here on the Boynton Pass Road, FR 152C. The paving soon ends, to be replaced by a good dirt road. Stop at the 8.9 mile *14.3 km* point, just before a cattle guard. Parking is on the right.

TRAILHEAD: The Bear Mt. Trail shares its parking space with the **Doe Mt. Trail**, and you will see signs for both trails there. Crawl through the "window frame" in the fence to begin the Bear Mt. Trail, #54.

DESCRIPTION: The first 0.25 miles *0.4 km* of the hike are across what seems to be flat land to the base of the mountain. In fact, the land is badly eroded and there are many gulches. You have to cross three of them. The trail is marked by cairns. Be sure to follow them, because this is cattle coun-try, and wherever the cattle wander in this dry soil they leave what appears to be a trail but is really an aimless meander.
   Bear Mountain will surprise you. As you climb, you keep thinking that you have reached the top. Actually, you will encounter five steppes or ter-races. You are climbing steeply almost all the way. The good news is that the beautiful views begin with the first steppe. The higher you go, the more of a panorama you get and the better the views are.
   At 2.2 miles *3.5 km*, you reach the base of steppe number five, the true top. It's a good stopping place. We quit here, but the trail goes on, making

what appears to be a hard climb over slickrock.

The bulk of the mountain is on steppe four. The surface here is eroded along crossbedding lines and a tiny amount of soil has formed in the cracks. Sparse vegetation grows in this soil, making the grasses and other plants form lines and rows that match the seams in the stone. In the right light, this causes fascinating patterns.

The top could well be called *Bare* Mountain rather than Bear Mountain, for there is precious little growing on it.

Friends tell us that from Capitol Butte you are supposed to be able to see a bear in the contours of the top of Bear Mountain. We have tried this from several viewpoints but were never able to see the bear. That's the way it is with these figures: sometimes you can see them and sometimes you can't, no matter how hard you try. According to our sources, the bear is lying down and it is his round ears that really make the formation.

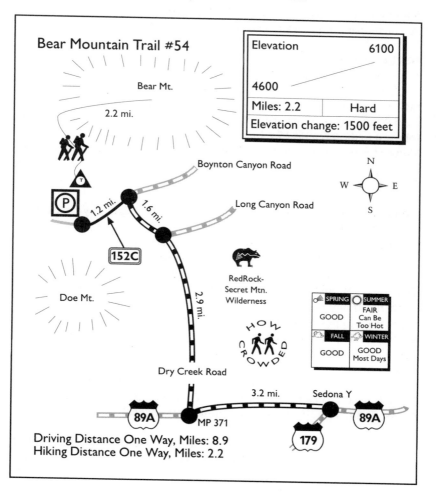

Bear Sign Trail #59

General Information
Location Map C4
Loy Butte and Wilson Mountain USGS Maps
Coconino Forest Service Map

Driving Distance One Way: 9.6 miles *15.4 km* (Time 45 minutes)
Access Road: Last 4.4 miles *7.0 km* bumpy unpaved road
Hiking Distance One Way: 3.25 miles *5.2 km* (Time 90 minutes)
How Strenuous: Moderate
Features: Secluded canyon, Beautiful redrocks

NUTSHELL: Located 9.6 miles *15.4 km* north of Sedona, this is a wilderness hike that follows a streambed to the base of the Mogollon Rim.

DIRECTIONS:
From the Sedona Y Go:
 Southwest on Highway 89A (toward Cottonwood) for 3.2 miles *5.1 km* (MP 371) to Dry Creek Road. Turn right on Dry Creek Road and proceed to the 5.2 mile *8.3 km* point. Turn right on FR 152, the Vultee Arch Road, and follow it to the 9.6 mile *15.4 km* point. Here there is a parking loop, with the **Vultee Arch** Trailhead at the tip. Curve around and head back, and you will see the parking for the Bear Sign and **Dry Creek** trails to your right, just a few yards beyond the Vultee parking area.

TRAILHEAD: At the parking area. There is a rusty sign: Dry Creek #52.

DESCRIPTION: You will walk across a little arroyo and around the toe of a hill for about 0.1 miles *0.16 km*, where you will encounter Dry Creek. At the entry point, the canyon cut by Dry Creek is rather shallow and wide. Turn right (N) and follow the trail up the creek—which usually *is* dry—northerly. If any appreciable amount of water is running in the creek, you might want to postpone this hike until the creek is dry, for the trail crosses the creek at least a dozen times.
 As you walk, the trail climbs, but this is gradual and you are barely conscious of it.
 At 0.63 miles *1.0 km*, you reach a point where the creek forks at a reef. The left-hand channel is the Bear Sign Trail, and the right fork is the **Dry Creek Trail**. There is a rusty sign in the left channel marked "Bear Sign #59."
 From this point, the canyon deepens and you are treated to the sight of giant redrock buttes on both sides of the creek. As you proceed, you will

notice a change in the flora, as the rise in elevation changes the life zones.

The trail ends where it intersects a channel running east and west. We are informed that this channel can be hiked. To the east, it would connect with Dry Creek Trail. Maps indicate that you could do a loop, going up the Bear Sign Trail and coming back via the Dry Creek Pack Trail, but we have not tried this.

Both the Bear Sign Trail and its neighboring Dry Creek Trail take you far away from habitation, and are nice if you want to get away into pristine country. Both trails head toward the Mogollon Rim and bump right against the base of it. The beauty of such trails is that even though they take you into wild and primitive country they are not dangerous. Stay in the canyons that define these trails and you won't get lost.

At the 3.1 mile *5.0 km* point, look to the left for the **David Miller Trail**, which connects Bear Sign to the **Secret Canyon Trail**.

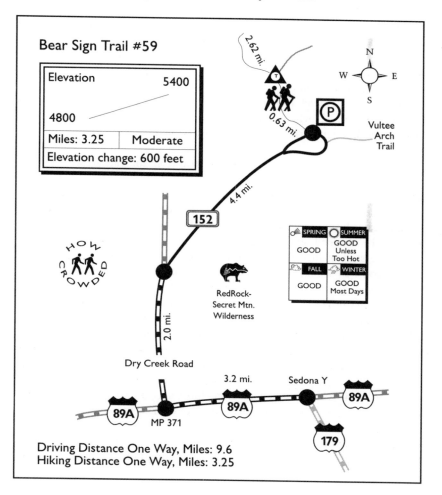

Beaverhead Route

General Information
Location Map G5
Casner Butte and Lake Montezuma USGS Maps
Coconino Forest Service Map

Driving Distance One Way: 11.2 miles *18.0 km* (Time 20 minutes)
Access Road: All cars, All paved
Hiking Distance One Way: 1.1 miles *1.8 km* (Time 45 minutes)
How Strenuous: Moderate
Features: Historic road, Views

NUTSHELL: Located 11.2 miles *18.0 km* south of Sedona, this hike climbs 1,000 feet to the top of the Mogollon Rim along an ancient Hopi trail that was converted into a wagon road in the 1870s.

DIRECTIONS:
From the Sedona Y Go:
    South on Highway 179 (toward Phoenix) for a distance of 11.2 miles *18.0 km* (MP 302.2) where you will see a gravel driveway to your left. Turn in on it, go left and park by the gate in the barbed wire fence.

TRAILHEAD: You will follow the old road from the gate.

DESCRIPTION: From the unlocked gate where you parked, walk up the dirt road a distance of 0.1 miles *0.16 km*. There you will see a road to your right that has been blocked by a dirt berm. Walk over the berm and you will pick up the old road, which you follow uphill.
    At the start of the hike, take a moment to look at your objective. High above, you will see a ridge with a long section of jagged cliffs. This is not an isolated ridge but a part of the Mogollon Rim. You are about to walk a short stretch of the Palatkwapi Trail, used by the Hopi Indians for more than 1,200 years. The trail starts at the Hopi mesas and ends at Camp Verde (with a branch to Jerome). The challenge to the pathfinders as they came off the high country was to find a gentle way down from the top of the Mogollon Rim to the Verde Valley. The route went from the Hopi mesas via Sunset Crossing (Winslow), Chavez Pass, Stoneman Lake, and Rattlesnake Canyon to the top of the Rim. As you walk along this trail, you can admire the choice that the ancients made. Except for being rocky, the route is excellent.
    Spanish explorers followed the trail in the late 1500s, then army scouts in the 1860s and then, when the army undertook to subdue hostile Indians, the old trail was improved as a wagon road linking Fort Whipple and Santa

Fe. Once established by the military, private operators became interested in the road and ran a stage line over it between 1876-1882. In 1884 a branch to Flagstaff was added. Until the Schnebly Hill Road was built in 1902, the Beaverhead Road was the only wagon road from Sedona to Flagstaff.

The road is easy to follow and the area has a pleasant feel. You soon climb high enough to get good views of the scenic surrounding country. At 0.75 miles *1.2 km* you will reach the beginning of an incredibly rocky passage. Many a wagon wheel must have broken here.

At 0.85 miles *1.4 km* you will reach the first top. In this area the old road looks almost like a trench, as it is deeply lined by the stones that were rolled to the sides. At 1.1 miles *1.8 km* you will be at the true top, where there are great views. The road veers away from the cliffs and continues its long journey northward (it is 145 miles long) from here over drab country.

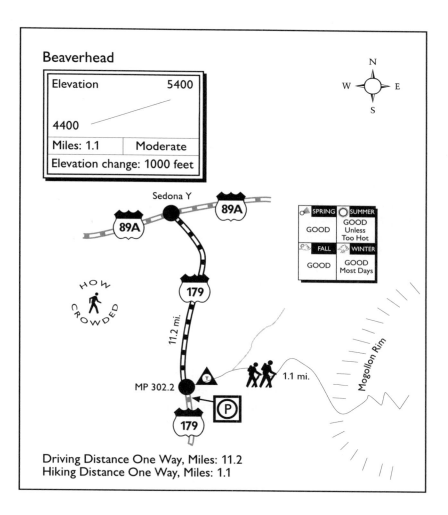

Bell Rock

VORTEX

General Information
Location Map F4
Sedona USGS Map
Coconino Forest Service Map

Driving Distance One Way: 5.2 miles *8.4 km* (Time 15 minutes)
Access Road: All cars, All paved
Hiking Distance One Way: 1.0 mile *1.6 km* (Time 45 minutes)
How Strenuous: Moderate
Features: Vortex Spot, Views

NUTSHELL: This landmark south of Sedona is one of the famed Vortex Spots. There is no defined trail. You explore as you wish.

DIRECTIONS:
From the Sedona Y Go:
South on Highway 179 (toward Phoenix) a distance of 5.2 miles *8.4 km* (MP 308.4). You will see parking areas on the opposite side of the road.

TRAILHEAD: Not a marked trail, but hundreds of visitors have worn an easy-to-see path up to the rock. At the rock there are some cairns.

DESCRIPTION: As you near the rock, there are many trails. Don't be concerned about these. Just pick out one that strikes your fancy. All of them go to Bell Rock. Once you are there, you may or may not see cairns marking trails going up onto the rock. If you see none, just pick a likely access and ascend. You are on your own.

You probably will encounter medicine wheels or other outlines on the rock made by New Agers. We know of no particular spot that is regarded as *the* vortex spot on Bell Rock. Different people get different responses. Other vortex spots covered in this book are shown in the Index, pages 252-254.

The redrock around Sedona was laid down in layers and has weathered in such a way that it has created ledges that are almost like stairsteps. This is especially true on Bell Rock, with its conical slopes. What you will do on this hike is look for likely ways to go up. Even the timid hiker should be able to get quite close to the top in comfort. Going to the absolute top is dangerous. As you wind your way around the rock, you are treated to great views.

The early settlers in the area were hard pressed to come up with names for all of the rock formations around Sedona, and there is controversy over the correct names for some of them. Nobody ever disagreed about Bell Rock, however. It *looks* like a bell. This is a very popular place because it is

so well known and easy to reach, and is on the road to Phoenix. So, you won't have a wilderness experience here, but it is a lot of fun, and you may even get a significant experience from the vortex power.

Bell Rock is often a busy site and it doesn't look very big. For those who like solitary places, its aspect is off-putting when you see people of all stripes, including whining infants and disrespectful teenagers assaying its slopes. A funny thing happens when you get to the rock, however. It suddenly seems much bigger than it looked from afar. You can pick out a way that no one else is using and before you know it, you are having an enjoyable peaceful experience in spite of the busy atmosphere. Give it a try in spite of the crowds.

An alternative, drive 6.2 miles *9.9 km* south from the Y and turn left at the entrance to the Bell Rock Pathway, a trail created in 1997. You then hike north to Bell Rock, about 0.75 miles *1.2 km.*

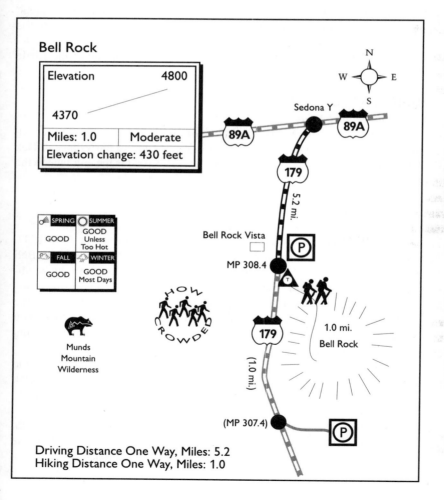

Bell Rock

Elevation	4800
4370	
Miles: 1.0	Moderate
Elevation change: 430 feet	

SPRING — GOOD SUMMER — GOOD Unless Too Hot
FALL — GOOD WINTER — GOOD Most Days

Munds Mountain Wilderness

Sedona Y

Bell Rock Vista

MP 308.4

1.0 mi. Bell Rock

(MP 307.4)

Driving Distance One Way, Miles: 5.2
Hiking Distance One Way, Miles: 1.0

Bell Rock Pathway Trail #96

General Information
Location Map F4
Sedona USGS Map
Coconino Forest Service Map

Driving Distance One Way: 6.2 miles *9.9 km* (Time 20 minutes)
Access Road: All cars, All paved
Hiking Distance One Way: 3.7 miles *5.9 km* (Time 2.0 hours)
How Strenuous: Moderate
Features: Views

NUTSHELL: This trail, new in 1997, was designed to connect the Village of Oak Creek with the trail system around Sedona. It starts just north of the Village of Oak Creek and winds its way north parallel to Highway 179, passing **Courthouse Butte** and **Bell Rock** along the way, to end at the **Little Horse** trailhead.

DIRECTIONS:
From the Sedona Y Go:
South on Highway 179 (toward Phoenix) for a distance of 6.2 miles *9.9 km* (MP 307.4) to a place south of Bell Rock, just short of the Village of Oak Creek, where you will see a road to your left. This road is the entrance to the parking lot for the Bell Rock Pathway. Turn into it and park.

TRAILHEAD: At the parking lot. It is signed.

DESCRIPTION: The Bell Rock Pathway was constructed in 1996-1997, and it is as wide as a road and makes for easy hiking. It runs north to Bell Rock parallel to Highway 179. At a point 0.6 miles *1.0 km* from the beginning, you will be almost to the base of Bell Rock. Here you will find a distinct but much narrower trail running to your right, toward Courthouse Butte. Take the fork to the left (W) here, circling the base of Bell Rock. You will pass very close to Bell Rock, along its shoulder, and will enjoy viewing the famous landmark.

A short distance beyond Bell Rock you enter the most scenic part of the trail, where you swing away from the highway onto some attractive redrock ledges. The views open up here and you will enjoy looking at Bell Rock, Courthouse Butte, and to the west, Little Park Heights.

Soon the trail moves over close to the road again, and continues north, toward Twin Buttes. The famous Chapel of the Holy Cross is located on the south face of Twin Buttes, and you can see it as you approach.

The trail ends at the trailhead for the Little Horse trail.

This is a nice trail and should serve its purpose. It has the earmarks of a trail that will prove to be very popular, so if you want a solitary hiking experience in the wilderness, look elsewhere. We were a bit bothered by its proximity to the busy (and noisy) Highway 179, but the convenience and easy approach made the hike worthwhile.

This would be a good hike after a storm, when the roads into the back country are too wet to travel.

The Bell Rock Pathway provides access to other trails mentioned in this book: Bell Rock, the Courthouse Butte Loop Trail, Little Horse Trail, and Big Park Loop Trail.

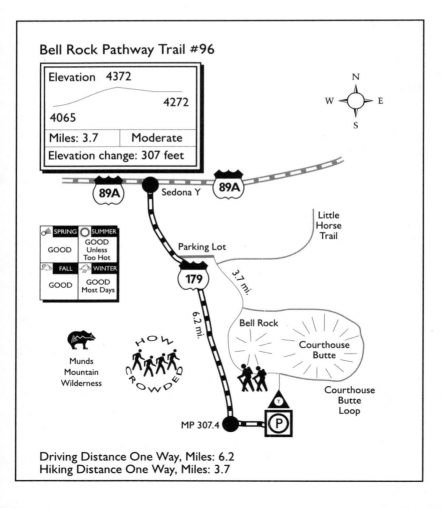

Bell Rock Pathway Trail #96

Elevation	4372	
Miles: 3.7	Moderate
Elevation change: 307 feet	

Driving Distance One Way, Miles: 6.2
Hiking Distance One Way, Miles: 3.7

Bell Trail #13 & Weir Trail #85

General Information
Location Map G6
Apache Maid and Casner Butte USGS Maps
Coconino Forest Service Map

Driving Distance One Way: 17.2 miles *27.6 km* (Time 30 minutes)
Access Road: All cars, Last 0.3 miles *0.5 km* gravel, in good condition
Hiking Distance One Way: Bell 3.25 miles *5.2 km* (Time 2 hours), Weir
2.5 miles *4.0 km* (1.25 hours)
How Strenuous: Moderate
Features: Permanent Stream, Rock Art

NUTSHELL: These trails follow the course of Wet Beaver Creek, 17.2
miles *27.6 km* southeast of Sedona. The trails are broad and easy, with many
attractions.

DIRECTIONS:
From the Sedona Y Go:
   South on Highway 179 (toward Phoenix) for 14.7 miles *23.5 km* (MP
298.9), to the I-17 intersection. Go straight rather than getting on I-17.
Follow paved FR 618 until you see a sign for the trailheads at 16.9 miles
27.1 km. Turn left. Park at 17.2 miles *27.6 km*.

TRAILHEAD: Start on the Bell Trail, which is well marked with signs at
the parking area.

DESCRIPTION: From the trailhead, the Bell Trail goes up the canyon
along Wet Beaver Creek. The trail is broad and easy to walk. It was built by
cattle rancher Charles Bell in 1932, as a means for taking his cattle to the top
of the Mogollon Rim in the spring. Charles Bell was a wealthy Easterner
who fell in love with the Beaver Creek area when he was a guest at one of
the dude ranches that flourished there from the 1920s through the 1940s. He
bought a ranch and got into the cattle business.
   At about 0.6 miles *1.0 km*, look for a large boulder on the left side of the
trail. On the side that faces away from you—rather faint; you will have to
look for them—are a number of interesting petroglyphs.
   At 1.5 miles *2.4 km* you will find the **White Mesa Trail #86** to your left.
At the 2.0 mile *3.2 km* point you will hit a fork where the **Apache Maid
Trail #15** branches to the left and climbs Casner Butte.
   Just beyond this fork you will find a signboard containing a map and dis-
cussion of the geology, plant and animal life of the area. The life is richer

than you might think. Just beyond the billboard is a trail going off to the right, down to the water. This is the **Weir Trail #85.** It is only 0.5 miles *0.8 km* long and goes down to an attractive pond formed by the weir, a low dam built to check the flow of water. Water gaging equipment is located here to measure runoff. There is an interesting cable car up the stream a short distance from the weir, and many blackberry bushes.

Bell Crossing is 1.25 miles *2.0 km* up the canyon from the signboard. There the trail narrows and crosses the creek. Along the creekside from the crossing are delightful places for a picnic. We recommend that you go upstream about 100 yards to check out a large pool known as The Crack.

From the crossing, the trail goes 2.75 miles *4.4 km* and 1200 feet up to the top of The Rim. The full hike is scenic, but is much longer and harder. We recommend stopping at the crossing for most day hikers.

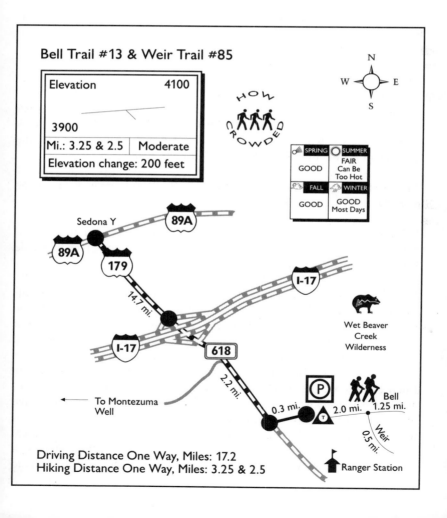

Bell Trail #13 & Weir Trail #85

Elevation 4100

3900

Mi.: 3.25 & 2.5 | Moderate

Elevation change: 200 feet

HOW CROWDED

N
W E
S

SPRING GOOD | SUMMER FAIR Can Be Too Hot
FALL GOOD | WINTER GOOD Most Days

Sedona Y
89A
89A
179
14.7 mi.
I-17
I-17
618
2.2 mi.
To Montezuma Well
0.3 mi.
P
2.0 mi.
Bell 1.25 mi.
Weir 0.5 mi.
Wet Beaver Creek Wilderness
Ranger Station

Driving Distance One Way, Miles: 17.2
Hiking Distance One Way, Miles: 3.25 & 2.5

Big Park Loop Trail

General Information
Location Map F5
Sedona USGS Map
Coconino Forest Service Map

Driving Distance One Way: 6.2 miles *9.9 km* (Time 20 minutes)
Access Road: All cars, All paved
Hiking Distance, Complete Loop: 2.6 miles *4.2 km* (Time 1.2 hours)
How Strenuous: Moderate
Features: Nice side trail from the Bell Rock Pathway.

NUTSHELL: This trail takes you along the Bell Rock Pathway area, starting at the Village of Oak Creek, But when it reaches Courthouse Rock, it skirts it to the east, and then loops back to the parking area.

DIRECTIONS:
From the Sedona Y Go:
    South on Highway 179 (toward Phoenix) for a distance of 6.2 miles *9.9 km* (MP 307.4) to a place south of Bell Rock, just short of the Village of Oak Creek, where you will see a road to your left. This road is the entrance to the parking lot for the Bell Rock Pathway. Turn into it and park.

TRAILHEAD: At the parking lot. While the Big Park Loop is shown on the map, the map is incorrect.

DESCRIPTION: Although the hike is depicted incorrectly on the trailhead map, it is correctly shown on the Forest Service publication given to people when they buy their Red Rock Pass.
    You start off on the main **Bell Rock Pathway Trail** and at 0.1 miles *0.16 km* reach the junction with the Big Park Loop Trail. Turn to the right, following the sign, but be careful, because it looks as if two paths go to the right. Take the one that curls up toward Courthouse Rock, even though it looks like the less-traveled trail. The area is cross-crossed with informal trails, so be sure to pay attention to the trail signs and cairns.
    At 0.6 miles *1.0 km* you reach the junction with the **Courthouse Butte Loop Trail**, at the base of Courthouse Rock. Turn to the right here. You will now enjoy a lovely walk along the base of this beautiful butte, and will have fine views of its highly sculpted faces. About midway along the rock, you will see a wide unmarked trail to your right going out across a flat open area. Ignore this and stay on the real trail. You will walk past the butte and into a streambed where the water has worn down to the red slickrock. Just on the

other side of this streambed you will find the place where you are to turn right. It is signed and marked with a cairn.

From this turn the nature of the trail changes and you walk through some heavy brush and low-growing trees across two ridges. You can't see out much because of the vegetation, though you will continue to have views of Courthouse Rock because it rises above the treetops.

At 2.4 miles *3.8 km* you come out of the trees onto an open flat place and meet a trail sign. From here you return to the starting sign for the Big Park Loop Trail. From this sign it is 0.1 miles *0.16 km* back to the trailhead, making a total walk of 2.6 miles *4.2 km*.

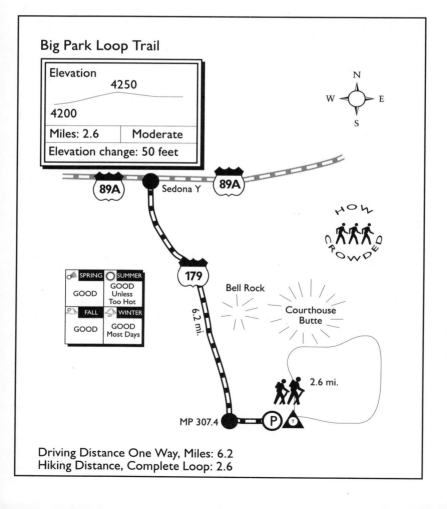

Boynton Canyon Trail #47

VORTEX

General Information
Location Map C3
Wilson Mountain USGS Map
Coconino Forest Service Map

Driving Distance One Way: 8.0 miles *13 km* (Time 20 minutes)
Access Road: All cars, All paved
Hiking Distance One Way: 3.25 miles *5.2 km* (Time 90 minutes)
How Strenuous: Moderate
Features: Indian Ruins, Vortex

NUTSHELL: This wonderful canyon is located just 8.0 miles *13 km* north-west of uptown Sedona, and is easily reached by paved roads. Its beauty is unsurpassed. **A personal favorite.**

DIRECTIONS:
From the Sedona Y Go:
Southwest on Highway 89A (toward Cottonwood) a distance of 3.2 miles *5.1 km* (MP 371), to the stoplight at Dry Creek Road, then make a right turn onto Dry Creek Road. Follow it to the 6.1 mile *9.8 km* point, where it joins Long Canyon Road. Take a left here, staying on FR 152C. At the 7.7 mile *12.3 km* point, you reach another junction. Go right. At 8.0 miles *13 km*, just before the gatehouse to the Enchantment Resort, you will see a parking area to the right.

TRAILHEAD: It is posted at the parking area.

DESCRIPTION: For the first mile this trail overlooks the Enchantment Resort. The trail winds along the east face of the canyon, hugging the towering ruin-dotted red cliffs so as to skirt the resort property.

One of the features of this lovely trail is no longer available—access to an alcove where Indian ruins are located in a cliff face. These ruins were being loved to death, receiving so many visitors that they were suffering damage, causing the Forest Service to close off access to them in order to protect them. At present there is no barrier at the entrance to the side trail that goes to the ruins, just some brush thrown across the trail, but plans are afoot to make one.

At just under 1.0 miles you will come downhill and will see the Enchantment fence to your left. From the Enchantment fence, the trail turns away from the cliffs and follows along the canyon floor. It is much wider and easier to walk from this point.

At 1.0 miles *1.6 km* you will cross a shallow wash, beyond which the vegetation changes as you go up canyon, because the elevation rises and the sheltering canyon walls make this part of the trail cooler.

At about 3.0 miles *4.8 km*, the trail pinches down as the canyon narrows. This is a good stopping place. However, you can bushwhack another 0.25 mile *0.4 km* to the head of Boynton, in a box against the side of Secret Mountain. The streambed forks here. Take the right fork and you will soon see a primitive path, almost a tunnel, through the lush growth at stream level. You will emerge into the box, ringed with towering cliffs.

Boynton Canyon is one of the Sedona Vortex spots. We have been to all of them, and this is the only one that really gives us any special feeling. The red cliffs here are really spectacular. We love them at about 4:00 p.m. on a winter's day. There is something about the angle, warmth and clarity of the light resonating on the beautiful red rocks that is really special then.

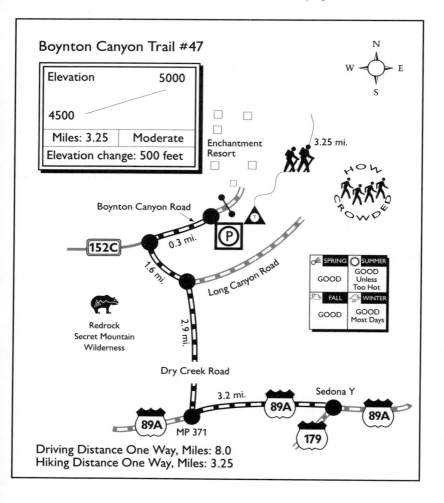

Boynton Canyon Trail #47

Elevation	5000
4500	
Miles: 3.25	Moderate
Elevation change: 500 feet	

Enchantment Resort

3.25 mi.

HOW CROWDED

Boynton Canyon Road

152C   0.3 mi.

P

1.6 mi.

Long Canyon Road

SPRING	SUMMER
GOOD	GOOD Unless Too Hot
FALL	WINTER
GOOD	GOOD Most Days

Redrock Secret Mountain Wilderness

2.9 mi.

Dry Creek Road

3.2 mi.   Sedona Y

89A   89A   89A

89A   179

MP 371

Driving Distance One Way, Miles: 8.0
Hiking Distance One Way, Miles: 3.25

Boynton Canyon Vista Trail

VORTEX

General Information
Location Map C3
Wilson Mountain USGS Map
Coconino Forest Service Map

Driving Distance One Way: 8.0 miles *13 km* (Time 20 minutes)
Access Road: All cars, All paved
Hiking Distance One Way: 0.33 miles *0.5 km* (Time 30 minutes)
How Strenuous: Moderate
Features: Vortex site, Views of Boynton Canyon

NUTSHELL: This wonderful canyon is located just 8.0 miles *13 km* northwest of uptown Sedona, and is easily reached by paved roads.

DIRECTIONS:
From the Sedona Y Go:
  Southwest on Highway 89A (toward Cottonwood) a distance of 3.2 miles *5.1 km* (MP 371), to Dry Creek Road, where you take a right turn onto Dry Creek Road. Follow it to the 6.1 mile *9.8 km* point, where it joins Long Canyon Road. Take a left here, staying on FR 152C. At the 7.7 mile *12.3 km* point, you reach another junction. Go right. At 8.0 miles *13 km*, just before the gatehouse to the Enchantment Resort, you will see a parking area to the right. Park there. There is also a small parking area on the left side of the road.

TRAILHEAD: It is posted at the parking area.

DESCRIPTION: The **Boynton Canyon Trail** and the Boynton Canyon Vista trail share a common trailhead. Posts painted with diamond markers indicate the trails. The Boynton Canyon Trail is designated by a gray diamond, while the Vista Trail has a green diamond.
  At the trailhead as you begin this hike, look up and to your right and you will see your destination, which is a large redrock formation with two spires that stick up from it. Between the spires is a saddle or gap. You will hike around to the back side of this formation, and up to the saddle.
  As you start the hike, both trails are together. You walk uphill a short distance, then veer off to the right on the Vista Trail, which climbs steadily as it goes to the top of the toe of the rock formation. It then winds around to the back side. On the back it is somewhat difficult to pick out the correct trail, as there are several maverick trails that meander through the area. Usually these side trails are blocked with a line of stones or brush to show the hiker

which trail to take.

If you get confused, it is not a problem, because your objective is always in plain sight. Take the trail that leads to the saddle, and you can't go wrong. Once you reach the top, you can see over into Boynton Canyon, which is mostly filled with the Enchantment Resort. There are views to the other side too, which are very nice. This is an easy little hike.

Some mystic types believe that the two spires are Vortex energy points, one positive and the other negative.

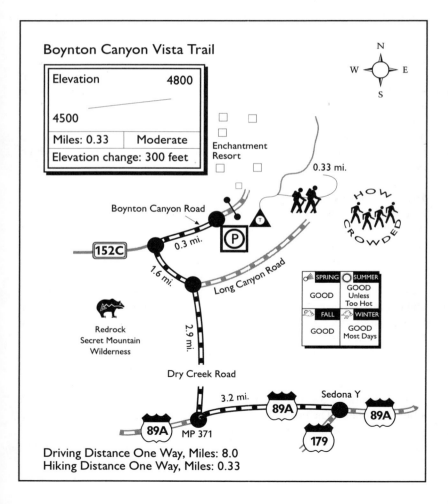

Boynton Canyon Vista Trail

Elevation	4800
4500	
Miles: 0.33	Moderate
Elevation change: 300 feet	

Enchantment Resort

0.33 mi.

HOW CROWDED

Boynton Canyon Road

0.3 mi.

152C

1.6 mi.

Long Canyon Road

Redrock Secret Mountain Wilderness

2.9 mi.

SPRING	SUMMER
GOOD	GOOD Unless Too Hot
FALL	WINTER
GOOD	GOOD Most Days

Dry Creek Road

3.2 mi.

Sedona Y

89A   89A   89A

179

MP 371

Driving Distance One Way, Miles: 8.0
Hiking Distance One Way, Miles: 0.33

Brewer Trail

General Information
Location Map E4
Sedona USGS Map
Coconino Forest Service Map

Driving Distance One Way: 1.5 miles *2.4 km* (Time 10 minutes)
Access Road: All cars, All paved
Hiking Distance One Way: 1.0 miles *1.6 km* (Time 45 minutes)
How Strenuous: Moderate
Features: Views from Airport Mesa

NUTSHELL: This trail takes you from Airport Mesa to Brewer Road.

DIRECTIONS:
From the Sedona Y Go:
　　Southwest on Highway 89A for 1.0 miles *1.6 km,* to Airport Road. Turn left onto Airport Road and drive uphill half a mile, to the 1.5 mile *2.4 km* point. Here you will see a parking lot to the left big enough for 12 cars.

TRAILHEAD: Through the gap in the cable fence on the east side of the parking lot. You will see a 3-panel trailhead sign with maps there. This hike is not shown on the map.

DESCRIPTION: From the parking lot walk through the gap in the cable fence and turn left, walking the trail that you will see running along next to the cables. There were no signs for this trail when we took it. It is easy to find, though, if you follow our directions.
　　Keep following the fence. There is a distinct path there, though not as heavily used as the other trails at the site. Don't worry. You never go uphill. Ignore all trails to your right that go uphill. You will walk around the knolls and come to a place where the trail seems to end and it looks impossible for it to go any farther. Keep looking. You will see your trail continuing along the face of the red knoll to your left. Trust it.
　　Walk out on this trail and you will soon see that it is going to be all right. It runs fairly level until it gets past the base of the knob and then begins to descend. You go from 4600 feet down to 4200 feet from this point.
　　At 0.8 miles *1.3 km* you will come into a clearing where there is an old stone water tank. The trail gets tricky here. Be sure to turn to your left before you walk past the tank. There are two false trails below the tank, which can confuse hikers. As you come to the place where the tank is located, turn to your left and you will see the true trail going through the shrubbery.

From the tank you go downhill even farther, reaching Brewer Road at 1.0 miles *1.6 km*. The point where the trail joins the road is 0.6 miles *1.0 km* from the junction of Brewer Road with Highway 89A. If coming in from the Highway 89A/Brewer Road junction, you drive Brewer Road, looking for the Wesleyan Church, which will be to your left. Just beyond the church there is a gravel parking apron on the left. The trail is just across Brewer Road, marked by a one-panel trailhead sign. Look sharp, for the sign blends into the bushes and is not easy to see.

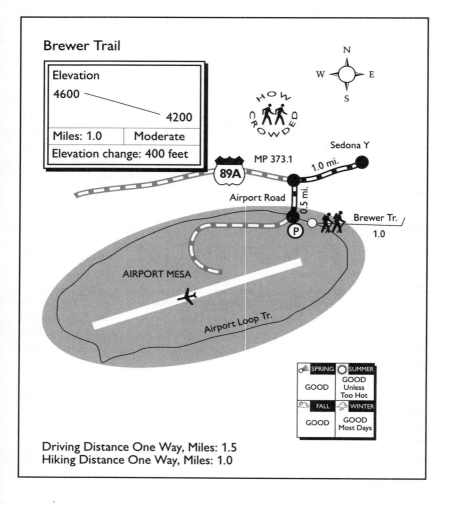

Brins Mesa Trail #119

General Information
Location Map D4
Wilson Mountain USGS Map
Coconino Forest Service Map

Driving Distance One Way: 1.7 miles *2.7 km* (Time 10 minutes)
Access Road: All cars, Last 0.4 miles *0.6 km* dirt road
Hiking Distance One Way: 4.5 miles *7.2 km* (Time 2.5 hours)
How Strenuous: Moderate
Features: Easy to reach, Good views

NUTSHELL: Starting at a point beyond the end of Jordan Road, you hike to the top of Brins Mesa, enjoy its fine views, then cross the mesa top and descend the other side, where the trail meets the Vultee Arch Road.

DIRECTIONS:
From the Y in Sedona, Go:

North on Highway on 89A (toward Flagstaff) for 0.3 miles *0.5 km* to Jordan Road, which is in the middle of uptown Sedona. Turn left (N) and take Jordan Road to its end, at 1.1 miles *1.8 km.* Turn left at the stop sign, onto West Park Ridge, a paved road, which ends at 1.3 miles *2.1 km.* Keep going on the unpaved road, which is rough but passable. You will reach the old Shooting Range gate at 1.7 miles *2.7 km.* Park at the gate. A new trailhead about 0.25 miles *0.4 km* inside the gate is under construction.

TRAILHEAD: Signed. Start at the gate (or new trailhead when it's ready).

DESCRIPTION: The first part of the trail is a gravel road. As you walk along the trail you will pass right by the trailheads for the **Jim Thompson Trail,** right, and **Cibola Trail**, left. The trail then becomes a jeep road that crosses over rolling hills on a moderate incline, taking you on an easy ramble to the foot of Brins Mesa in 1.25 miles *2.0 km.* Now the trail gets strenuous as you climb the mesa, a 500-foot rise. As you go up, look behind you to enjoy views that get better and better as you rise. You'll reach the top at 1.75 miles *2.8 km.* There is a trail to the right here, but ignore it and go straight ahead.

On top out of the mesa, you'll have great views. One thinks of a mesa as being a flat, broad tableland, but Brins Mesa is neither flat nor broad. Keep following the main trail (which is shown as a pack trail on the USGS map, but looks like a jeep road) as it continues across the mesa to the west. To your left as you walk along, you can tell that there is a canyon. This is the

Soldier Pass area. At 2.4 miles *3.8 km* there is a signpost without a sign, marking the turn for a connector going 0.25 miles *0.4 km* to join the **Soldier Pass Trail** from here (the wilderness part of the Soldier Pass Trail was blocked in 2002). Go straight.

At 2.8 miles *4.5 km* the Brins Mesa trail begins to drop strongly, winding down through a lovely Arizona Cypress forest to join the Vultee Arch Road, where there is a second Brins Mesa trailhead. This creates the opportunity to do a two-car hike, parking a car at each end. To get to the second trailhead from the Y, drive SW on Highway 89A for 3.2 miles *5.1 km* (MP 371) then turn right on Dry Creek Road and proceed to the 5.2 mile *8.4 km* point, where you turn right on FR 152, the Vultee Arch Road, and follow it to the 7.7 mile *12.4 km* point. Pull off to the right into the big parking area, where you will see a Brins mesa trailhead sign, and park. Be sure each car displays a Red Rock Pass.

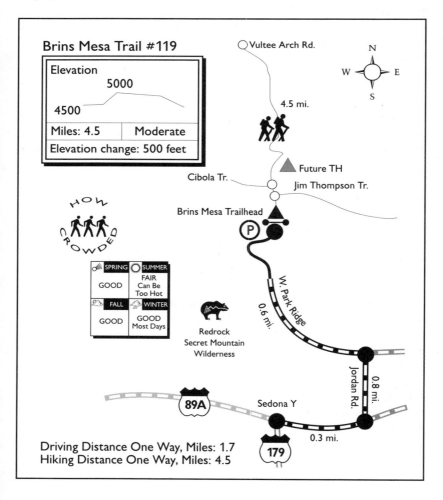

Broken Arrow Trail #125

General Information
Location Map E5
Sedona USGS Map
Coconino Forest Service Map

Driving Distance One Way: 2.1 miles *3.4 km* (Time 10 minutes)
Access Road: All cars, Last 0.1 mile *0.16 km* good dirt road
Hiking Distance One Way: 1.5 miles *2.4 km* (Time 60 minutes)
How Strenuous: Moderate
Features: Redrocks, Views, Sinkhole

NUTSHELL: This trail is located in Sedona's "backyard" at the south end of Marg's Draw. It winds around redrock cliffs and canyons, ending at Chicken Point, with a stop at Devil's Dining Room along the way. **A Personal Favorite**

DIRECTIONS:
From the Sedona Y Go:
South on Highway 179 (toward Phoenix) for 1.4 miles *2.3 km* (MP 312.1) to Morgan Road in the Broken Arrow Subdivision. Turn left (E) on Morgan Road and follow it to its end, at 2.0 miles *3.2 km*; then go another 0.1 miles *0.16 km* to the parking area.

TRAILHEAD: At the parking lot.

DESCRIPTION: There is a large parking lot for the Broken Arrow Trail, but as the trail is very popular, parking can be scarce on busy days. Before an official hiking trail was created here, hikers had to walk down the road, dodging tour jeeps. This trail was designed to take you off the road, but it does more than that: it is a great trail in its own right.

From the parking lot, you walk southwest across the road and follow the markers and cairns west and south. The trail soon moves over near the base of the nice redrock cliffs of Battlement Mesa and climbs up onto a ledge, winding around the base of the mesa.

At 0.5 miles *0.8 km* you will come downhill to a sinkhole protected by a fence. This is the Devil's Dining Room, a local landmark. At 0.75 miles *1.2 km* you will reach a trail junction. From this point the trail to the left goes down to **Submarine Rock**, while the trail to the right goes to Chicken Point. Take the right fork. You will now do some climbing, but nothing too strenuous. You will come to several very nice viewpoints, one of which looks down on Submarine Rock.

From this trail junction the Broken Arrow trail winds around the base of Twin Buttes heading south. The trail moves over near some gorgeous red spires and sculptures that are very fine, and we think you will especially enjoy this last leg of the hike. At 1.45 miles *2.3 km* you come to a gap in the butte, where you have a great view. From here it is a short drop down to Chicken Point, where you can go out onto a red slickrock and enjoy even more views.

The Broken Arrow Trail gets its name from the nearby Broken Arrow Subdivision, which gets its name from a Western movie filmed here, a big-budget film titled *Broken Arrow*, released in 1950. The movie starred Jeff Chandler and Jimmy Stewart. The film was a commercial success and is still available on videotape. Rent it and you will be amazed to see how things have changed around Sedona in the intervening years.

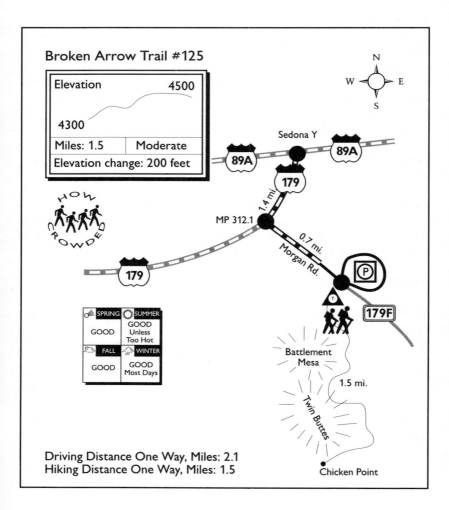

Carroll Canyon Trail

General Information
Location Map E4
Sedona USGS Map
Coconino Forest Service Map

Driving Distance One Way: 2.6 miles *4.2 km* (Time 10 minutes)
Access Road*:* All cars, All paved
Hiking Distance, Complete Loop*:* 4.3 miles *6.9 km* (Time 2 hours)
How Strenuous*:* Moderate
Features*:* Connects to other trails around Airport Mesa

NUTSHELL: This trail in the Airport Mesa area reaches Carroll Canyon at a point where it is deep and scenic, then curves around to the base of Airport Mesa, where you join the Ridge Trail, following it back to the starting point.

[Note: older editions of this book included a Carroll Canyon Trail that went along the bottom of the canyon. The use of that trail was causing disturbance to ecologically sensitive areas. The Forest Service has now created the trail described in this edition, which ties in with other system trails in the area. The use of the old trail should be stopped].

DIRECTIONS:
From the Sedona Y Go:

Southwest on Highway 89A for 2.1 miles *3.4 km,* to a stoplight. Turn left on Shelby Drive. Continue on Shelby for 0.5 miles *0.8 km* (just past Stanley Steamer Drive) and turn right into the parking lot of a building known as La Entrada, at 2155 Shelby Drive. At the back of the paved parking lot you will see three trailhead parking signs. Park at one of them.

TRAILHEAD: Orphan. Access via the **Old Post Trail**.

DESCRIPTION: Take the footpath going into the trees from the parking area. Almost immediately you will see a sign for the Old Post Trail. Turn right and follow this trail, which is a connector to the desired trail. At 0.5 miles *0.8 km* you will come to the trail junction, where you turn left on the Carroll Canyon Trail, which heads off into the trees. At 0.7 miles *1.1 km* you will come to a sign showing that the Carroll Canyon Trail splits. We suggest that you take the left fork.

At 1.3 miles *2.1 km* you reach a T-junction where you meet the **Ridge Trail** at the base of Airport Mesa. Go right here, on the joint Ridge-Carroll Canyon trails. At 1.6 miles *2.6 km* turn right where the Carroll Canyon Trail veers away from the Ridge Trail. The Ridge Trail goes uphill while the

Carroll Canyon Trail goes down, crossing the canyon at a shallow place. Soon after you make the crossing, Carroll Canyon, which has been nothing more than a wash up to now, deepens, with attractive cliffs lining both sides.

You will walk along the rim of the cliffs on the north bank for a while, and then veer away from the canyon to the west. As you come over a ridge, you will meet the **Old Post Trail** at 2.6 miles *4.2 km*. Turn right.

From here the Old Post and Carroll Canyon trails are combined, following the old road over which mail was carried in years past. This old mail road ends at the 2.8 miles *4.5 km* point. You then follow the Old Post Trail as a footpath back to the parking lot.

Note: There is another trailhead, coming in from Golden Eagle, but it requires driving a very rough dirt road. We think it is better to hike a little farther and use a trailhead that all vehicles can reach.

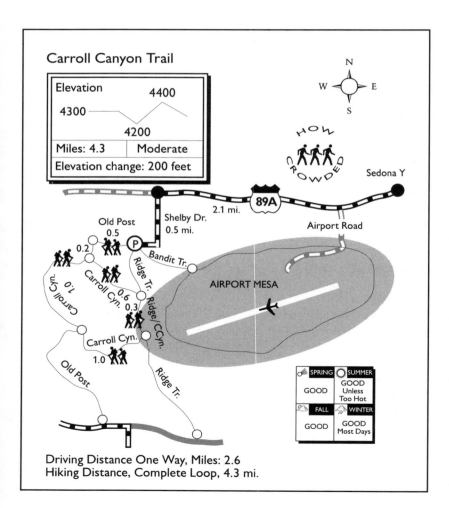

Carruth Trail

General Information
Location Map D4
Sedona USGS Map
Coconino Forest Service Map

Driving Distance One Way: 2.1 miles *3.4 km* (Time 10 minutes)
Access Road: All cars, All paved
Hiking Distance, Complete Loop: 0.9 miles *1.4 km* (Time 20 minutes)
How Strenuous: Easy
Features: Easy to reach, Views

NUTSHELL: This little trail is just what the doctor ordered for many hikers. It is very easy to find on good paved roads and requires only a short drive. The trail itself is gentle and short, but interesting. On one section there is even a flight of steps supported by a handrail. There is also a shaded picnic table. A very nice urban trail that should see lots of use.

DIRECTIONS:
From the Sedona Y Go:
Southwest on Highway 89A (toward Cottonwood) for a distance of 1.5 miles *2.4 km* (MP 371.3), to Posse Ground Road. Turn right onto Posse Ground Road. Follow it to the 1.8 mile point *2.9 km* where the road splits at a V intersection in front of the community park. Take the right-hand fork. At 2.1 miles *3.4 km* you will intersect Carruth Drive. Turn right and drive about ten yards. You will see the lath-type trail marker on the left (N) side of the road. Park on the shoulder.

TRAILHEAD: At the parking place. It is signed.

DESCRIPTION:
This is a short hike and not a wilderness experience. In fact, you are in a pocket of land surrounded by subdivisions and are close to a park; so there are houses and people in sight and hearing at all times. Nevertheless, the trail provides a very pleasant walk. It is just the thing for someone limited by physical condition or age who wants to have a hike or for someone who is more fit but who doesn't have time to get out into the boonies. It would be a great leg stretcher after work.

The trail heads in a northerly direction, toward Coffee Pot Rock. It hugs a high ridge so you have good views all along the trail, looking down into a basin.

At the 0.25 mile *0.4 km* point, you will find a short flight of stairs with a

handrail, a thoughtful touch, meeting the special needs of some hikers. At the top of the little climb you will find a shaded picnic table off to the side of the trail. This would make a great place to stop for a while and enjoy the views. At the 0.33 mile *0.5 km* point you reach a sign indicating that the trail becomes a loop. You can go in either direction and return at the same point. We went to the right and soon came upon a nice stone bench, a great place to sit and enjoy the nice views.

In preparing this hike book, we have included trails to suit the needs and tastes of all kinds of hikers. Some trails are very difficult, requiring steep climbs, pathfinding experience, bushwhacking, etc. Such hikes are far beyond the abilities of many hikers. This one is for those on the other end of the spectrum, who want to hike but must take it easy. We salute the City of Sedona for providing this excellent trail.

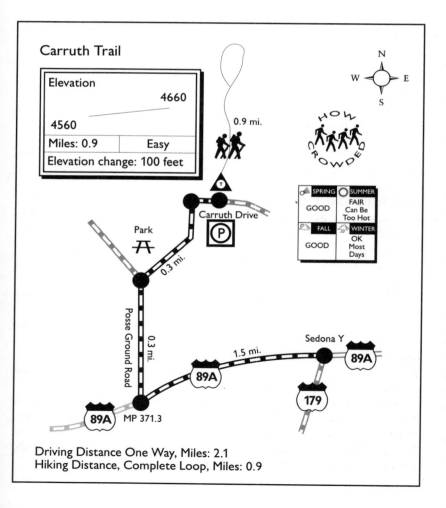

Carruth Trail

Elevation
4660
4560

Miles: 0.9	Easy
Elevation change: 100 feet	

0.9 mi.

HOW CROWDED

	SPRING	SUMMER
	GOOD	FAIR Can Be Too Hot
	FALL	WINTER
	GOOD	OK Most Days

Carruth Drive

P

Park

0.3 mi.

Posse Ground Road

0.3 mi.

Sedona Y

89A

1.5 mi.

89A

179

89A MP 371.3

Driving Distance One Way, Miles: 2.1
Hiking Distance, Complete Loop, Miles: 0.9

Casner Canyon Trail #11

General Information
Location Map D5
Munds Park USGS Map
Coconino Forest Service Map

Driving Distance One Way: 2.6 miles *4.2 km* (Time 10 minutes)
Access Road: All cars, All paved
Hiking Distance One Way: 2.0 miles *3.2 km* (Time 75 minutes)
How Strenuous: Hard
Features: Views

NUTSHELL: Located just north of Sedona, this trail takes you across Oak Creek, then up Casner Canyon to a point on the Schnebly Hill Road just north of Schnebly Hill Vista.

DIRECTIONS:
From the Sedona Y Go:
    North on Highway 89A (toward Flagstaff) a distance of 2.6 miles *4.2 km* (MP 376.8) where you park at the mouth of a closed road.

TRAILHEAD: Walk down the old road a few feet and you will see a rusty sign reading, "Casner Canyon #11" where the trail goes downhill left.

DESCRIPTION: Follow the path down to Oak Creek, where you must wade across. We like to bring a towel along to dry our feet when we get to the other side. This is not a hike you would want to do while wearing wet tennies. A good method is to pack a pair of Tevas or other sandals, as walking the creek is tricky. Use the sandals for crossing the creek, then dry your feet and switch back to your hiking shoes on the other shore. You don't want to fall in. Count on wading, because even though there may be stepping stones, our experience is that they are unreliable.
    Once you are across the water and have dry shoes on, you will see Casner Canyon. You head right up the canyon on its right (S) side. Soon the trail lifts out of the canyon and climbs the north wall of the canyon, meaning that you are on a southern exposure. There is no shade and you are fully exposed to sun. Don't do this hike on a hot day.
    From the point where you rise above the crowns of the trees that grow in the bottom of the canyon, the trail goes to the top in a very businesslike way, cutting a straight diagonal line from the bottom of the canyon to the top of Schnebly Hill. There is no scenery along the trail. In fact, it is quite drab, though you do climb high enough to get sweeping views.

You reach the top at a place that is close to the Schnebly Hill Vista, going through a gate in a barbed wire fence; so one way to do this hike is to use the two-car switch, parking one at Schnebly Hill Vista and the other at the Casner Canyon Trailhead. The easy way to do the hike is to start at the top, from Schnebly Hill. It is easy to recognize the start of the trail there by looking for the gate in the fence.

When you stand at the Schnebly Hill Vista you can see the Casner Canyon Trail. Sometimes, when the light is just right, it looks like a road and you wonder what on earth it can be, because no car could drive straight up the mountain as the trail goes. The trail was built by the Casner ranching operation as a livestock trail in the late 1890s.

The Casner family left its name in several areas: **Casner Mountain,** NW of Sedona, Casner Butte (see **White Mesa Trail**) in the Wet Beaver Creek Country, Casner Canyon Draw near Woody Mountain and others.

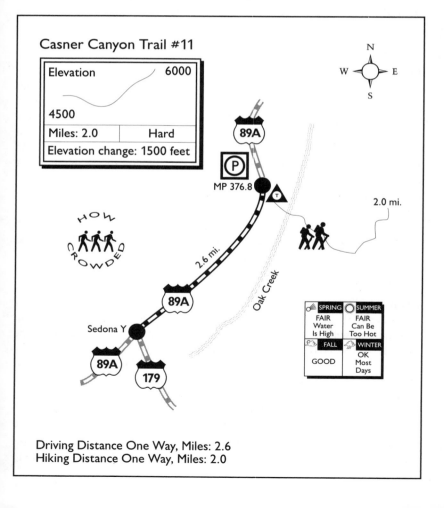

Casner Canyon Trail #11

Elevation	6000
4500	
Miles: 2.0	Hard
Elevation change: 1500 feet	

MP 376.8

2.0 mi.

HOW CROWDED

2.6 mi.

Oak Creek

Sedona Y

SPRING	SUMMER
FAIR Water Is High	FAIR Can Be Too Hot
FALL	WINTER
GOOD	OK Most Days

Driving Distance One Way, Miles: 2.6
Hiking Distance One Way, Miles: 2.0

Casner Mountain South Trail #8

General Information
Location Map C1
Loy Butte and Clarkdale USGS Maps
Coconino Forest Service Map

Driving Distance One Way: 19.6 miles *31.4 km* (Time 30 minutes)
Access Road: All cars, Last 10.0 miles *16 km* good dirt road
Hiking Distance One Way: 2.0 miles *3.2 km* (Time 1.5 hours)
How Strenuous: Hard
Features: Views

NUTSHELL: This hike takes you to the top of a mountain overlooking Sycamore Canyon and the Sedona back country.

DIRECTIONS:
From The Y in Sedona Go:
Southwest on Highway 89A (toward Cottonwood) a distance of 9.6 miles *15.4 km* (MP 364.5) to the Red Canyon Road. Turn right on Red Canyon Road, also known as FR 525, and follow it to the 12.4 mile *19.8 km* point where FR 525C branches to the left. Turn left on FR 525C and stay on it to the 15.6 mile *25 km* point, the next major junction. Here FR 761, the Bill Gray Road, goes to the left—don't take it. Stay on FR 525C, the right fork, and follow it to the 19.6 mile *31.4 km* point, where you will see a trail sign marked "Casner Mtn. #8." There is a parking spot big enough for one car at the trailhead.

TRAILHEAD: The trailhead is marked with a sign. The trail follows the power line up the south face of Casner Mountain, and you can see clearly from the start of the hike where the trail goes.

DESCRIPTION: Casner Mountain is bare of shade trees except for a few junipers and the trail takes you up its south face. Because of that, you are in full sunlight with no shade, so take a hat and plenty of water and don't try this hike on a hot day. The trail follows along a jeep road created for the construction of the power line. You will climb about 0.4 miles *0.65 km* to join the power line, then hike across a gradually rising shelf. From there you will begin the steepest ascent. Look over to your right (E) and you will see the rounded red butte known as **Robber's Roost.**

The payoff for this hike is the viewing. Casner is a tall mountain and is situated so that you can see into some beautiful country. To the south you see the Black Hills and Jerome. To the east you will see many of the Sedona

landmarks and parts of the town. As you climb higher you will begin to see the red towers of Sycamore Pass to your left (W).

From the end of the shelf, the trail goes straight up the mountain to about the halfway point, where the pitch becomes quite steep, and from there the trail serpentines. At the 1.6 mile *2.6 km* point you come to a sharp switchback at the west edge of the mountain where you break over a shoulder so that you can suddenly see into the whole of Sycamore Canyon. It is a vast and soul-stirring view, worth the trip all by itself.

From this point you will make the final push and stop at the top, at the highest point. Though Casner Mountain looks like a free-standing mountain when you start the hike, it is attached to the Mogollon Rim by Buck Ridge. The power line runs across this ridge and you can continue hiking the power line road for 4.0 miles *6.4 km* to the rim. We describe the hike from Casner's summit to the rim in *Flagstaff Hikes*, as Casner Mountain North.

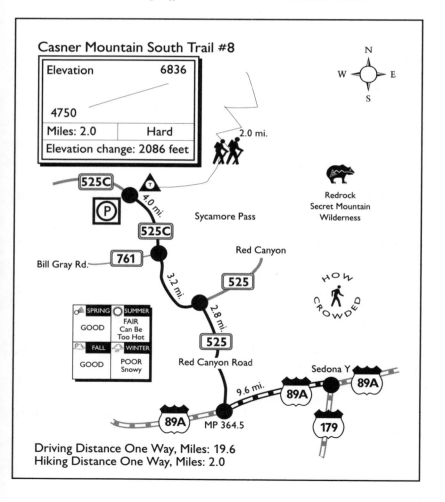

Casner Mountain South Trail #8

Elevation	6836
4750	
Miles: 2.0	Hard
Elevation change: 2086 feet	

2.0 mi.

525C

P

525C

Bill Gray Rd. — 761

Red Canyon

525

Sycamore Pass

Redrock
Secret Mountain
Wilderness

HOW CROWDED

	SPRING		SUMMER
	GOOD		FAIR Can Be Too Hot
	FALL		WINTER
	GOOD		POOR Snowy

4.0 mi.

3.2 mi.

2.8 mi.

525

Red Canyon Road

Sedona Y

89A

89A

89A

179

9.6 mi.

89A   MP 364.5

Driving Distance One Way, Miles: 19.6
Hiking Distance One Way, Miles: 2.0

Cathedral Rock Trail #170

VORTEX

General Information
Location Map F4
Sedona USGS Map
Coconino Forest Service Map

Driving Distance One Way: 4.1 miles *6.6 km* (Time 15 minutes)
Access Road: All cars, All paved
Hiking Distance One Way: 0.7 miles *1.1 km* (Time 45 minutes)
How Strenuous: Hard
Features: Views, Redrocks

NUTSHELL: This trail provides an exciting but hard climb to a saddle on Cathedral Rock, from which there are superb views.

DIRECTIONS:
From the Sedona Y Go
   South on Highway 179 a distance of 3.4 miles *5.5 km* (MP 310.2) to the Back O' Beyond road. Turn right onto this paved road and follow it to the 4.1 mile *6.6 km* point, where you will see a marked and fenced parking area to your left.

TRAILHEAD: At the parking lot.

DESCRIPTION: From the parking lot you will cross a little streambed and then make a 150 foot climb to the Vista, a bare redrock shelf which offers wonderful views. A short distance up the trail from the Vista you will intersect the **Templeton Trail** running to the left and right. Go to the right, on the Templeton Trail, following the cairns. In a few paces, the Cathedral Rock Trail will take you to the left, uphill, away from the Templeton Trail. From this point the hike changes character: the climb is much steeper and there are places where you have to scramble up rock faces. There are toeholds cut into key places and we found the ascent to be thrilling rather than daunting.
   The route makes a sharp climb to the saddle between two major clusters of spires on top of the Cathedral Rock. The sign at the entry warns that this hike is for experienced hikers only and requires some strenuous climbing. It is a steep, rough trail and makes considerable demands on hikers. We have seen some very unathletic people make the hike, however. Some of them protested a bit at the climbing required, but they made it. Timid or out-of-shape hikers, may be satisfied to stop at the Vista.

There are several places as you climb the high part of the trail where you encounter level open spaces and can pause to enjoy the great views, which improve as you get higher. Although the pitch of the upper trail is steep, it is short. Follow the cairns carefully and you will have a most rewarding pay-off. Once the saddle is in sight, you will be spurred to finish the climb so that you can see what is on the other side.

The saddle is magnificent. There is room to move around, with wonderful views to the east and west and mighty cliffs framing the north and south sides. There are some perfectly placed rocks, made to order for sitting, viewing and meditating. This is one of the major vortex sites.

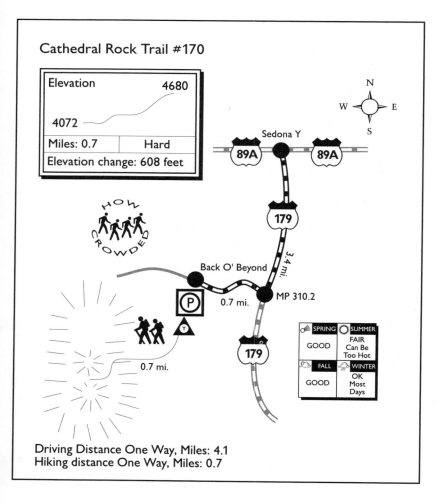

Cathedral Rock Trail #170

Elevation

4680

4072

Miles: 0.7 | Hard

Elevation change: 608 feet

Sedona Y

89A · 89A

179

3.4 mi.

Back O' Beyond

0.7 mi.

MP 310.2

0.7 mi.

179

SPRING	SUMMER
GOOD	FAIR Can Be Too Hot
FALL	WINTER
GOOD	OK Most Days

Driving Distance One Way, Miles: 4.1
Hiking distance One Way, Miles: 0.7

Chapel Trail

General Information
Location Map E5
Sedona USGS Map
Coconino Forest Service Map

Driving Distance One Way: 3.6 miles *5.8 km* (Time 10 minutes)
Access Road: All cars, All paved
Hiking Distance One Way: 2.4 miles *3.84 km* (Time 1.2 hours)
How Strenuous: Moderate
Features: Views, Redrocks, "Back door" to world-famed Chapel of the Holy Cross

NUTSHELL: This unmaintained trail branches off from the maintained Little Horse Trail at the base of Twin Buttes and takes you along a scenic route to the parking lot at the foot of the Chapel of the Holy Cross.

DIRECTIONS:
From the Sedona Y Go:
   South on Highway 179 (toward Phoenix) for a distance of 3.6 miles *5.8 km* (MP 309.8).Turn left into the **Little Horse Trail** parking lot. This was ready for use in May 1998 to serve as the parking lot for both the Little Horse Trail and the **Bell Rock Pathway.**

TRAILHEAD: At the parking lot, with signs.

DESCRIPTION: There is a nicely developed trailhead at the parking place, with informative signs, a map and—most welcome at times—a toilet. If you examine the map you will see that it features the Little Horse Trail, but it does show the Chapel Trail branching off from Little Horse near its end. So the thing to do is simply to hike the Little Horse Trail, which is signed and marked with cairns, to the trail junction.
   The Little Horse Trail is really a connector to the Chapel Trail, when viewed in light of making the Chapel Trail hike. The Little Horse Trail up to the junction is nothing special. You do not have any sweeping views, as you are down in the trees. You will find the trail junction at the 1.5 mile *2.4 km* point, which is at the base of Twin Buttes. There is a cairn at the trail junction. The Forest Service seems to have mixed feelings about the Chapel Trail, because even though they show it on their trailhead maps, it is not marked or identified on the ground. Indeed, it even looks as if someone tried to block it.
   Because the trail is not marked in any way, a certain amount of pathfind-

ing ability is needed, but if you stay alert, you should be able to follow it comfortably. Soon after you start on the trail, you will see the Chapel in the distance, which will serve to orient you.

The trail goes up on redrock ledges in places, where you are up high enough to see over the screen of trees, and for the first time on this hike you can enjoy views, primarily to the south, where you will see Bell Rock, Courthouse Butte and Cathedral Rock. Near at hand, you can look up to your right onto the gorgeous cliff faces of Twin Buttes. We really enjoy this part of the hike—by far the best part. The trail gets a little tricky as you near the Chapel. The best advice we can give about this is: don't go down into the gully, stay high.

The trail ends at the lower parking lot, from where it is a simple matter to walk up to the Chapel and enjoy its unique beauty and tranquillity.

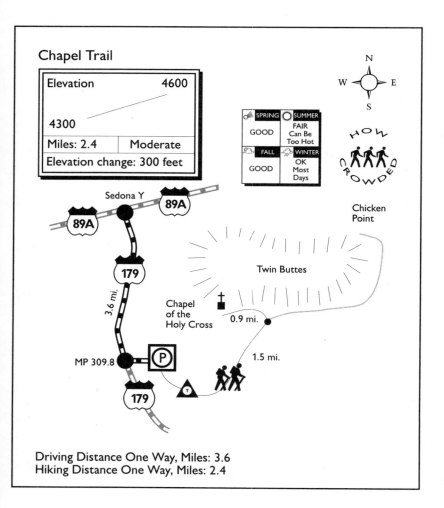

Chapel Trail

Elevation	4600
4300	
Miles: 2.4	Moderate
Elevation change: 300 feet	

	SPRING	SUMMER
	GOOD	FAIR Can Be Too Hot
	FALL	WINTER
	GOOD	OK Most Days

HOW CROWDED

Sedona Y

89A 89A

179

3.6 mi.

Chapel of the Holy Cross

MP 309.8

P

179

Chicken Point

Twin Buttes

0.9 mi.

1.5 mi.

N
W E
S

Driving Distance One Way, Miles: 3.6
Hiking Distance One Way, Miles: 2.4

Chimney Rock Pass Trail

General Information
Location Map D4
Sedona and Wilson Mountain USGS Maps
Coconino Forest Service Map

Driving Distance One Way*:* 4.3 miles *6.9 km* (Time 15 minutes)
Access Road*:* All cars, All paved
Hiking Distance, Complete Loop: 2.25 miles *3.6 km*
How Strenuous: Moderate
Features: Rock formations, Views

NUTSHELL: Chimney Rock is a prominent landmark in Sedona. This trail takes you to the top of the ridge from which the spire rises for wonderful views.

DIRECTIONS:
From the Sedona Y Go:
    Southwest on Highway 89A (toward Cottonwood) for 3.2 miles *5.1 km* (MP 371) to Dry Creek Road. Turn right on Dry Creek Road and proceed to the 3.7 mile *5.9 km* point. Turn right Thunder Mountain Road at the entrance to the Thunder Mountain subdivision. Drive to the 4.3 miles *6.9 km* point, then turn left into the trail parking lot.

TRAILHEAD: At the parking area. There is a 3-panel sign with a map of the trails in the area.

DESCRIPTION: We formerly had a hike to Chimney Rock that required some pathfinding. Now, with the Thunder Mountain Trail system on line, this fine loop hike can be made much better than the old way.
    From the parking area, walk north, toward the redrock buttes. At 0.2 miles *0.32 km* you reach a trail junction with a sign, where the **Thunder Mountain Trail** goes to the right. Go straight here.
    You will climb to the top of a little pass at 0.35 miles *0.56 km*. The **Summit Route Trail** goes to the left just beyond here. The Lower Chimney Rock Trail goes downhill. Turn to the right.
    From now on you will ascend to the ridge where Chimney Rock is located. The trail has been well designed so that the climb is easy to make. We find this approach to be very scenic and really enjoy it. As you get near the top, keep your eyes open for the sidetrail to the right that goes over to the base of Chimney Rock. The main trail does not take you there. The trail to the Chimney is just below the crest and is the only one going off in that

direction; so even though it is not marked, it is easy to find.

The top of the ridge is a fine place, giving you good views from both sides. We enjoy just sitting here, looking and thinking.

When you are ready to finish the hike, go down the other side. You will come to a trail junction in about 0.25 miles *0.4 km*, where you turn right. In another 0.15 miles *0.24 k*m you will reach a trail junction where a trail goes down to your left to a big green water tank, to a parking area off Andante Drive. Pass this by and continue straight ahead.

You will complete your loop when you reach the junction with the trail from the parking lot, marked with a signpost, where you turn left and go back to your car.

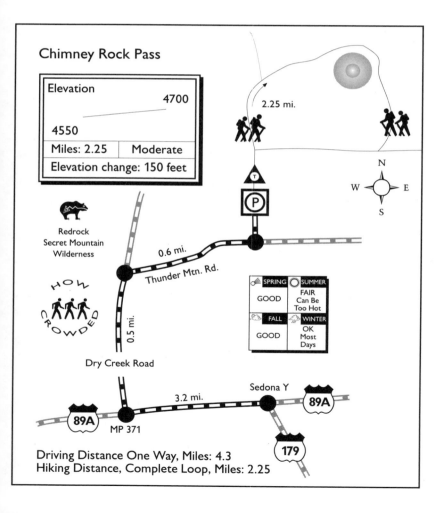

Chimney Rock Pass

Elevation		4700
4550		
Miles: 2.25	Moderate	
Elevation change: 150 feet		

2.25 mi.

N
W E
S

Redrock
Secret Mountain
Wilderness

0.6 mi.

Thunder Mtn. Rd.

HOW CROWDED

0.5 mi.

Dry Creek Road

SPRING	SUMMER
GOOD	FAIR Can Be Too Hot
FALL	WINTER
GOOD	OK Most Days

Sedona Y

89A

3.2 mi.

89A
MP 371

179

Driving Distance One Way, Miles: 4.3
Hiking Distance, Complete Loop, Miles: 2.25

Cibola Pass Trail

General Information
Location Map D4
Munds Park, Wilson Mountain USGS Maps
Coconino Forest Service Map

Driving Distance One Way: 1.7 miles *2.7 km* (Time 10 minutes)
Access Road: All cars. Last 0.4 miles *0.6 km* dirt road
Hiking Distance One Way: 1.0 miles *1.6 km* (Time 40 minutes)
How Strenuous: Easy
Features: Easy to reach, all-weather road, pleasant hike near town, good views

NUTSHELL: Starting from the old shooting range at the end of Jordan Road, this trail branches west, climbs over a pass on Cibola Ridge and goes over to connect to the **Jordan Trail.**

DIRECTIONS:
From the Y in Sedona Go:
    North on Highway on 89A (toward Flagstaff) for 0.3 miles *0.5 km* to Jordan Road, in the middle of uptown Sedona. Turn left (N) and take Jordan Road to its end, at 1.1 miles *1.8 km.* Turn left at the stop sign, onto Park Ridge Drive, a paved road, which goes through a subdivision and ends at 1.3 miles *2.1 km.* Keep going past the subdivision on the unpaved road, which has been improved since our last edition. At the 1.7 mile *2.7 km* point, you will come to the parking area outside the gate of the old shooting range. A new trailhead about 0.25 miles *0.4 km* inside the gate is under construction.

TRAILHEAD: Walk through the gate and up the road 0.1 miles *0.16 km* where you will see the **Jim Thompson Trailhead** to your right. Keep going another 25 yards and you will come to the Cibola Pass Trailhead to your left, marked with a signpost.

DESCRIPTION: Although this trail was designed as a connector, linking the **Brins Mesa** and **Soldier Pass** areas, it is a nice little trail in its own right.
    The trail at first dips down into the bottom of a little wash, and then begins to climb, passing through an attractive forest of Arizona cypress as it does so. As you begin to climb, you will ascend high enough so that you have views out over the Brins Mesa area, which is quite scenic, rimmed by beautiful red and white cliffs.
    At about the 0.5 mile *0.8 km* point, you will come to the top of Cibola Ridge, where there is a barbed wire fence. Piles of brush have been placed

along the fence to prevent hikers from going to the north or south ends of the ridge, confining traffic to the path. Take a moment here to enjoy the nice views on each side of the ridge.

Turn right at the fence and follow it for about 30 paces to a gate (left). You pass through the gate and then descend the other side of the ridge, hiking through another cypress forest and finally reaching a junction with the **Jordan Trail** at 0.9 miles *1.44 km.* This is the end of the Cibola Pass Trail. You now have an opportunity to mix and match. You can turn right and hike another 0.4 miles *0.64 km* to **Devil's Kitchen**. Or you can turn left and follow the Jordan Trail back to the parking lot, a hike of about 1.0 miles *1.6 km.* We usually make this hike as a loop, turning to the left when we get to the Cibola-Jordan trail junction and returning home on the Jordan Trail. It gives the hiker a very nice view of the impressive red cliffs on the edge of Cibola Ridge.

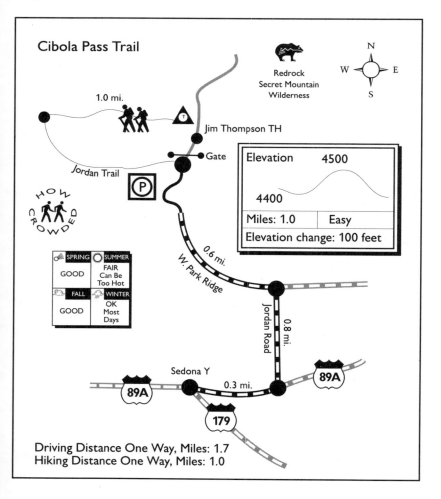

Cockscomb Butte Route

General Information
Location Map D3
Wilson Mountain USGS Map
Coconino Forest Service Map

Driving Distance One Way: 10.7 miles *17.1 km* (Time 20 minutes)
Access Road: All cars, Last 3.0 miles good dirt roads
Hiking Distance One Way: 0.75 miles *1.2 km* (Time 1.0 hour)
How Strenuous: Moderate
Features: Views

NUTSHELL: The Cockscomb is one of the southernmost redrock buttes in the Sedona area. After a short, level approach, you make a 400 foot climb to enjoy exploring the top and take in the wonderful views.

DIRECTIONS:
From the Sedona Y Go:
    Southwest on Highway 89A a distance of 3.2 miles *5.1 km* (MP 371) to Dry Creek Road and turn right onto Dry Creek Road. Follow it to the 6.1 mile *9.8 km* point, where it joins Long Canyon Road. Turn left here, staying on FR 152C. At the 7.7 mile *12.3 km* point, turn left on FR 152C, which is now a dirt road. At the 9.7 mile *15.5 km* point, turn left on FR 9583 and follow it to the 10.7 mile *17.1 km* point, where you will find a locked gate. There are no designated parking spaces. Park on the shoulder of the road in such a way that you do not block access through the gate.

TRAILHEAD: There are non-system signs. Walk up to the gate, (but not throught it) turn right, and follow the barbed wire fence. You will soon see a well-worn path that follows around the ranch fence.

DESCRIPTION: This area is under development, which may change the access.
    The ranch, the boundaries of which you will follow, is known to Sedona old-timers as the Tree Farm, but there are plans afoot to change it into a major golf course subdivision. As you walk around the fence, you will see some patches of cultivated trees.
    At about the 0.35 mile *0.6 km* point the trail will move away from the fence, bearing southeast, as it begins heading toward the Cockscomb. You are almost at the foot of the Cockscomb at this point, and will meet the system **Cockscomb Trail** here. From the place where you can no longer see the fence, look for a path going to the right (S) and heading uphill. It is usually

marked with cairns. We measured this point as being at 0.43 miles *0.7 km*. This is a hiker-made trail, and receives enough use so that the path is well worn and easily discernible.

The trail has been level up to here. You will now climb 400 feet to the top. Look carefully. We have never had any trouble following this trail, but you want to keep checking the cairns, because there is only one route to the top. The trail winds up the face and "around the corner" where you will find some natural stairsteps and some hiker-built steps to the top. The top is small, easy to explore, and has many clear areas for excellent views out over the area.

Bikers love this area and there are informal trails all over the place. Keep your eyes open and the objective in mind and you should be able to pick the correct route, the one that will take you to the top.

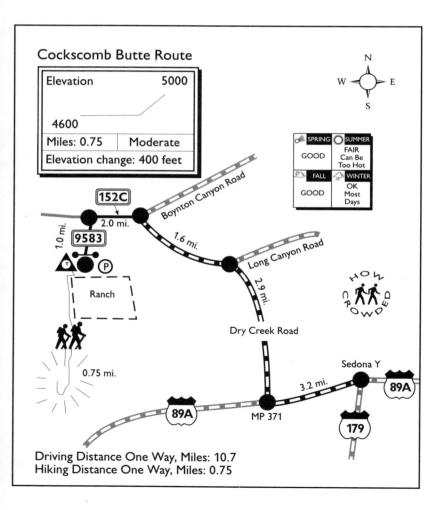

Cockscomb Butte Route

Elevation	5000
4600	
Miles: 0.75	Moderate
Elevation change: 400 feet	

SPRING	SUMMER
GOOD	FAIR Can Be Too Hot
FALL	WINTER
GOOD	OK Most Days

152C

Boynton Canyon Road

2.0 mi.

1.6 mi.

9583

1.0 mi.

Long Canyon Road

2.9 mi.

Ranch

0.75 mi.

Dry Creek Road

HOW CROWDED

Sedona Y

3.2 mi.

89A

89A

MP 371

179

Driving Distance One Way, Miles: 10.7
Hiking Distance One Way, Miles: 0.75

Cockscomb Trail

General Information
Location Map D3
Wilson Mt. USGS Map
Coconino Forest Service Map

Driving Distance One Way: 8.7 miles *13.9 km* (Time 25 minutes)
Access Road: All cars, Last mile fair dirt road
Hiking Distance One Way: 2.5 miles *4.0 km* (Time 1.25 hours)
How Strenuous: Moderate
Features: Views of Doe Mountain and the Cockscomb

NUTSHELL: This trail, new to the system in 2001, is easy to reach and takes the hiker into some interesting backcountry around Doe Mountain and the Cockscomb. If you want to hike to the top of the Cockscomb, take the **Cockscomb Butte Route** described in this book.

DIRECTIONS:
From the Sedona Y Go:
Southwest on Highway 89A (toward Cottonwood) for a distance of 3.2 miles *5.1 km* (MP 371) to Dry Creek Road. Turn right onto Dry Creek Road and follow it to the 6.1 mile *9.8 km* point, where it intersects the Long Canyon Road, where you turn left on FR 152C. Stay on FR 152C to the 7.7 mile *12.3 km* point, where it intersects the Boynton Canyon Road. Here you will turn left onto the Boynton Pass Road. It is paved for a short distance and then becomes unpaved. At the 8.2 mile *13.1 km* point you will see the driveway to the parking area for the **Fay Canyon Trail**, to your right. Drive past this turnoff for a few feet. You will see a sign reading, "Fay Canyon Tr. Overflow Parking," and find a turn to the left just beyond it. Turn left onto FR 9586. The design is to drive in 0.5 miles *0.8 km* to the trailhead, but the last 0.1 miles *0.16 km* is very rough. Go as far as you feel comfortable and park.

TRAILHEAD: There are "trail" signs along FR 9586 and a "Cockscomb Trail" sign where the trail starts at a gate in a barbed wire fence.

DESCRIPTION: At the end of the access road there is a gate in a barbed wire fence, where there is a trail sign. Go through the gate. The trail at this point is a footpath running under a power line. The trail rises modestly and affords some nice views into scenic country around Thunder Mountain and the Dry Creek areas.
At 1.0 miles *1.6 km* the **Dawa Trail** comes in from your left on an old

jeep road and joins you for a few yards, then branches off to the left. The Cockscomb Trail now turns and runs along the base of Doe Mountain. In this area the trail is an old jeep road, so it is wide and easy to walk. We enjoy the views of Doe Mountain from this side, a vantage point from which the attractive mesa is seldom seem. We always find bike tracks on this part of the trail, an indication that bikers like this part of the trail, and we can see why: it is scenic and easy to ride, free of overhanging branches, boulder fields and other obstacles.

At 2.5 miles *4.0 km* the trail ends for now at a fence corner, where there is a sign for the **Rupp Trail**. Forest Service officials told us in April 2002 that they were not certain about the course of the Cockscomb Trail from this point, because certain decisions hinge on the development of the old Tree Farm property that runs south from Doe Mountain. The fence corner where the trail stops is a boundary of that land.

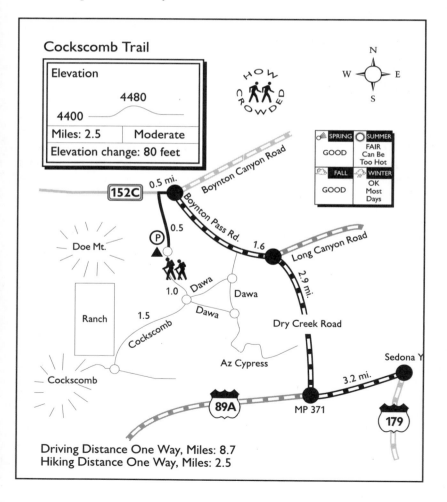

Cockscomb Trail

Elevation

4480

4400

Miles: 2.5 — Moderate

Elevation change: 80 feet

	SPRING	SUMMER
	GOOD	FAIR Can Be Too Hot
	FALL	WINTER
	GOOD	OK Most Days

152C 0.5 mi. Boynton Canyon Road

Boynton Pass Rd.

0.5

1.6 Long Canyon Road

Doe Mt.

P

1.0 Dawa Dawa

2.9 mi.

Ranch 1.5 Dawa

Cockscomb Dry Creek Road

Az Cypress

Sedona Y

Cockscomb 89A 3.2 mi. 179

MP 371

Driving Distance One Way, Miles: 8.7
Hiking Distance One Way, Miles: 2.5

Coffee Pot

General Information
Location Map D4
Sedona and Wilson Mt. USGS Maps
Coconino Forest Service Map

Driving Distance One Way: 2.85 miles *4.6 km* (Time 10 minutes)
Access Road: All cars, All paved
Hiking Distance One Way: 1.0 miles *1.6 km* (Time 45 minutes)
How Strenuous: Easy
Features: Rock formations, Views

NUTSHELL: Coffee Pot Rock is one of the most familiar Sedona land-marks. This trail allows you easy access to its base. You walk to a point under the "spout" where you enjoy great views.

DIRECTIONS:
From the Sedona Y Go:
Southwest on Highway 89A (toward Cottonwood) for a distance of 1.9 miles *3.0 km* (MP 372.7) to Coffee Pot Drive (at stoplight by Basha's Shopping Center). Turn right onto Coffee Pot Drive. Follow it to the 2.5 mile *4.0 km* point where you turn left on Sanborn and proceed west to the 2.65 mile *4.2 km* point, where you turn right on Little Elf Drive. At the end of Little Elf, the 2.85 mile *4.6 km* point, turn right on Buena Vista and drive a few yards, turning left into the first road you see, which goes into an unmarked parking lot.

TRAILHEAD: At the parking area, but the sign does not show this trail.

DESCRIPTION: The access we previously used, off of Mountain Shadows-Fabulous Texan Way, is no longer available, but there is a convenient substitute, which is using the **Thunder Mountain Trail.**
At the parking area, if you look to the northeast, you will see Coffee Pot Rock in the distance. From the parking area, you walk north. The trail immediately splits and even though there are some signs, there are so many official and unofficial trails running through the area that you may easily be confused. Go right at the first fork and keep moving north toward the distant cliffs. You will reach a power line at 0.5 miles *0.8 km* where there is a T intersection with the Thunder Mountain Trail, where you turn right.
Next you will come to a signpost for the **Sugarloaf Loop Trail**. Go past it, and shortly beyond, at 0.6 miles *1.0 km* you will see the unmarked trail junction for the Coffee Pot Trail. It is not signed, but a circle of stones sur-

rounds a bush here. Turn left and follow the trail. Even though it is unofficial, it is well traveled and easy to follow, using an old jeep road.

Once you get confidently established on this old road, the rest of the hike is easy. Whenever you come to a side path (and there are several of them), just remember where Coffee Pot Rock is and keep moving toward it.

The trail goes to the base of the cliffs and then moves right along a ledge toward Coffee Pot. You will enjoy looking at the cliffs here, as they are very colorful and highly sculptured. As the trail nears Coffee Pot it becomes rougher and you have to watch carefully to see where it goes. Eventually the ledge you walk on will reduce down to the point where you can't walk it any farther. Here you can look up and see the spout of Coffee Pot towering above your head. It will seem that you are right under it, though you will be a little west of it. You will have some great views there.

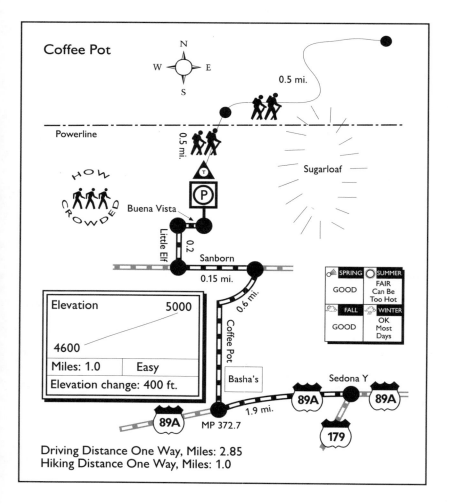

Cookstove Trail #143

General Information
Location Map B5
Mountainaire USGS Map
Coconino Forest Service Map

Driving Distance One Way: 12.7 miles *20.4 km* (Time 20 minutes)
Access Road: All cars, All paved
Hiking Distance One Way: 0.75 miles *1.2 km* (Time 45 minutes)
How Strenuous: Hard
Features: Views

NUTSHELL: This is a marked and posted trail located just across Highway 89A from the Pine Flat Campground 12.7 miles *20.4 km* north of Sedona. It climbs the east wall of Oak Creek Canyon.

DIRECTIONS:
From the Sedona Y Go:

   North on Highway 89A (toward Flagstaff) for a distance of 12.7 miles *20.4 km* (MP 386.9) to the Pine Flat Campground. On your left at the upper end of the campground on the shoulder of the highway, you will see a structure about 5 feet high and 4 feet square made of round stones that houses a spring. You will see water flowing out of a pipe that sticks out the back of the structure. Park anywhere near here. There are wide aprons on both shoulders in this area.

TRAILHEAD: On the east side of the road just across Highway 89A from the spring. It is marked by a rusty sign reading, "Cookstove Trail #143."

DESCRIPTION: The water in the spring at Pine Flat is pure, and you will see people filling bottles and jugs there, as we do ourselves. There is a caution about this water, however: even though it is pure, it contains microbes that *your* system may not handle well, whereas local residents can drink it with no trouble.

   The Cookstove Trail is typical of all trails in upper Oak Creek Canyon that climb the east wall of the canyon: namely, it goes virtually straight up with little finesse. Similar trails are **Harding Spring, Purtymun, Thomas Point** and Thompson's Ladder**.** They are all strenuous hikes.

   The trail starts by the road and immediately begins to climb. At first the trail parallels Cookstove Draw. At 0.1 miles *0.16 km* you get a great view down into the draw, where there is a small waterfall during snow melt and after hard rains. Then the trail veers away from Cookstove Draw as it rises.

The forest through which this trail passes is typical for upper Oak Creek Canyon, with pine at the beginning, changing into mixed pines and firs as you climb and the elevation increases.

The trail does a little zigging and zagging. When you top out, you are in a spot where you get good views of the west wall of Oak Creek Canyon, but the views are not as good as the views you get at the top of the Harding Spring trail.

The elevation at the rim is about 6,600 feet, almost as high as Flagstaff, and the climate is similar to Flagstaff's climate. These hikes can often be pleasant in summer when hiking in Sedona would be too hot.

On the rim the country is flat and not scenic. The old-timers who built these trails would travel to Flagstaff once they got to the top, and did not build trails for the scenery. We like to walk along the rim looking for viewpoints, which are plentiful.

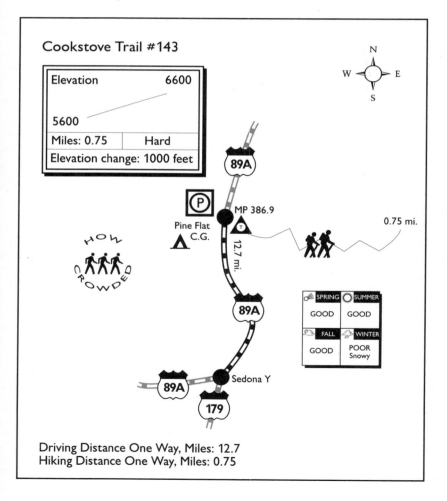

Cookstove Trail #143

Elevation	6600
5600	
Miles: 0.75	Hard
Elevation change: 1000 feet	

89A

MP 386.9

Pine Flat C.G.

12.7 mi.

0.75 mi.

HOW CROWDED

89A

🌱 SPRING	☀ SUMMER
GOOD	GOOD
🍂 FALL	❄ WINTER
GOOD	POOR Snowy

89A

Sedona Y

179

Driving Distance One Way, Miles: 12.7
Hiking Distance One Way, Miles: 0.75

Courthouse Butte Loop Trail

General Information
Location Map F5
Sedona and Munds Mt. USGS Maps
Coconino Forest Service Map

Driving Distance One Way: 6.2 miles *9.9 km* (Time 20 minutes)
Access Road: All cars, All paved
Hiking Distance, Complete Loop: 4.3 miles *6.9 km* (Time 2.0 hours)
How Strenuous: Moderate
Features: Views

NUTSHELL: This easy trail features Courthouse Butte, a landmark located south of Sedona.

DIRECTIONS:
From the Sedona Y Go:
    South on Highway 179 (toward Phoenix) for a distance of 6.2 miles *9.9 km* (MP 307.4) to a place south of Bell Rock, just short of the Village of Oak Creek, where you will see a road to your left. This road provides access to the Bell Rock Pathway, a trail created in 1997. There is parking and the Pathway provides access to the Courthouse Butte Trail.

TRAILHEAD: Use the Bell Rock Pathway as the trailhead.

DESCRIPTION: The Bell Rock Pathway is a welcome addition to the Sedona trail system, and it is as wide as a road, making for easy hiking. There is a nice shelter with map at the parking area showing the details of the network of trails. Walk the Bell Rock Pathway north to a point 0.5 miles *0.8 km* from the beginning, where you will find a signed trail junction. The Courthouse Butte Loop starts here, a much narrower trail running to your right. From this point, the trail makes a circle around Courthouse Butte, hugging the base of this beautiful formation. Since a formal trail has been created, this path is now much easier to follow than the hike we described in the first three editions of this book.
    At 1.5 miles *2.4 km* from the point of beginning, you will come to a streambed, where the soil has been washed off, down to the native red bedrock. At this point you are in the Munds Mountain Wilderness Area, and the Forest Service is reluctant to spoil the natural look by posting signs. As you walk out onto the streambed, turn left (N) and walk about 75 paces along the far side. Here you will find the trail again, coming off of the rock and running along a shelf of soil a few yards away from the stream bottom.

This area is our favorite part of the hike, because it is quiet, scenic and natural, quite different from the bustle around Bell Rock. You will make a climb on the next leg of the hike, but it is not very steep, finally emerging on a ridge top where there is a round redrock knob just to your right. We suggest a small detour to climb up to the top of this knob for superb views, especially of Rabbit Ears off to the east.

From this point, you walk west along the north side of the butte, rejoining the Bell Rock Pathway. From this point, you are near Highway 179 and there are always a lot of people around. You simply turn south and walk back to the parking place.

What is now called Courthouse Butte was originally called Cathedral Rock and *vice versa*. A government map maker confused the two and switched names. It doesn't seem to matter much, as either name seems appropriate, but some old-timers were pretty irate about the change.

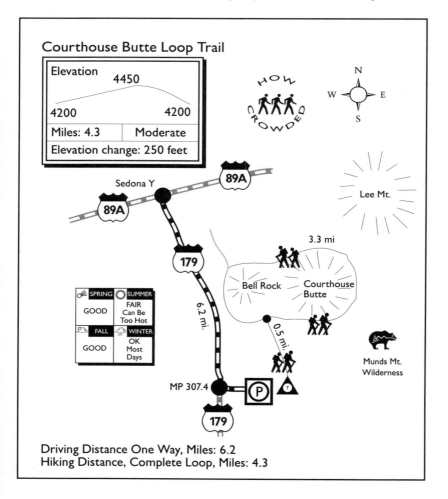

Courthouse Butte Loop Trail

Elevation
4450
4200   4200
Miles: 4.3 | Moderate
Elevation change: 250 feet

HOW CROWDED

N W E S

Lee Mt.

Sedona Y
89A
89A
179

3.3 mi

Bell Rock — Courthouse Butte

6.2 mi.

	SPRING		SUMMER
	GOOD		FAIR Can Be Too Hot
	FALL		WINTER
	GOOD		OK Most Days

0.5 mi.

Munds Mt. Wilderness

MP 307.4

P   T

179

Driving Distance One Way, Miles: 6.2
Hiking Distance, Complete Loop, Miles: 4.3

Cow Pies

VORTEX

General Information
Location Map E5
Munds Mt. and Munds Park USGS Maps
Coconino Forest Service Map

Driving Distance One Way: 3.8 miles *6.1 km* (Time 20 minutes)
Access Road: High clearance cars, Last 2.5 miles *4.0 km* rough dirt road
Hiking Distance One Way: 1.5 miles *2.4 km* (Time 40 minutes)
How Strenuous: Easy
Features: Views, Fascinating rock formations and sculptures, Vortex

NUTSHELL: An ugly name for a beautiful area. The Cow Pies are redrock formations just west of the Schnebly Hill Road, only 3.8 miles *6.1 km* east of uptown Sedona. If you like redrocks, you will love the Cow Pies. **A personal favorite**.

DIRECTIONS:
From the Sedona Y Go:
      South on Highway 179 (toward Phoenix) for a distance of 0.3 miles *0.5 km* (MP 313.1) to the Schnebly Hill Road. It is just across the bridge past Tlaquepaque. Turn left onto the Schnebly Hill Road. It is paved for the first 1.0 mile *1.6 km* and then turns into a dirt road that is so bad that a sign warns that it is unsuitable for passenger cars. At the 3.8 mile *6.1 km* point, there is a marked parking area to the right; pull over and park.

TRAILHEAD: There is a trail sign at the parking area.

DESCRIPTION: What's in a name? Many Sedona landmarks have grand names, such as the Crimson Cliffs. This hike takes place on a formation known by the ugly name, Cow Pies. The name does describe the appearance of the rock formations, but utterly fails to convey a sense of how beautiful and interesting they are. The "pies" look like hardened blobs of soft warm red mud, dropped into Bear Wallow Canyon the way you'd drop cookie dough onto a baking sheet. They are a unique Sedona experience, easy to reach and hike on. We prefer to call these formations "muffins."
      At 0.2 miles *0.3 km* you will come to the first muffin, a redrock shelf that had a very thin crust of volcanic basalt on top. This crust has broken up into small black stones which New Agers often arrange into a giant medicine wheel. This place is one of the fabled Sedona Vortex spots.
      At 0.43 miles *0.7 km* you reach the next muffin. The trail you have been following continues in a straight line (for a hike called **Mitten Ridge**). You

want to quit the trail here and turn to the left. Now you will get a better idea of the muffins. They are mounds of slickrock with many ridges and levels. Walk west, to your left, on the level area to the end of this muffin, where at 0.52 miles *0.8 km* you will find a land bridge linking it to the largest muffins, which sit by themselves in the bottom of the gorge.

You will top out on the Master Muffin at about 0.59 miles *1.0 km*. There is usually a cairn marking this spot. Take note of it, since it will help you find your way down on the return trip. From this point there is no trail. You just walk around and explore. In fact, it is so easy to walk around on these formations that you won't realize how substantial they are until you get to their edges and look down

The farthest extension of these rocks takes you out about 1.5 miles *2.4 km* from the parking place.

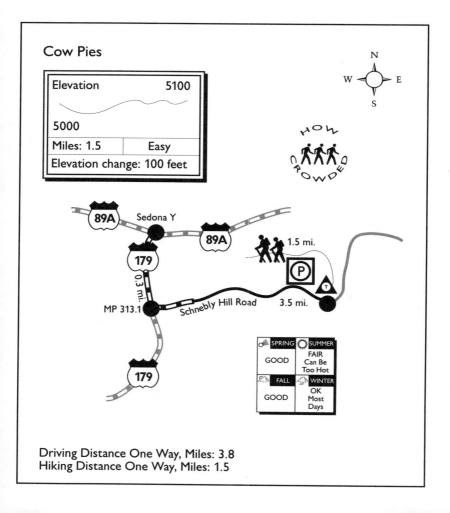

Driving Distance One Way, Miles: 3.8
Hiking Distance One Way, Miles: 1.5

Crescent Moon Creek Walk

General Information
Location Map F4
Sedona USGS Map
Coconino Forest Service Map

Driving Distance One Way: 7.0 miles *11.2 km* (Time 20 minutes)
Access Road: All cars, All paved
Hiking Distance One Way: 1.0 miles *1.6 km* (Time 30 minutes)
How Strenuous: Easy
Features: Easy to reach, Views of Cathedral Rock, Creekside stroll

NUTSHELL: You drive to Crescent Moon Ranch, then walk along the banks of Oak Creek in the shadow of Cathedral Rock.

DIRECTIONS:
From the Sedona Y Go:
   Southwest on Highway 89A (toward Cottonwood) a distance of 4.2 miles *6.8 km* (MP 368.9) to the Upper Red Rock Loop Road. Turn left and follow the Loop to the 6.0 mile *9.6 km* point, where you turn left, heading toward Crescent Moon Ranch Park on a paved road. Follow the paved road to Crescent Moon Ranch Park, a total of 7.0 miles *11.2 km*. You must pay a fee at the entrance booth. Park inside.

TRAILHEAD: There is no marked trailhead or trail, but you will see a pink concrete sidewalk running parallel to the creek.

DESCRIPTION: The site of this park is one of the most famous in Sedona, one that made its beauties known to the world. Originally this place was called Baldwin's Crossing, a name that was later changed to Red Rock Crossing. Travelers used to ford Oak Creek here, where a redrock shelf gave firm footing. The crossing is no longer used, though hotly contested plans to build a bridge here are still under discussion.
   It doesn't much matter where you park, though we suggest you try to park near the entrance booth. Follow the pink sidewalk down toward the creek, at the west end of the park. Here you find the famous vantage point from which all the photos were taken.
   Then turn and walk along the pink sidewalk easterly, There are several places where benches have been placed so that you can take your time, sit and meditate or just enjoy the experience of being in this lovely place. The sidewalk ends about 0.25 miles *0.4 km* from its beginning, and a dirt footpath continues from there.

You enter into the site of the old Chavez Ranch next, with some interesting old buildings. Of particular interest is a water wheel. From this point, the trail moves nearer the creek. We particularly enjoyed an area where the trail moves across a broad redrock shelf. Keep following the trail. There are many side paths, but it doesn't matter, they all go to the same place, confined by the creek on one side and an irrigation ditch on the other.

The trail ends at a big curve, where the creek splits and a power line crosses it. This is a very pleasant, easy walk that people of all ages can enjoy. It can be taken at almost any time of year, except for very cold days in winter and very hot days in summer.

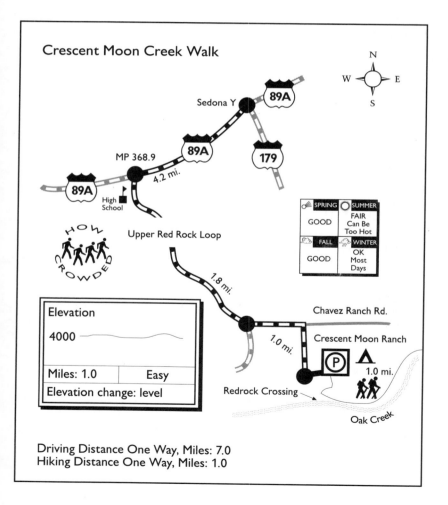

Crescent Moon Creek Walk

Driving Distance One Way, Miles: 7.0
Hiking Distance One Way, Miles: 1.0

David Miller Trail

General Information
Location Map C4
Wilson Mt. USGS Map
Coconino Forest Service Map

Driving Distance One Way: 8.6 miles *13.8 km* (Time 30 minutes)
Access Road: Most cars, Last 3.4 miles *5.4 km* rough dirt road
Hiking Distance, Complete Loop: 7.3 miles *11.7 km* (Time 4 hours)
How Strenuous: Hard
Features: Views, Remote canyons, Variety of terrain

NUTSHELL: The David Miller Trail is a connector that links the **Secret Canyon Trail** to the **Bear Sign Trail,** creating a welcome new loop hike in some of Sedona's most scenic, wildest backcountry.

DIRECTIONS:
From the Sedona Y Go:
Southwest on Highway 89A (toward Cottonwood) for 3.2 miles *5.1 km* (MP 371) to Dry Creek Road. Turn right on Dry Creek Road and proceed to the 5.2 mile *8.3 km* point. Turn right on FR 152, the Vultee Arch Road, and follow it to the 8.6 mile *13.8 km* point, where you will see a road sign pointing to the Secret Canyon trail turnoff. Make a sharp turn to your left into the parking area.

TRAILHEAD: There is a signboard and map at the trailhead.

DESCRIPTION: You will first hike the Secret Canyon Trail to the 2.1 mile *3.4 km* point, a place where the Secret Canyon Trail makes a sharp turn west. The signed David Miller Trail joins here, to your right (N).
This trail, new in 1999, takes you uphill along an unnamed canyon through a dense forest of oak and cypress. At the 2.6 miles *4.2 km* point you break out above the forest and are delighted by truly superb vistas. Before you is a notch at the top of a ridge between two buttes—your target, requiring a very steep climb. This is wild country, almost inaccessible before the David Miller Trail was built, and constructing this trail obviously required a tremendous amount of hard work.
You reach the top of the pass at the 2.9 mile *4.6 km* point, a place where you might want to sit a while, enjoy the views, and rest. From this point you begin an immediate descent into Bear Sign Canyon. While steep, the trail down to the Bear Sign bottom is not as long as the climb up the other side. You will be struck by the difference in vegetation, passing from desert into

alpine landscape. The trail winds down through cool pines and firs, to the sign at the Bear Sign/David Miller junction at 3.2 miles *5.2 km*. Turn right here, for a 3.1 mile *5.0 km* walk to the Bear Sign/Dry Creek Trailhead. From there you walk along the road south 1.0 mile *1.6 km* to the Secret Canyon Trailhead.

This makes for quite a long, tiring hike, so we like to use a two-car shuttle. The way to do this is to drive both cars to the Bear Sign Trailhead, which is at the 9.6 mile *15.4 km* point on FR 152, all the way to its end. Park one car here. Then everybody piles into the second car, which is driven to the Secret Canyon Trailhead and parked there.

David Miller was a young Forest Service employee who went out hiking by himself in 1997 and disappeared. In spite of the massive manhunt that was launched to find him, he was never found, and his location is a mystery.

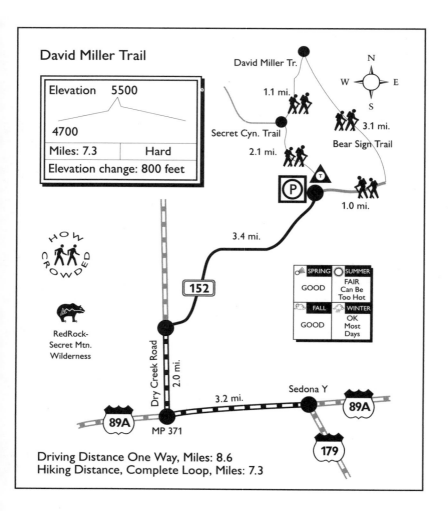

David Miller Trail

Elevation	5500
4700	
Miles: 7.3	Hard
Elevation change: 800 feet	

David Miller Tr.

1.1 mi.

Secret Cyn. Trail

3.1 mi.

Bear Sign Trail

2.1 mi.

1.0 mi.

3.4 mi.

HOW CROWDED

152

RedRock-
Secret Mtn.
Wilderness

SPRING	SUMMER
GOOD	FAIR Can Be Too Hot
FALL	WINTER
GOOD	OK Most Days

Dry Creek Road

2.0 mi.

3.2 mi.

Sedona Y

89A

89A

MP 371

179

Driving Distance One Way, Miles: 8.6
Hiking Distance, Complete Loop, Miles: 7.3

Dawa Trail

General Information
Location Map D3
Wilson Mt. USGS Map
Coconino Forest Service Map

Driving Distance One Way: 6.7 miles *10.7 km* (Time 15 minutes)
Access Road: All cars, All paved
Hiking Distance, Complete Loop: 2.9 miles *4.6 km* (Time 2.5 hours)
How Strenuous: Moderate
Features: Connections to other trails

NUTSHELL: The Dawa Trail has no pretensions to greatness, but makes a nice circle in the Doe Mountain area, connecting to three other trails in its course.

DIRECTIONS:
From the Sedona Y Go:
Southwest on Highway 89A (toward Cottonwood) for a distance of 3.2 miles *5.1 km* (MP 371) to the Dry Creek Road. Turn right onto Dry Creek Road and follow it to the 6.1 mile *9.8 km* point, where there is a stop sign. The paved road to your right is the Long Canyon Road. Turn left instead, and drive to the 6.7 mile *10.7 km* point, where you see a wide apron in front of a gap in a barbed wire fence to your left. Park.

TRAILHEAD: On the other side of the fence, where there is a 2-panel trail-head sign.

DESCRIPTION: Follow the trail from the sign. At 0.1 miles *0.16 km* you come to a V-fork. Go straight here. The **OK Trail** goes to the left at this junction. The Dawa Trail is an old road, which appears on the Wilson Mt. 7.5 topo map. In the area where you will now walk there are many old roads, so keep a lookout, as the road you are to walk does not stand out from the other roads. Because this trail is popular with bikers, the best way to tell where the trail is will be to look for bike tracks

At 1.3 miles *2.1 km*, near Doe Mountain, you come to a T-shaped trail junction, where the Dawa joins the **Cockscomb Trail**. Turn left, as the Dawa and the Cockscomb run together for a short distance. In about ten yards, turn left, as the Dawa leaves the other trail.

From now on you will walk along the course of a power line. At times you will see the line overhead and at other times it seems to be underground, but you will see green metal power boxes sticking up out of the ground

along the trail on this part of the loop.

At 2.3 miles *3.7 km* you reach Dry Creek and go across. On the other side, a few yards from the bank, is a T-trail junction with the **Arizona Cypress Trail**. Turn left here. At 2.5 miles *4.0 km* you will cross Dry Creek again, at a point where it has two channels. On the far side of the second channel is a T-junction with the OK Trail. Turn left and hike the OK Trail back to the parking place.

Many of the trails in the Sedona area are named after pioneers or landmarks; so we have wondered about "Dawa," as it seems different from the other trail names. It is different. "Dawa" is a Hopi word, meaning "sun".

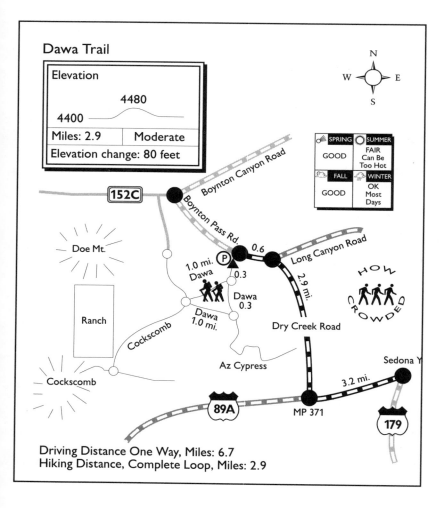

Dawa Trail

Elevation

4480

4400

Miles: 2.9	Moderate
Elevation change: 80 feet	

SPRING	SUMMER
GOOD	FAIR Can Be Too Hot
FALL	WINTER
GOOD	OK Most Days

Boynton Canyon Road

152C

Boynton Pass Rd.

Long Canyon Road

0.6

Doe Mt.

1.0 mi. Dawa

0.3

Dawa 0.3

2.9 mi.

Dawa 1.0 mi.

Cockscomb

Dry Creek Road

Ranch

Az Cypress

HOW CROWDED

Cockscomb

Sedona Y

3.2 mi.

89A

MP 371

179

Driving Distance One Way, Miles: 6.7
Hiking Distance, Complete Loop, Miles: 2.9

Dead Horse Ranch State Park Trails

General Information
Location Map F1
Clarkdale USGS Map
Coconino Forest Service Map

Driving Distance One Way: 21.5 miles *34.4 km* (Time 45 minutes)
Access Road: All cars, All paved
Hiking Distances: Tavasci Marsh 1.0 miles *1.6 km*, one-way, Verde River
Greenway 2.0 mile 3.2 *km* loop
How Strenuous: Moderate (both trails)
Features: Easy to reach, Verde River access, Birdwatching, Toilets and
other amenities

NUTSHELL: This state park, located near Cottonwood, has nice facilities,
including trails. Upon entrance to the park, visitors are given a map showing a number of hiking trails. Most of these are simply intra-park trails
designed to move visitors from one part of the park to another. Two of the
trails, the Tavasci Marsh and the Verde River Greenway trails, are worthy
of an entry in this article. Two other trails originating in the park, the **Lime
Kiln Trail** and the **Raptor Hill Trail**, are given full chapters.

DIRECTIONS:
From the Sedona Y Go:
   Southwest on Highway 89A for 18.6 miles *29.8 km*, to the first stoplight
in Cottonwood. Go straight on Highway 89A. You'll reach a second stop-
light at 19.2 miles *30.7 km*. Go straight on Historic Highway 89A (Main
Street). At 20.6 miles *33.0 km*, just past the cemetery, turn right on 10th
Street, which is signed for the park. The entrance to the park is at 21.5 miles
34.4 km, where you must pay an entrance fee.

TRAILHEADS:
   (1) Verde River Greenway Trail—make the second turn to the right,
into the Mesquite Day Use Area, and drive to first striped parking area to the
left. The trail starts at the head of the handicapped parking space. There is a
nice toilet here.
   (2) Tavasci Marsh Trail—Turn left at the second road to the left, where
you will see a Tavasci Marsh sign. Drive to the parking lot at the end.

DESCRIPTIONS:
   (1) Verde River Greenway Trail. 2.0 miles *3.2 km*. Level. Moderate.
At the start there is no trailhead sign, only a lath-type marker with a hiker

symbol. The trail takes you downhill to a streambed which you cross three times on plank bridges. Then you climb stairsteps and emerge onto a parking lot west of the Lagoon. From here the trail is close to the river but never goes to the river's edge, staying on the cliffs above. At the Lagoon take the right fork and then the left. The trail is away from the riverbank but there are many places to walk a few paces to the right and see the river. Then the trail moves away from the river and becomes a sandy path through stands of tall cottonwoods and sycamores, an excellent birding area. Deep sand here makes walking hard. At 1.0 miles *1.6 km* is a trail fork; go left. Soon there is another fork where you go left on a dirt road looping back to the start.

(2) Tavasci Marsh Trail. 1.0 miles *1.6 km*. Fairly level. Moderate. Takes you to an observation deck at a marsh, the Verde's best bird watching spot. At the start, you can take the River Route, downhill left, or the Road Route, uphill through the gate. The paths merge. This is a good hike for kids.

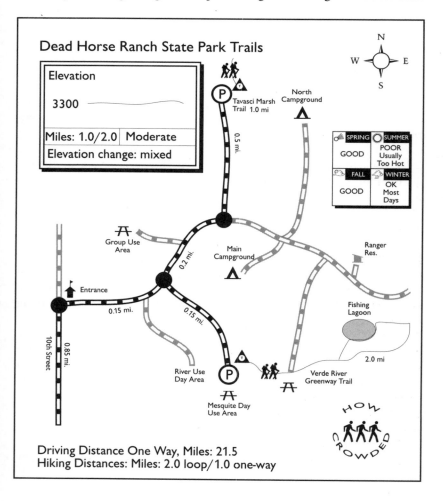

Deadman Pass Trail

General Information
Location Map C3
Wilson Mountain USGS Map
Coconino Forest Service Map

Driving Distance One Way: 7.9 miles *12.6 km* (Time 20 minutes)
Access Road: All cars, All paved
Hiking Distance One Way: 1.4 miles *2.2 km* (Time 45 minutes)
How Strenuous: Moderate
Features: Easy to reach, Redrock views, uncrowded

NUTSHELL: You hike along an old jeep trail through dense thickets of manzanita, admiring the buttes of Boynton on one side and Mescal Mountain on the other, then joining the Long Canyon Trail.

DIRECTIONS:
From the Sedona Y Go:
   Southwest on Highway 89A (toward Cottonwood) a distance of 3.2 miles *5.1 km* (MP 371), to Dry Creek Road, where you take a right turn onto Dry Creek Road. Follow it to the 6.1 mile *9.8 km* point, where it joins Long Canyon Road. Take a left here, staying on FR 152C. At the 7.7 mile *12.3 km* point, you reach another junction. Go right. At 7.9 miles *12.6 km*, just before the **Boynton Canyon Trail** parking lot, you will see a road, the entrance to which is blocked by a cable. Park here.

TRAILHEAD: No official trailhead yet. Hike the old road.

DESCRIPTION: We don't know how Deadman Pass got its name, as it is not listed in *Arizona Place Names*. The pass is a natural corridor leading between the buttes that form the east side of Boynton Canyon and the west side of **Mescal Mountain**. At its end, the Deadman Pass trail joins the **Long Canyon Trail.**
   The USFS is planning to build a larger trailhead-parking area to serve both the Boynton Canyon and Deadman trails, so we are not sure what the situation on the ground will be by the time you read this. Whether you start at the old entry point or the new one, you will see a powerline running north-easterly through the pass. At its beginning, the trail runs along under this line. In time, the trail swings away from the line slightly, but it is never very far away, and you can see the line off to your right at all times.
   The trail carves a path through thick forests of manzanita and other desert shrubs, which are incredibly dense here. On your left, you will enjoy

enchanting views of the cliffs of a large butte. We particularly admire some spectacular sheer red cliffs on this face of this butte, though it features pillars and alcoves as well.

To your right you will see Mescal Mountain. Its cliffs are not nearly so impressive, but it is still very scenic. The trail undulates, following the natural curvature of the terrain—no cuts or fills here—gradually climbing to a high point at the end of Mescal Mountain. From here you will enjoy sweeping views out to the north, which are very fine. From the high point, the trail curls around the tip of Mescal Mountain and descends, crossing under the powerline, then joins the Long Canyon Trail on the flat. There is a sign at the trail junction. Just beyond the junction, to your left, the Long Canyon Trail enters the Red Rock Secret Mountain Wilderness.

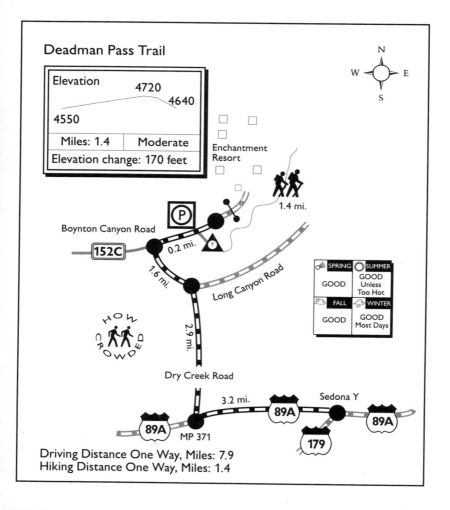

Deadman Pass Trail

Elevation
4720
4640
4550

| Miles: 1.4 | Moderate |
| Elevation change: 170 feet | |

Enchantment Resort

1.4 mi.

Boynton Canyon Road

152C

0.2 mi.

1.6 mi.

Long Canyon Road

2.9 mi.

Dry Creek Road

HOW CROWDED

SPRING	SUMMER
GOOD	GOOD Unless Too Hot
FALL	WINTER
GOOD	GOOD Most Days

3.2 mi.

Sedona Y

89A   89A   89A

179

MP 371

Driving Distance One Way, Miles: 7.9
Hiking Distance One Way, Miles: 1.4

Devil's Bridge Trail #120

General Information
Location Map D4
Loy Butte and Wilson Mt. USGS Maps
Coconino Forest Service Map

Driving Distance One Way: 6.5 miles *10.4 km* (Time 30 minutes)
Access Road: All cars, Last 1.3 miles *2.1 km* bumpy dirt road
Hiking Distance One Way: 1.0 miles *1.6 km* (Time 30 minutes)
How Strenuous: Moderate
Features: Views, Arch

NUTSHELL: Located 6.5 miles *10.4 km* northwest of Sedona, this is a short hike to a fascinating arch.

DIRECTIONS:
From the Sedona Y Go:
  Southwest on Highway 89A (toward Cottonwood) for a distance of 3.2 miles *5.1 km* (MP 371) to the Dry Creek Road. Turn right onto Dry Creek Road and follow it to the 5.2 mile *8.3 km* point, where FR 152 branches off to the right. The road is paved to this point. FR 152 is a dirt road that has been improved since the first edition of this book. Ordinary passenger cars can make it, though it can be rough. At 6.5 miles *10.4 km* you will turn right on the signed dirt road to the parking lot.

TRAILHEAD: This is a marked and maintained trail. There is a rusty sign where you park reading "Devil's Bridge #120."

DESCRIPTION: You will walk up an old road for about 0.4 miles *0.7 km*, to a point where the hiking path forks off to your right. You will see that it leads up toward a red ledge on the east face of Capitol Butte. The path is steep but fairly short, being about 0.4 miles *0.7 km* from the fork.
  When you reach a point about halfway up the trail from the fork you will begin to see the arch off to your left in the red ledge. It is hidden from your sight until you get to this point.
  The path itself is very interesting as it begins to climb up the cliff. The Forest Service has used some natural stairsteps made by erosion and has added to these by cementing in some sandstone slabs to form stair steps.
  At the top you have great views into colorful backcountry. You come out behind the arch. You can follow the trail to the end of the arch and loop around to stand on the arch if you are daring. The trail places you in a spot where you are above the arch looking down on it.

To get under the arch, go back down to the bottom of the trail and look for cairns about 100 yards from the bottom, marking a small trail going off to your right. The trail goes down into a wash. You walk up the wash and find yourself under the arch.

This is a fine hike but attracts so many visitors that the large numbers may lessen the quality of your experience if you like solitude. Devil's Bridge is generally regarded as the largest of the natural arches around Sedona, and is an impressive sight.

After you have reached the top and walk down to the arch, you will see a side trail to your right which is worth a look for the adventurous.

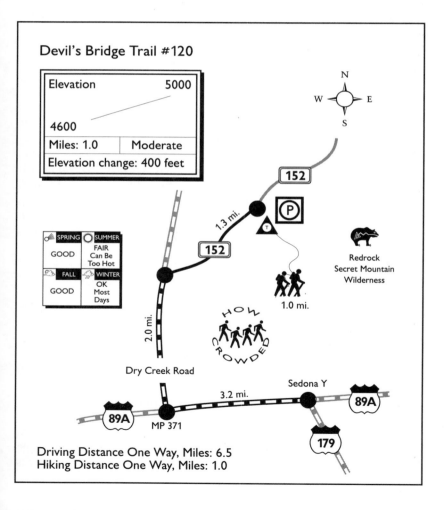

Devil's Bridge Trail #120

Elevation	5000
4600	
Miles: 1.0	Moderate
Elevation change: 400 feet	

N
W — E
S

152

P

1.3 mi.

152

Redrock
Secret Mountain
Wilderness

SPRING	SUMMER
GOOD	FAIR Can Be Too Hot
FALL	WINTER
GOOD	OK Most Days

1.0 mi.

HOW CROWDED

2.0 mi.

Dry Creek Road

Sedona Y

3.2 mi.

89A

89A

MP 371

179

Driving Distance One Way, Miles: 6.5
Hiking Distance One Way, Miles: 1.0

Doe Mountain Trail #60

General Information
Location Map D3
Wilson Mt. USGS Map
Coconino Forest Service Map

Driving Distance One Way: 8.9 miles *14.3 km* (Time 20 minutes)
Access Road: All cars, Last 1.2 miles *1.9 km* good dirt road
Hiking Distance One Way: 1.8 miles *2.9 km* (Time 1 hour)
How Strenuous: Moderate
Features: Views

NUTSHELL: This small mesa, 8.9 miles *14.3 km* west of uptown Sedona, is fairly easy to climb. Its weathered cliffs are a delight to explore and it provides great views. **A personal favorite**

DIRECTIONS:
From the Sedona Y Go:
Southwest on Highway 89A (toward Cottonwood) for 3.2 miles *5.1 km* (MP 371) to Dry Creek Road. Go right on Dry Creek Road to the 6.1 mile *9.8 km* point, where Dry Creek Road joins the Long Canyon Road, both paved. Turn left here, on FR 152C, and go to the 7.7 mile *12.3 km point*, where it joins the Boynton Canyon Road. Turn left here on the Boynton Pass Road, FR 152C. The paving soon ends, to be replaced by a good dirt road. Stop at the 8.9 mile *14.3 km* point, just before a cattle guard. The parking area is on the right. This is also the parking place for the **Bear Mountain** hike.

TRAILHEAD: You will see a rusty sign across the road reading "Doe Mountain #60."

DESCRIPTION: Doe Mountain is a small mesa standing by itself. It is one of the most southerly redrock formations in the west-of-Sedona area. Only the **Cockscomb** is farther south. The trail zigzags to the top of the mesa, climbing steadily. After the second edition of this book was published, the trail was improved. It is now a bit longer, but it climbs up on more gradual grades.
The top of Doe Mountain is not bare rock as you might think when you see it from a distance. Soil has formed through weathering and in some places is deep enough to support low growing junipers and shrubs. The best part of this hike once you are on the top is to walk around the rim, the edge of which is mostly bare redrock. This bareness means that there are no trees

to obstruct your views; so Doe Mountain is a terrific viewpoint and it is situated so that there are interesting things to look at. The views of the town of Sedona are particularly good from here.

In addition to the views of far off objects, you will see some wonderful things on Doe Mountain itself, where erosion has worked the cliff faces into some really fantastic rock sculptures. The Sedona Westerners report that there are Indian ruins on the top of the mesa but in our trips we have never seen any.

For many years there was a tree farm at the base of Doe Mountain, but that has closed and the land as we write this is being prepared for a large subdivision.

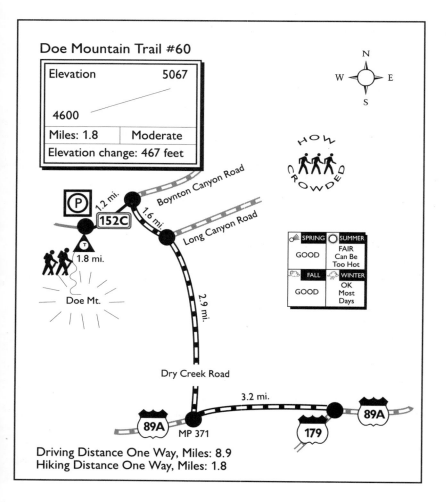

Driving Distance One Way, Miles: 8.9
Hiking Distance One Way, Miles: 1.8

Dogie Trail #116

General Information
Location Map C1
Loy Butte and Clarkdale USGS Maps
Coconino Forest Service Map

Driving Distance One Way: 20.7 miles *33 km* (Time 45 minutes)
Access Road: All cars, Last 11.1 miles *17.8 km* good dirt road
Hiking Distance One Way: 4.0 miles *6.4 km* (Time 2.5 hours)
How Strenuous: Moderate
Features: Sycamore Canyon access, Views

NUTSHELL: This hike provides access into Sycamore Canyon at Sycamore Pass, located 20.7 miles *33 km* northwest of Sedona.

DIRECTIONS:
From The Y in Sedona Go:
Southwest on Highway 89A (toward Cottonwood) a distance of 9.6 miles *15.4 km* (MP 364.5) to the Red Canyon Road. Turn right on Red Canyon Road, also known as FR 525, and follow it to the 12.4 mile *19.8 km* point where FR 525C branches to the left. Turn left on FR 525C and stay on it to the 15.6 mile *25 km* point where it meets FR 761, the Bill Gray Road. Your destination is Sycamore Pass. Go right here, staying on FR 525C to the 19.7 mile *31.5 km* point, where it meets FR 9529. Turn left here and go to the 20.7 mile *33 km* point, where the road meets FR 9528. Park near this intersection. Don't try to drive on FR 9528.

TRAILHEAD: At the intersection beyond your parking spot you will see a road sign reading, *"Sycamore Pass, Dogie Trail"* with an arrow pointing to the right. Follow the arrow and walk down the road. You will reach a fork in the road, where you should take the right hand path. From there you will walk down a jeep road to the trailhead. Distance from the parking area to the trailhead is 0.5 miles *0.8 km.*
At the trailhead you will see a sign: *"Sycamore Canyon 5 miles, Sycamore Basin Trail 5.5 miles, Road 525C 0.5 miles, Dogie Trail #116."*

DESCRIPTION: From the beginning, this trail slopes gradually toward Sycamore Canyon. You will walk down an old stock trail that is very rocky, but the grade is gentle. After hiking a few hundred yards, the landscape will open up to some great views ahead of you, where you will see redrock spires and buttes that are just as impressive as those nearer Sedona.
There are two cattle tanks on this trail. To get to the first one, you must

detour to your left. The path goes right around the rim of the second one.

We recommend that you stop at about the 3.0 mile *4.8 km* or 4.0 mile *6.4 km* point rather than going all the way into Sycamore Canyon, for it is a very strenuous hike to go to the bottom. By staying on top you will have a fine hike and enjoy tremendous views. Remember that the return leg of this hike is all uphill.

Sycamore Canyon is a huge wild place. Even experienced hikers should not attempt a multi-day trip through it unless they are thoroughly prepared and know what they are doing. The brief sight of the canyon you get on a day hike like this is misleading and understates the rigors of the place. It is very beautiful and deserves to be better known and visited, as we hope to encourage in this book, but please do not overextend yourself.

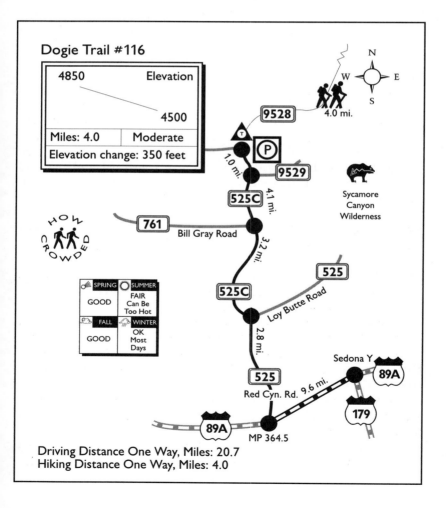

Dry Creek Trail #52

General Information
Location Map C4
Loy Butte and Wilson Mt. USGS Maps
Coconino Forest Service Map

Driving Distance One Way: 9.6 miles *15.4 km* (Time 45 minutes)
Access Road: Most cars, Last 4.4 miles *7.0 km* bumpy unpaved road
Hiking Distance One Way: 2.0 miles *3.2 km* (Time 1 hour)
How Strenuous: Moderate
Features: Scenic canyon

NUTSHELL: Located 9.6 miles *15.4 km* north of Sedona, this is a wilderness hike that follows the course of Dry Creek to its head at the base of the Mogollon Rim.

DIRECTIONS:
From The Y in Sedona Go:
   Southwest on Highway 89A (toward Cottonwood) for 3.2 miles *5.1 km* (MP 371) to Dry Creek Road. Turn right on Dry Creek Road and proceed to the 5.2 mile *8.3 km* point. Turn right on FR 152, the Vultee Arch Road, and follow it to its end at the 9.6 mile *15.4 km* point. Here there is a parking loop, with the **Vultee Arch** Trailhead at the tip. Curve around and head back, and you will see the parking for the **Bear Sign** and Dry Creek trails to your right, just a few yards beyond the Vultee Arch parking spot.

TRAILHEAD: The parking area is in a grove of trees. Walk west across a little gully. There you will see a rusty sign marked "Dry Creek #52."

DESCRIPTION: Since the first edition of this book came out, FR 152 has been improved and can now be driven by any car with reasonable clearance if you keep a lookout for rocks and ruts.
   From the parking place, walk across a little arroyo and around the toe of a hill for about 0.10 miles *0.16 km* where you will encounter Dry Creek. Where you enter it, the canyon cut by Dry Creek is rather shallow and wide. The trail follows up the creek (which usually is *dry*, living up to its name) in a northerly direction.
   If there is any appreciable amount of water in the creek, you might want to postpone this hike for another day when the creek is dry because the trail crosses the creekbed at least a dozen times.
   As you walk, the trail gains elevation but this is a gradual climb and you are barely conscious of it. The walking is pretty easy and the trail is good.

At 0.63 miles *1.0 km* you reach a point where the creek forks at a reef. The left hand channel is the **Bear Sign Trail** and the right fork is the Dry Creek Trail. There is a rusty sign in the left channel marked "Bear Sign #59." From this point the canyon deepens and you are treated to the sight of giant redrock buttes on both sides of the creek. As you proceed you will notice a change in the vegetation as the increase in elevation causes changes in the life zones.

The trail ends where it intersects a channel running east and west. We are informed that this channel can be hiked but it would be very steep and rugged, for advanced hikers only. To the east, it appears to go all the way to the top of the rim to East Pocket, where the East Pocket fire lookout tower is located.

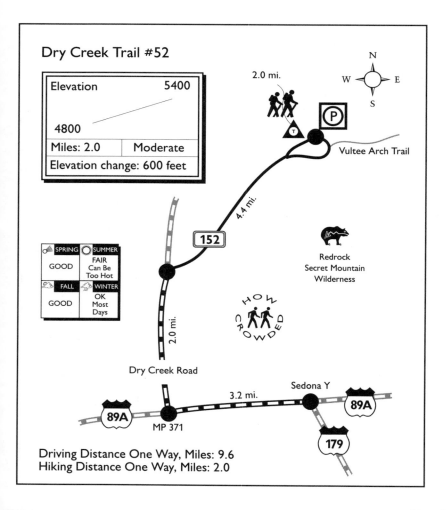

Dry Creek Trail #52

Elevation 5400
4800
Miles: 2.0 | Moderate
Elevation change: 600 feet

2.0 mi.

Vultee Arch Trail

4.4 mi.

152

Redrock Secret Mountain Wilderness

SPRING | SUMMER
GOOD | FAIR Can Be Too Hot
FALL | WINTER
GOOD | OK Most Days

HOW CROWDED

2.0 mi.

Dry Creek Road

Sedona Y

3.2 mi.

89A

89A

MP 371

179

Driving Distance One Way, Miles: 9.6
Hiking Distance One Way, Miles: 2.0

Fay Canyon Trail #53

General Information
Location Map C3
Wilson Mt. USGS Map
Coconino Forest Service Map

Driving Distance One Way: 8.2 miles *13.1 km* (Time 20 minutes)
Access Road: All cars, Last half mile good dirt road
Hiking Distance One Way: 1.2 miles *1.9 km* (Time 30 minutes)
How Strenuous: Moderate
Features: Views, Arch, Indian ruins

NUTSHELL: This is an easy hike 8.2 miles *13.1 km* northwest of uptown Sedona, featuring a lovely canyon on the side of Bear Mountain with a natural arch and Indian ruins. **A personal favorite.**

DIRECTIONS:
From the Sedona Y Go:
    Southwest on Highway 89A (toward Cottonwood) for a distance of 3.2 miles *5.1 km* (MP 371) to Dry Creek Road. Turn right onto Dry Creek Road and follow it to the 6.1 mile *9.8 km* point, where it intersects the Long Canyon Road, where you turn left on FR 152C. Stay on FR 152C to the 7.7 mile *12.3 km* point, where it intersects the Boynton Canyon Road. Here you will turn left onto the Boynton Pass Road. It is paved for a short distance and then becomes unpaved. At the 8.2 mile *13.1 km* point you will reach the driveway to the parking area, which is off to your right. Pull in and park there.

TRAILHEAD: You will see a rusty sign at the gate: "Fay Canyon #53."

DESCRIPTION: The trail is gentle and wide. You will find a forest of oaks, many of them quite sizable. Though the canyon is short, about one mile long, it is broad and very scenic. There are impressive red cliffs on both sides with buff colored cliffs rimming the back of the canyon.
    At just over 0.5 miles *0.8 km*, a side trail branches off to the right (E) and makes a sharp climb up the east side of the canyon to Fay Arch. This trail is usually marked with cairns. The path to the arch is nothing like the main trail. It seems to have just been scratched out of the side of the canyon haphazardly. It is steep and there are places where the footing is tricky. Aunt Maude would have no trouble with the main trail along the canyon floor but the climb to the arch would be too much for her.
    Canyon wrens, tiny birds with a glorious call, live in this cliff face, and if you are lucky you may hear one.

There is a narrow slot between the arch and the wall from which it has broken away. You can stand underneath the gap and look up through it for an interesting view. The clamber up the side of the canyon would be worthwhile for the views even if there were no arch. Spectacular.

After visiting the arch, return to the main trail and continue up the canyon. Near its end it forks around a redrock fin that sticks out like the prow of a ship. You can quit right where you are for a 1.2 mile *1.9 km* hike or you can climb up on the fin. You can go in either direction around the fin, but we recommend the left hand fork. It will take you up and out on a slick-rock shelf where you will find a few shallow caves in an undercut ledge.

We like this trail and find that we can hike it even when the roads are muddy and the weather is poor, because it is easy to reach, on good roads, and the canyon shelters the trail. A fine little hike.

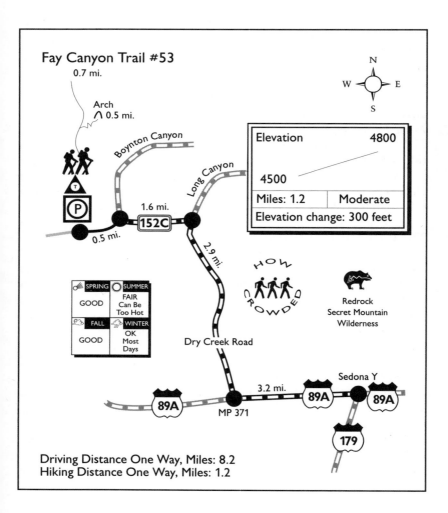

Fay Canyon Trail #53

Elevation	4800
4500	
Miles: 1.2	Moderate
Elevation change: 300 feet	

Redrock Secret Mountain Wilderness

SPRING	SUMMER
GOOD	FAIR Can Be Too Hot
FALL	WINTER
GOOD	OK Most Days

HOW CROWDED

Dry Creek Road

Driving Distance One Way, Miles: 8.2
Hiking Distance One Way, Miles: 1.2

Girdner Trail

General Information
Location Map E3
Sedona USGS Map
Coconino Forest Service Map

Driving Distance One Way: 4.4 miles *7.0 km* (Time 10 minutes)
Access Road: All cars, All paved
Hiking Distance One Way: 5.0 miles 8.*0 km* (Time 2.5 hours)
How Strenuous: Hard
Features: Views, A means of enjoying Dry Creek's glorious hidden canyon

NUTSHELL: This trail, new to the system in 1999, takes off from the Sedona Cultural Park and winds around through an area of backcountry hills, dipping into the canyon of Dry Creek, a hidden oasis surrounded by development, and following the channel of the creek for some distance before swinging away to end at a point on Dry Creek Road.

DIRECTIONS:
From the Sedona Y Go:
    Southwest on Highway 89 (toward Cottonwood) for 4.1 miles *6.6 km* (MP 369.9); then turn right onto Cultural Park Place. As you drive in, there is a series of parking lots to your right. Go to the farthest lot, one of the Upper Parking East group, where you see a picnic table under a big roof with massive pillars. There is a 3-panel trailhead sign here. Pull in and park.

TRAILHEAD: The trail starts at the sign.

DESCRIPTION: This trail takes is named for the Girdner family, early day ranchers in the area. You will notice lots of old cans, broken glass, etc. on the first few yards of this hike since the trail goes through the old Sedona Dump. The trail heads off through a typical juniper forest, with homes and other construction visible. Soon, however, you are out of sight of manmade things and are able to enjoy a nice "out in the country" feeling.
    You may be surprised, as we were, to find a hidden system of hills and valleys carved by unnamed tributaries of Dry Creek in the area that you hike, even though you are very close to developed areas full of subdivisions and shopping centers. Portions of the trail are high enough so that you have nice views in the first part.
    The trail at about the 1.0 mile *1.6 km* point begins to work its way down to Dry Creek and soon joins an old jeep road. You will cross a feeder creekbed first and soon reach Dry Creek at the 1.25 mile *2.0 km* point. Dry

Creek will be your companion for the next 2.0 miles *3.2 km*. The trail crosses the creek a dozen times, so don't try this when water is high.

Dry Creek's canyon is very pretty and we enjoy this hike along its banks immensely. The Forest Service has done a nice job building the trail so that it follows the terrain in an intelligent manner. At 2.6 miles *4.2 km* you will pass through a gate with supports high enough to allow a mounted horse rider to ride through. At 3.0 miles *4.8 km* The **Rupp Trail** comes in from your left on an old jeep road. The Girdner Trail becomes a jeep road. You cross the creek again and then begin to swing away from it as the old road lifts out of the canyon, allowing you to see out again. The trail goes to a good high viewpoint and then descends.

At 3.7 miles *5.9 km* the **Arizona Cypress** Trail branches to the left. At 3.8 miles *6.1 km* the **Two Fences** trail branches to the right. The trail ends at the Dry Creek Road just opposite the Vultee Arch junction.

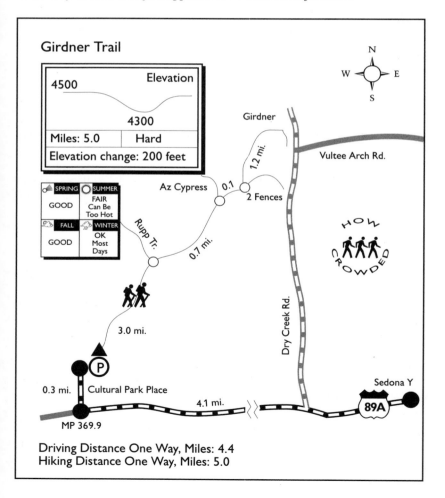

Goosenecks

General Information
Location Map F3
Sedona USGS Map
Coconino Forest Service Map

Driving Distance One Way: 7.3 miles *11.7 km* (Time 15 minutes)
Access Road: All cars, All paved
Hiking Distance One Way: 1.8 miles *2.9 km* (Time 1.0 hours)
How Strenuous: Moderate
Features: Views, Picnic site on the banks of Oak Creek, Easy to reach

NUTSHELL: This hike follows a horse trail from the Lower Red Rock Loop Road to the Goosenecks of Oak Creek through pretty back country.

DIRECTIONS:
From the Sedona Y Go:
   Southwest on Highway 89 (toward Cottonwood) for a distance of 5.5 miles *8.8 km* (MP 368.6) to the Lower Red Rock Loop Road. Turn left on the Lower Red Rock Loop Road and follow it to the 7.3 miles *11.7 km* point, where you will see a gravel parking apron to your right big enough for about four cars.

TRAILHEAD: Walk back the way you came for about 170 paces, where you will see a trail to your left (W). It is marked with a lath bearing a horse symbol, as this is primarily a horse trail.

DESCRIPTION: This is a horse trail and you may encounter some riders coming over from the stables to the west. If you look at the lath marking the trail you will see that the letter S has been added to it. You will first follow Trail S.
   Hike the horse trail up and down some low red hills until at 0.6 miles *1.0 km*, you come to a red dirt road, FR 9845. Keep walking straight ahead, where you will see horse Trail S take up again after crossing the road. At this point you will walk for a time behind a subdivision, just outside the fence that encloses it. At the 1.0 mile *1.6 km* point you will reach a trail junction. Go left here (S), turning away from the fence. You will go over a rise and soon will be out of sight of the works of man.
   From now on you will be in a terrain that is scenic with hills and cliffs; so there is a bit of going up and down, but nothing strenuous. At the 1.3 mile *2.1 km* point you will meet a jeep road. In a few steps the trail veers away from the road only to join it again a short distance beyond, then move away

from it and join it again. Hike on the horse trail wherever you meet the road—don't follow the road. The horse trail switches numbers in this area and becomes Trail A.

At the 1.5 mile *2.4 km* point you will come to a viewpoint where you can see down into Oak Creek, where the stream makes a couple of recurving goosenecks against a high wall of red cliffs. The trail forks here, with one branch going down to the creek and the other going up over a hill. Take the left fork, going downhill.

You will now encounter the most strenuous part of this trail, which drops 250 feet in 0.3 miles *0.5 km*, but it is well worth the effort. When you reach the bottom you will find that you have come to a secluded bend in the river where the creek forms a long pool against red cliffs. This is a very pretty, quiet spot, perfect for a picnic.

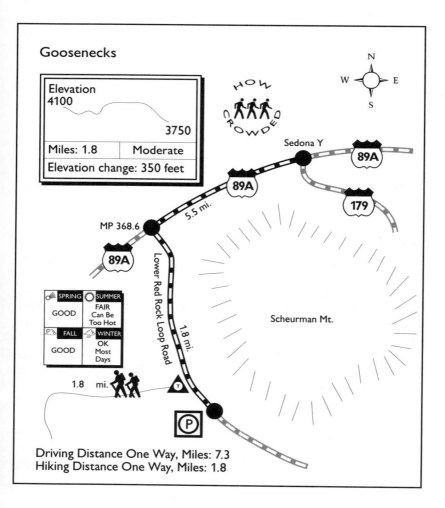

Harding Spring Trail #51

General Information
Location Map B5
Mountainaire and Munds Park USGS Maps
Coconino Forest Service Map

Driving Distance One Way: 11.4 miles *18.2 km* (Time 20 minutes)
Access Road: All cars, All paved
Hiking Distance One Way: 0.8 miles *1.3 km* (Time 45 minutes)
How Strenuous: Hard
Features: Views

NUTSHELL: This is a marked and posted trail located just across Highway 89A from the Cave Spring Campground 11.4 miles *18.2 km* north of Sedona. It climbs the east wall of Oak Creek Canyon.

DIRECTIONS:
From the Sedona Y Go:
North on Highway 89A (toward Flagstaff) for a distance of 11.4 miles *18.2 km* (MP 385.6) to the entrance to the Cave Spring Campground, which is on your left (west). Pull in to the Cave Spring driveway and take an immediate right into a small parking area.

TRAILHEAD: On the east side of Highway 89A just across from the Cave Spring Campground entrance. It is marked by a rusty sign reading, "Harding Spring Trail #51."

DESCRIPTION: Since you will be so near the Cave Spring Campground after you park, you might as well walk into the campground and take a look at Cave Spring, as it is an interesting place.

Like the other trails climbing the east wall of upper Oak Creek Canyon, the Harding Spring trail goes virtually straight up with little finesse. You start in a pine and spruce forest, reach a more open area as you climb above tree line, then get into a region of pine forest again at the top.

The trail zigzags in such a way that it isn't a killer, like the **Purtymun Trail** or Thompson's Ladder. It is more like the **Cookstove Trail** or the **Thomas Point Trail.**

The trail was built in the 1890s to provide access to the canyon rim by O. P. Harding, who lived in the Cave Spring area, so that he could get to the top and go to Flagstaff. Harding came to Flagstaff in 1884 and worked as a contractor, building some of the historic buildings in downtown. He was very secretive about his past and would never talk about it. In those days

there were many people who had come West for reasons of which they were not proud, and it was considered impolite to pry. In 1893 Harding moved to an Oak Creek homestead and took up fruit ranching, planting some 600 trees on the flat shelf of land around today's Troutdale.

Harding was quite a hiker himself, and in 1910—for a lark—walked from Cave Spring to Flagstaff at the age of 76. Only after he died in June 1915 did Harding's family reveal his secret: he had been a distinguished Brigadier General in the Union Army during the Civil War, leading Pennsylvania troops in several battles. He was so horrified by his wartime experience that he came to Arizona to get as far away as possible from the battlefields and the reminders of his past.

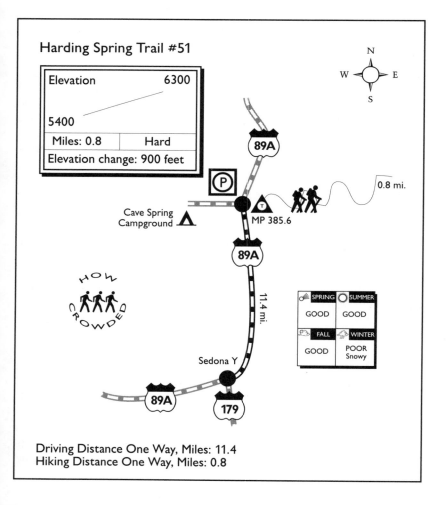

Driving Distance One Way, Miles: 11.4
Hiking Distance One Way, Miles: 0.8

Herkenham Trail

General Information
Location Map E4
Sedona USGS Map
Coconino Forest Service Map

Driving Distance One Way: 6.2 miles *9.9 km* (Time 20 minutes)
Access Road: All cars, All paved
Hiking Distance One Way: 2.0 miles *3.2 km* (Time 1 hour)
How Strenuous: Moderate
Features: Easy to reach, Views

NUTSHELL: This trail runs from the Chavez Ranch Road through a little pocket of Forest Service land up to the Sedona Red Rock High School.

DIRECTIONS:
From the Sedona Y Go:
Southwest on Highway 89A (toward Cottonwood) a distance of 4.2 miles *6.8 km* (MP 368.9) to the Upper Red Rock Loop Road. Turn left and follow the Upper Red Rock Loop Road to the 6.0 mile *9.6 km* point, where you turn left, heading toward Crescent Moon Ranch Park on a paved road. At the 6.2 mile *9.9 km* point you will see a parking apron and 2-panel trailhead sign to your left. Park there.

TRAILHEAD: At the trail sign.

DESCRIPTION: You begin this hike by walking along an old road that has been converted into the **Old Post Trail**. At the 0.66 mile *1.1 k*m point you reach a V-fork where the **Herkenham Trail** branches off to the left. Take the left fork.

This trail has been designed as a Class 2 trail, with low to moderate use and limited signage. If you only have time to hike a few trails in Sedona, this one would not be on your list. If you have hiked the major trails and are the kind of hiker (as we are) who wants to do all the trails, then this one does have something to offer.

After the trail leaves the old jeep road it becomes strictly a footpath, with most of its length freshly located. It has no history. You are heading toward Schuerman Mountain, which you can see from many points on the trail, following through country dotted with low-growing pinons and junipers.

At 0.8 miles *1.3 km* the trail veers to the right. It doesn't look correct, as it is fainter than the trail that you leave, but by the time this book appears there should be markers to guide you. We hiked this while it was still being

developed and had to follow orange ribbons and paint splotches. The real trail does not go into a ravine. If you go into a ravine, backtrack and look again. The trail works its way toward the Upper Red Rock Loop Road, and from the 1.5 mile *2.4 km* point is very near it. You can hear cars going by overhead to your left, but you can't see them until you are quite near the end of the trail. Eventually it comes to a point where it meets the road just across from the high school, at Scorpion Drive, at 2.0 miles *3.2 km*.

The trail is named for long-time trail supporter Norm Herkenham.

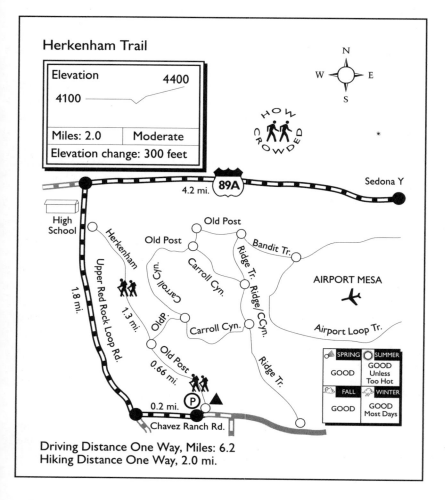

Herkenham Trail

Elevation
4400
4100

Miles: 2.0 | Moderate
Elevation change: 300 feet

N
W · E
S

HOW CROWDED

89A
4.2 mi.
Sedona Y

High School

Upper Red Rock Loop Rd.
Herkenham
Old Post
Old Post
Carroll Cyn.
Carroll Cyn.
Ridge Tr.
Bandit Tr.
Ridge/ CCyn.
AIRPORT MESA
Airport Loop Tr.

1.8 mi.
1.3 mi.
Old P.
Carroll Cyn.
Old Post
0.66 mi.
Ridge Tr.

0.2 mi.
P
Chavez Ranch Rd.

	SPRING	SUMMER
	GOOD	GOOD Unless Too Hot
	FALL	WINTER
	GOOD	GOOD Most Days

Driving Distance One Way, Miles: 6.2
Hiking Distance One Way, 2.0 mi.

Hidden Cabin

General Information
Location Map F3
Sedona USGS Map
Coconino Forest Service Map

Driving Distance One Way: 7.3 miles *11.7 km* (Time 15 minutes)
Access Road: All cars, All paved
Hiking Distance One Way: 2.5 miles *4.0 km* (Time 1.5 hours)
How Strenuous: Moderate
Features: Views, Picnic site on the banks of Oak Creek, Cabin ruins

NUTSHELL: This hike follows a horse trail from the Lower Red Rock Loop Road to the hidden ruins of a cabin beside the banks of Oak Creek.

DIRECTIONS:
From the Sedona Y Go:
    Southwest on Highway 89 (toward Cottonwood) for a distance of 5.5 miles *8.8 km* (MP 368.6) to the Lower Red Rock Loop Road. Turn left on the Lower Red Rock Loop Road and follow it to the 7.3 miles *11.7 km* point, where you will see a gravel parking apron to your right.

TRAILHEAD: Walk back the way you came for about 170 paces, where you will see a trail to your left (W). It is marked with a horse symbol.

DESCRIPTION: You will follow a series of horse trails on this hike and you may encounter some riders coming over from the stables to the west. Laths mark the trails and you will see trails S and A on this adventure. You will first follow Trail S.
    Hike the horse trail up and down some low red hills until at 0.6 miles *1.0 km*, you come to a red dirt road, FR 9845. Keep walking straight ahead, where you will see horse Trail S take up again after crossing the road. At this point you will walk for a time behind a subdivision, just outside the fence that encloses it. At the 1.0 mile *1.6 km* point you will reach a trail junction. Go left here (S), turning away from the fence. You will go over a rise and soon will be out of sight of the works of man.
    From now on you will be in a terrain that is scenic with hills and cliffs; so there is a bit of going up and down, but nothing strenuous. At the 1.3 mile *2.1 km* point you will meet a jeep road. In a few steps the trail veers away from the road only to join it again a short distance beyond, then move away from it and join it again. Hike on the horse trail wherever you meet the road—don't follow the road: go on horse Trail A.

At the 1.5 mile *2.4 km* point you will come to a viewpoint where you can see down into Oak Creek, where the stream makes a couple of recurving goosenecks against a high wall of red cliffs. The trail forks here, with the **Gooseneck Trail** going down to the creek. You want to take the other fork, the one going straight up over a hill.

The trail climbs steeply for a while, to the high point, then follows hilltops and ridges until it turns down toward the creek. You will come to a "major" road, where you turn left (E) on the road itself. In a few yards Horse Trail A forks, going downhill. Stay on the horse trail, going left from the road. Soon you will see how the trail meets the road again and goes downhill to Oak Creek, following an old ranch road. When you come to a gate in the barbed wire fence, go on through. At the end of the road you will find the ruins of the cabin. The trail makes a short turn to the left to the water. The road runs on another 0.2 miles *0.3 km*, then ends.

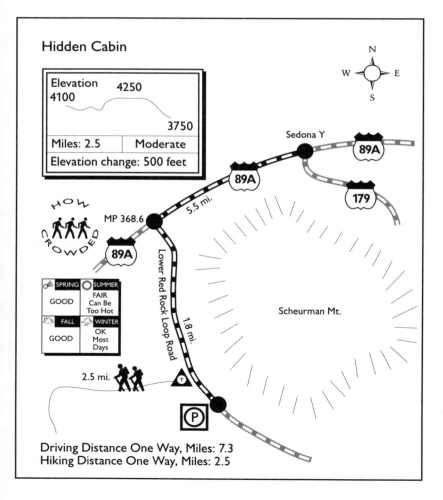

Hidden Cabin

Elevation
4100
4250
3750

| Miles: 2.5 | Moderate |

Elevation change: 500 feet

Sedona Y

89A

89A

179

MP 368.6

89A

5.5 mi.

Lower Red Rock Loop Road

1.8 mi.

HOW CROWDED

SPRING	SUMMER
GOOD	FAIR Can Be Too Hot
FALL	WINTER
GOOD	OK Most Days

Scheurman Mt.

2.5 mi.

Driving Distance One Way, Miles: 7.3
Hiking Distance One Way, Miles: 2.5

Honanki

General Information
Location Map C1
Loy Butte and Page Springs USGS Maps
Coconino Forest Service Map

Driving Distance One Way: 16.2 miles *25.9 km* (Time 45 minutes)
Access Road: All cars, Last 8.5 miles *13.6 km* good dirt road
Hiking Distance One Way: 0.25 miles *0.4 km* (Time 10 minutes)
How Strenuous: Easy
Features: Best Indian ruins in the Sedona area

NUTSHELL: Located 16.2 miles *25.9 km* northwest of Sedona, this is a short hike to excellent Indian ruins.

DIRECTIONS:
From The Y in Sedona Go:
   Southwest on Highway 89A (toward Cottonwood) a distance of 3.2 miles *5.1 km,* to the Dry Creek Road. Turn right on the Dry Creek Road and drive to the stop sign at 6.1 miles *9.8 km.* Turn left on the paved road and drive to the 7.7 mile *12.3 km* point, where the road to Enchantment Resort forks right. Go left here, on the unpaved road FR 152C, to Boynton Pass. You will come to a road junction at 11.7 miles *18.7 km,* where you turn right on FR 525. Near the end of this road you will come to the Hancock Ranch. The road goes through it and soon reaches the parking area for Loy Butte at the 16.2 mile point *25.9 km.*

TRAILHEAD: Marked with signs. There is an entrance booth, and beyond it, the trail is clearly visible.

DESCRIPTION: Don't be alarmed by the Hancock Ranch signs as you drive into the region of the ruins. An easement for the road runs through the ranch and you are welcome to drive through so long as you stay on the road and abide by the rules: no shooting, no hunting, no wandering around on the private property, etc.
   Note: since 1997, an admission fee has been charged to visit this site. The ruins—the official name for which is the Honanki Ruins—are located in a large cave in the cliff face. Before 1997 there was no caretaker for them and over the years careless and malicious visitors have caused some damage. In recent years the Forest Service has done some work to stabilize the ruins, and they are well preserved and definitely worth a visit. You will see names carved and painted on the walls, some of them fairly old. The

Smithsonian Institution did a survey of Indian ruins in northern Arizona many years ago, headed by Dr. Jesse Walter Fewkes. He spent some time at this ruin and thought that it was a major find. In spite of his glowing reports, the government did little about the ruins except to preserve public access to them. They were little known and not very frequently visited until lately. Now they seem to be on the menus for all the jeep tours.

It is fun to explore the ruins and walk along the cliff face on both sides of the ruins. Try to imagine yourself as an occupant of the place centuries ago when the tribe of Indians lived there and picture the life you would have led. There is a small streambed running along the cliff bottom but it seldom carries water. Maybe in the days when these ruins were inhabited, water ran in the stream year around.

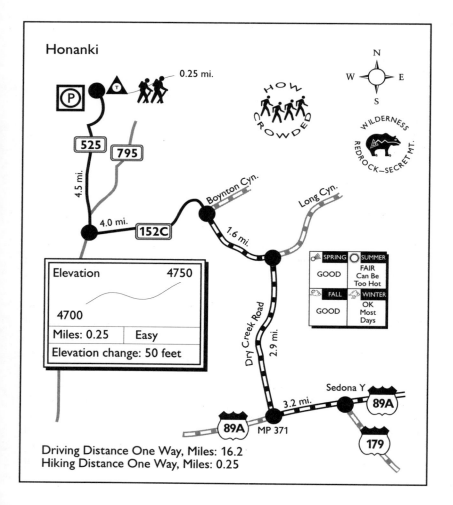

Honanki

0.25 mi.

HOW CROWDED

WILDERNESS
REDROCK–SECRET MT.

525   795

4.5 mi.

4.0 mi.   152C

Boynton Cyn.

Long Cyn.

1.6 mi.

Elevation	4750
4700	
Miles: 0.25	Easy
Elevation change: 50 feet	

☀ SPRING	☀ SUMMER
GOOD	FAIR Can Be Too Hot
☁ FALL	❄ WINTER
GOOD	OK Most Days

Dry Creek Road

2.9 mi.

Sedona Y

3.2 mi.   89A

89A   MP 371

179

Driving Distance One Way, Miles: 16.2
Hiking Distance One Way, Miles: 0.25

Hot Loop Trail #94

General Information
Location Map F5
Munds Mountain USGS Map
Coconino Forest Service Map

Driving Distance One Way: 9.55 miles *15.3 km* (Time 15 minutes)
Access Road: All cars, Last 0.25 miles *0.4 km* good dirt road
Hiking Distance One Way: 3.0 miles *4.8 km* (Time 2 hours)
How Strenuous: Hard
Features: Views

NUTSHELL: This trail starts at a corral on the Jack's Canyon Road, skirts a subdivision, climbs over a saddle, and rises to the top of Wild Horse Mesa.

DIRECTIONS:
From the Sedona Y Go:
    South on Highway 179 (toward Phoenix) for a distance of 7.2 miles *11.5 km* (MP 306.2) to Jack's Canyon Road (stoplight). Turn left (E) onto Jack's Canyon Road and follow it to the 9.3 miles *14.9 km* point, where there is a road to your right going to a corral. Go through the gate and drive an additional 0.25 miles *0.4 km* and park by the trailhead sign.

TRAILHEAD: Rusty sign at the end of the access road.

DESCRIPTION: For the first 0.6 miles *1.0 km*, the trail moves around a subdivision. Do not take any of the branch trails to your right, as they lead to private corrals. Keep moving uphill, toward the mountain.
    As the trail passes the last house, it begins to rise significantly. You can see a low saddle on the ridge ahead of you, your first target. Look behind you as you climb, for good views.
    You will reach the top of the saddle in about 1.1 miles *1.8 km*. From this vantage point you will have excellent views to the north, into the Village of Oak Creek area and its surroundings. A particularly nice feature about this hike is that just over the other side of the ridge, the landscape changes entirely—going from urban to wild in just a few steps.
    The trail dips down below the ridge and moves east. You will pass through some nice redrocks, with thrilling views. The big canyon you can see here is Woods Canyon. Your trail winds down and comes to a side canyon where you cross a slickrock face. On the other side of this you will intersect a larger trail, at 1.75 miles *2.8 km*. To the right is the old (now bypassed) part of the Hot Loop Trail, coming up from the **Woods Canyon**

Trail. From this point you turn left and climb to the top of Wild Horse Mesa. The trail to the top is difficult, where it goes over loose lava stones, and is a steep climb of 700' in about 0.75 miles *1.2 km*.

When you finally struggle to the top of Wild Horse Mesa, the trail improves, with more soil and fewer rocks. At the 3.0 mile point *4.8 km* it is obvious that the rim of the mesa is to your left. Walk over to it and enjoy the view—a great vantage point from which to see Pine Valley, Jacks Canyon and Lee Mountain. For a day hike, this is a good stopping point, though the trail continues some 7.0 miles *11.2 km* to Jack's Point.

When the first homesteaders came into the Sedona area in 1876 (after the Apaches had been subdued by troops from Camp Verde) they found many wild horses. Some men made money trapping and selling these horses. Wild Horse Mesa was the location for a sizable horse herd and that is how it got its name. It is also called Horse Mesa. A Hot Loop was a branding iron.

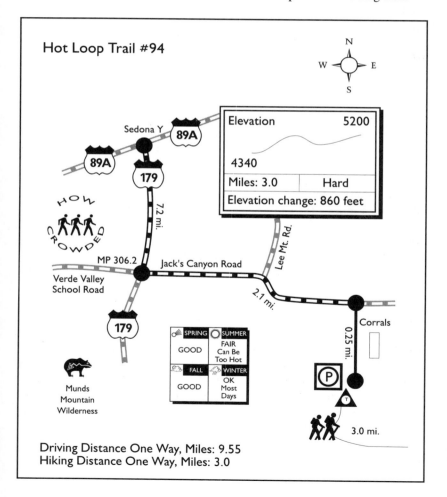

HS Canyon Trail #50

General Information
Location Map C4
Loy Butte and Wilson Mt. USGS Maps
Coconino Forest Service Map

Driving Distance One Way: 8.6 miles *13.8 km* (Time 30 minutes)
Access Road: Last 3.4 miles *5.4 km* rough dirt
Hiking Distance One Way: 2.0 miles *3.2 km* (Time 70 minutes)
How Strenuous: Moderate
Features: Views, Remote side canyon

NUTSHELL: This beautiful canyon, 8.6 miles *13.8 km* northwest of
uptown Sedona, provides a delightful hike.

DIRECTIONS:
From the Sedona Y Go:
   Southwest on Highway 89A (toward Cottonwood) for 3.2 miles *5.1 km*
(MP 371) to Dry Creek Road. Turn right on Dry Creek Road and proceed to
the 5.2 mile *8.3 km* point. Turn right on FR 152, the Vultee Arch Road, and
follow it to the 8.6 mile *13.8 km* point. At the place where you turn, you will
see a road sign pointing to the Secret Canyon trail turnoff. Make a sharp turn
to your left into the parking area.

TRAILHEAD: Hike the Secret Canyon Trail, which starts at the parking
area, for 0.6 miles *1.0 km* to reach the HS Canyon trailhead.

DESCRIPTION: The access road, FR 152, road is often rough, but it does
receive periodic maintenance. Unless there has been a recent washout, we
think most ordinary passenger cars, unless they are very low slung, can
make it.
   Once you get to the trailhead, you hike the **Secret Canyon Trail**. It goes
immediately over to Dry Creek and then proceeds along the Dry Creek
drainage. If water is running in Dry Creek you may not be able to make this
hike because the trail winds across the creekbed several times.
   At 0.6 miles *1.0 km* you will see a trail going off to the left marked with
a rusty sign reading, "H S Canyon #50." Take this trail. H S Canyon is narrow. It goes mostly to the west toward the north face of Maroon Mountain,
and you can see a huge fin of Maroon Mountain in the distance. H S Canyon
is a pretty little canyon and not very well known. We have never encoun-
tered any other hikers on this trail, but usually find them on the better known
Secret Canyon Trail.

An easy walk, the trail is mostly shaded by a pleasant forest. It climbs but the climb is so gradual that it is not exhausting. There are great views. The canyon walls here are lower than those flanking some of the other hikes in this book. As a result they seem to be on a more human scale, and consequently the canyon has a nice friendly feeling.

The trail takes you to the base of Maroon Mountain where it ends in a box canyon surrounded by thousand foot high white cliffs—truly an impressive place. The end of the trail gives a false appearance of climbing out of the canyon but that is an illusion, for it plays out against the mountain.

The old cowboys who named many of the Sedona landmarks were an earthy bunch. They called this place Horse Shit Canyon, but that was too salty for the map makers, who have sanitized it to HS Canyon.

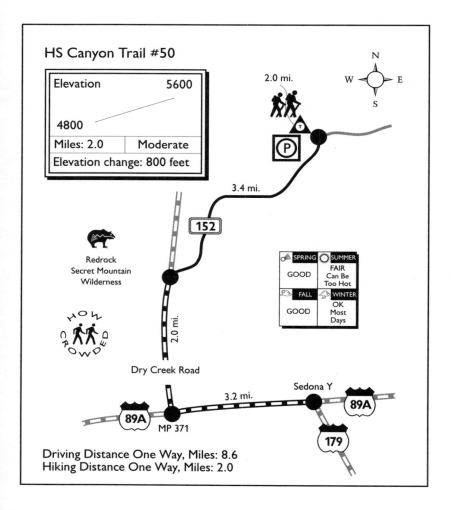

H. T. Trail

General Information
Location Map F5
Munds Mountain and Sedona USGS Maps
Coconino Forest Service Map

Driving Distance One Way: 3.6 miles *5.8 km* (Time 10 minutes)
Access Road: All cars, All paved
Hiking Distance One Way: 1.25 miles *2.0 km* (Time 45 minutes)
How Strenuous: Easy
Features: Easy to reach, Interesting passage under Highway 179.

NUTSHELL: This short trail departs from the Bell Rock Pathway, crosses under Highway 179 and heads toward Cathedral Rock, to end where it meets the **Templeton Trail**.

DIRECTIONS:
From the Sedona Y Go:
   South on Highway 179 (toward Phoenix) for a distance of 3.6 miles *5.8 km* (MP 309.8). Turn left into the trailhead parking lot, which is well posted on the highway. This is a major trailhead, with all facilities, including toilets.

TRAILHEAD: At the parking lot (at least, you begin the hike there).

DESCRIPTION: When you start hiking, within a few steps you will come to a trail sign which shows that the **Little Horse Trail** and **Bell Rock** are to your right and the **Mystic Trail** is to your left. Turn right. At 0.3 miles *0.5 km* you will reach a V-fork where the Little Horse Trail turns off to your left. Go right here.
   At 0.5 miles *0.8 km* you will walk over a wooden bridge. On the other side of the bridge, to your right, is the actual H. T. trailhead. The H. T. Trail itself is only 0.75 miles *1.2 km* long, but you have to walk 0.5 miles *0.8 km* to reach it. There is a small trail sign where the trail begins. Turn right onto the H. T. Trail, which is much narrower than the trail you have been walking.
   The trail goes down into a wash and then passes through a short tunnel under Highway 179. We are told that H. T. stands for Highway Tunnel. You will note that the older half of the tunnel is made of native stone and the newer half, built when the road was widened, is made of concrete. On the other side of the tunnel you soon move up out of the drainage and onto a low ridge, moving south parallel to Highway 179 and very close to it.

You have nice views of Cathedral Rock and the Transept from this area. Soon you will be walking on an old jeep road, moving away from the highway. Look carefully at 0.9 miles *1.4 km*, where the trail turns to the right, off of the road, at a point where the road starts downhill. The place is marked with cairns.

At 1.0 miles *1.6 km* you cross a streambed and begin to walk again on a jeep road, heading toward Cathedral Rock. The trail goes up over another ridge, and where it comes down on the other side, it ends, at 1.25 miles *2.0 km*, where it meets the Templeton Trail.

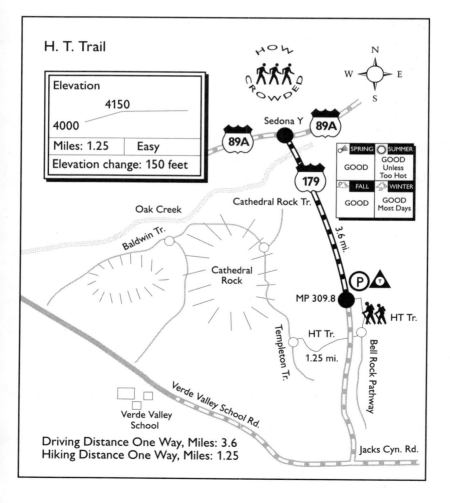

Huckaby Trail

General Information
Location Map D5
Sedona, Wilson Mtn., Munds Mtn.
& Munds Park USGS Maps
Coconino Forest Service Map

Driving Distance One Way: 1.3 miles *2.1 km* (Time 7 minutes)
Access Road: All cars, All paved
Hiking Distance One Way: 3.0 miles *4.8 km* (Time 2.0 hours)
How Strenuous: Moderate or Hard (see below)
Features: Views, Hike into inner gorge of Oak Creek Canyon, Variety

NUTSHELL: This fine trail runs between Schnebly Hill and Midgley Bridge. Both ends are elevated, while the center part runs along the banks of Oak Creek. **A personal favorite.**

DIRECTIONS:
From the Sedona Y Go:
    South on Highway 179 (toward Phoenix) for a distance of 0.3 miles *0.5 km* (MP 313.1) to the Schnebly Hill Road. It is just across the bridge past Tlaquepaque. Turn left onto the Schnebly Hill Road. Drive to the 1.3 mile *2.1 km* point, where you will see a sign for the trailhead parking to your left. Pull in and park. This is a major trailhead with signs, maps, and a toilet.

TRAILHEAD: At the parking area.

DESCRIPTION: This relatively new trail, finished in 1998, was a welcome addition to the Sedona trail system and instantly became one of our personal favorites.
    As you begin the hike you will reach a trail fork where the **Marg's Draw** and Huckaby Trails go to the left and a trail to a Vista goes to the right. Take the left fork (the Vista is not a real trail, just a path running a few yards to a lookout point). At 0.2 miles *0.3 km* the Marg's Draw Trail splits off to the left. The trail has been fairly level to here, but soon starts downhill on a steep old jeep road. You will cross Bear Wallow Canyon on a redrock shelf at 0.5 miles *0.8 km* and start up the other side. You will climb steeply to the 1.0 mile *1.6 km* point. Along the way the trail departs from the jeep road and becomes a footpath, twisting up and around rolling hills. You can't see out in this area. You will also find a nice bench at the side of the trail, a great place to rest and view the backcountry.
    Soon after you leave the bench, still climbing, you begin to have fine

views of Sedona, and at 1.1 miles *1.8 km* begin walking above bluffs over-looking the creek and the town. The high point is reached at 1.25 miles *2.0 km* and from here you can see an area burnt by a forest fire below. Holding this same contour, the trail continues, entering the burnt zone at 1.5 miles *2.4 km*. Shortly after this the trail winds downhill at a steep angle to creek level.

You will now head north along the east bank of the creek, a very nice part of the trail, until you come to a footbridge which allows you to cross the creek. Mighty Midgley Bridge looms over you here. The trail then corkscrews up under the bridge, giving you an unusual view of the structure, and you emerge at the parking lot. This is a moderate hike if you use two cars, parking one at the bridge; but parking at the bridge is very limited and often crowded, so timing is everything if you use this ploy.

Huckaby was an engineer who worked on the Midgley Bridge project and road building jobs around Sedona.

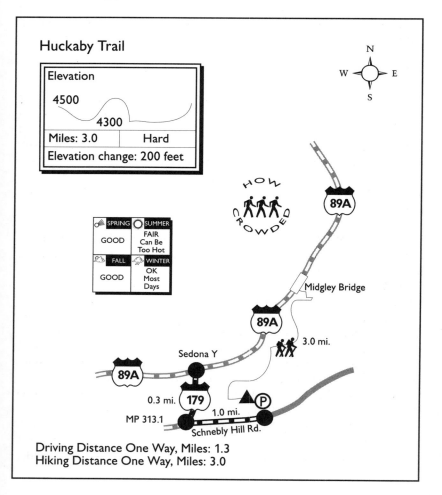

Huckaby Trail

Elevation	
4500	
4300	
Miles: 3.0	Hard
Elevation change: 200 feet	

HOW CROWDED

SPRING	SUMMER
GOOD	FAIR Can Be Too Hot
FALL	WINTER
GOOD	OK Most Days

89A

Midgley Bridge

89A

3.0 mi.

Sedona Y

89A

0.3 mi. 179

1.0 mi.

MP 313.1

Schnebly Hill Rd.

Driving Distance One Way, Miles: 1.3
Hiking Distance One Way, Miles: 3.0

Jack's Canyon Trail #55

General Information
Location Map F5
Munds Mountain and Sedona USGS Maps
Coconino Forest Service Map

Driving Distance One Way: 9.4 miles *15.0 km* (Time 15 minutes)
Access Road: All cars, Last 0.1 mile *0.16 km* good dirt road
Hiking Distance One Way: 5.0 miles *8.0 km* (Time 2.5 hours)
How Strenuous: Moderate to Hard
Features: Old cattle trail, Views

NUTSHELL: Located 9.4 miles *15.0 km* south of the Sedona Y, this old cattle trail starts in an inhabited area. It then proceeds into some remote back country.

DIRECTIONS:
From the Sedona Y Go:
   South on Highway 179 (toward Phoenix) for a distance of 7.2 miles *11.5 km* (MP 306.2) to Jack's Canyon Road (stoplight). Turn left (E) onto Jack's Canyon Road and follow it to the 9.3 miles *14.9 km* point, where you turn right onto an unpaved road into a corral area. Go through the fence and park at the 9.4 mile *15.0 km* point, next to a brown metal gate.

TRAILHEAD: You will see a pole gate and rusty sign reading, "Jack's Canyon #55."

DESCRIPTION: The first 2.5 miles *4.0 km* of the hike are not very attractive because you are always in sight of the houses. For a time you will feel as if you are walking through people's backyards.
   Jack's Canyon runs between Lee Mountain on your left (W) and the lower (Wild) Horse Mesa on your right and curves around Lee Mountain going to the north. Eventually it climbs up to the top of the Mogollon Rim at Jack's Point, where it meets the **Munds Mt. Trail**. The rim in that location is quite flat and open and makes a good grazing area for cattle. This trail provided a means of taking cattle herds up to the top of the rim in the summer and bringing the critters back to the low country in the winter.
   The trail reaches Jacks Tank at 2.5 miles *4.0 km* point. Just beyond the tank the jeep road ends and your route turns into a foot path that branches off to the right, down into the canyon floor. The canyon curves at the tank and begins a northerly course from there. (The jeep road continues about 0.5 miles *0.8 km* from Jacks Tank parallel to the canyon but up on the shoulder

of the hill. It terminates at a pasture—not worth hiking).

The hiking trail is more interesting from Jacks Tank onward, especially if there is water running in the canyon. You don't want a lot of water, just a bit, since you will be walking across the canyon bottom.

Over many centuries the intermittent flow of water has worn the soil in the channel down to redrock and in many places the water has carved interesting sculptures in the soft stone. The canyon is narrow and scenic.

We recommend stopping at the 5.0 mile *8.0 km* point, which is where the trail leaves the canyon bottom and begins its steep ascent to the rim, which requires a climb of over 1200 feet in 2.0 miles *3.2 km*. The trail tops out on Munds Ridge, near the Munds Mt. Trailhead.

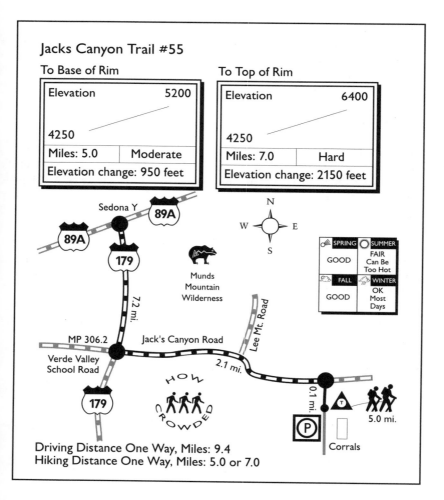

Jacks Canyon Trail #55

To Base of Rim

Elevation	5200
4250	
Miles: 5.0	Moderate
Elevation change: 950 feet	

To Top of Rim

Elevation	6400
4250	
Miles: 7.0	Hard
Elevation change: 2150 feet	

Sedona Y — 89A

89A — 179

Munds Mountain Wilderness

N
W — E
S

SPRING	SUMMER
GOOD	FAIR Can Be Too Hot
FALL	WINTER
GOOD	OK Most Days

MP 306.2 — Jack's Canyon Road

Verde Valley School Road

Lee Mt. Road

7.2 mi.

2.1 mi.

0.1 mi.

HOW CROWDED

179

P — Corrals

5.0 mi.

Driving Distance One Way, Miles: 9.4
Hiking Distance One Way, Miles: 5.0 or 7.0

Jail Trail

General Information
Location Map F1
Clarkdale USGS Map
Coconino Forest Service Map

Driving Distance One Way: 20.1 miles *32.2 km* (Time 45 minutes)
Access Road: All cars, All paved
Hiking Distance One Way: 0.5 miles *0.8 km,* with an extension available
How Strenuous: Easy
Features: Easy to reach, Verde River access, Nature walk with identified plants

NUTSHELL: This trail, opened in June 2001, starts at the old Cottonwood Jail, goes down to the Verde River on a wide old road, then follows the bank of the river to a bridge, where it officially ends. However, a river walk extends along the Verde from the bridge, allowing hikers to enjoy a river-side ramble for 2.0 miles *3.2 km* or so.

DIRECTIONS:
From the Sedona Y Go:
   Southwest on Highway 89A for 18.6 miles *29.8 km*, to the first stoplight in Cottonwood. Go straight on Highway 89A. You'll reach a second stop-light at 19.2 miles *30.7 km*. Go straight on Historic Highway 89A (Main Street). At 20.1 miles *32.2 km*, you will see a trail sign in front of a small building constructed of river rock. Pull in and park in the lot beside the building.

TRAILHEADS: At the parking lot. You will see a trail sign at the side of a gate. Below the sign there is a metal box containing beautifully printed nature walk brochures. Be sure to take one, as the plant identification adds to the enjoyment of the hike. The little river-rock building is an information center; so if there are no brochures in the box you may be able to get one inside.

DESCRIPTIONS: This is an easy walk. You go through the gate and fol-low an old road down to the river level. Along the way you will find some nicely executed metal signs shaped like a leaf. Each sign bears a number that is keyed in to the brochure. The signs allow you to identify the plants. There are the expected cottonwoods and willows, along with a number of other species. For people who have recently moved to the area, this is an excellent way to become acquainted with the native flora.

Once you reach the river level, you will walk along the south bank. There are heavy growths of cattails and other plants between you and the water in most places, but there are some breaks where you could go over and dip your toes in the aqua if you are so inclined. The trail here goes along river sand, not the best footing, but there are plans to put some kind of fill to make a harder surface.

The trail meanders along the river until it comes to the bridge where Tenth Street crosses the Verde on its way to **Dead Horse State Park**. Officially the trail hooks to the right, goes through a little pass-through stockade fence, and rises up to Tenth Street at the side of the bridge. Ignore this. You can stop at the bridge for a gentle but interesting hike. You also have the option of continuing to walk along the Riverwalk Trail, which continues along the riverbank for about 0.75 miles *1.2 km* over to the Riverfront Park.

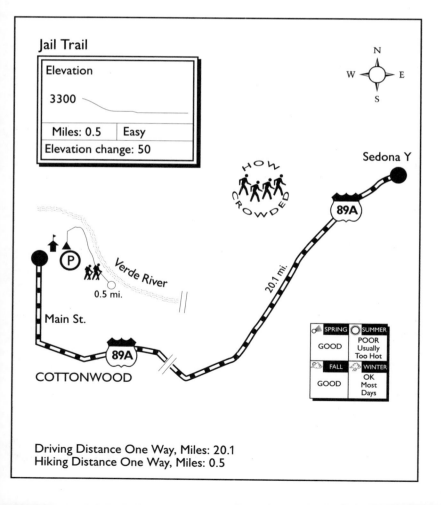

Driving Distance One Way, Miles: 20.1
Hiking Distance One Way, Miles: 0.5

Jim Thompson Trail #124

General Information
Location Map D5
Munds Park, Wilson Mountain USGS Maps
Coconino Forest Service Map

Driving Distance One Way: 1.7 miles *2.7 km* (Time 10 minutes)
Access Road*:* All cars. Last 0.4 miles *0.6 km* dirt road
Hiking Distance One Way*:* 3.0 miles *4.8 km* (Time 1.5 hours)
How Strenuous*:* Moderate
Features*:* Historic road, Good views

NUTSHELL: This historic road is easy to reach and provides superb views while you hike around the base of Steamboat Rock.

DIRECTIONS:
From the Y in Sedona Go:
   North on Highway on 89A (toward Flagstaff) for 0.3 miles *0.5 km* to Jordan Road, in the middle of uptown Sedona. Turn left (N) and take Jordan Road to its end, at 1.1 miles *1.8 km.* Turn left at the stop sign, onto Park Ridge Drive, a paved road, which goes through a subdivision and ends at 1.3 miles *2.1 km.* Keep going past the subdivision on the unpaved road, which has been improved since our last edition. At the 1.7 mile *2.7 km* point, you will come to the parking area outside the gate of the old shooting range.

TRAILHEAD: Walk through the gate and up the road 0.1 miles *0.16 km.* The trailhead is now well marked. (Note: a new trailhead 0.25 miles *0.4 km* inside the gate is under construction).

DESCRIPTION: The trail goes to your right, south, following the cairns. You will follow along this access, created in 1997, over mostly level terrain.
   At 0.14 miles *0.2 km*, you will intersect the Old Jim Thompson Road. Turn left here and go uphill. The downside leg of the road is blocked where it enters private property.
   You will come to a gate at 0.4 miles *0.6 km*, and at this point will have climbed high enough to begin to enjoy the wonderful views that are available on this hike.
   Soon after this, you will stop climbing at the 4,800 foot level and from this point the old road is wide and easy to walk. You will move right over to the base of Steamboat Rock and curve around it.
   At the 1.0 mile *1.6 km* point, you will walk under a power line. Here a private hiking trail takes off to the right, going down to the Red Rock Lodge

in 1.0 miles *1.6 km.*

At 2.0 miles *3.2 km* you will be just below Steamboat Tank, which you can identify by the deciduous trees sticking up from it. A short detour to it is worthwhile. The road ends where it comes down to **Wilson Canyon.**

Jim Thompson was the first settler in Oak Creek, arriving at Indian Gardens in 1876. Later he established a second homestead in Sedona. He built this road to link his two homes. First it ran along the creek banks, but it was washed away by floods, causing him to build this road, far from the creek, in 1887.

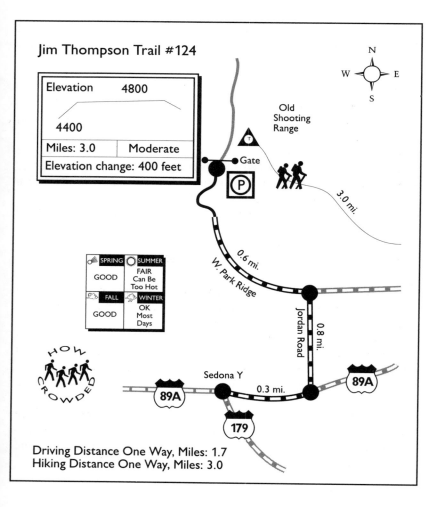

Jordan Trail

General Information
Location Map D4
Munds Park, Wilson Mountain USGS Maps
Coconino Forest Service Map

Driving Distance One Way: 1.7 miles *2.7 km* (Time 10 minutes)
Access Road: All cars. Last 0.4 miles *0.6 km* dirt road
Hiking Distance One Way: 1.5 miles *2.4 km* (Time 50 minutes)
How Strenuous: Moderate
Features: Easy to reach, all-weather road, pleasant hike near town, good views

NUTSHELL: Starting from the end of Jordan Road, this trail curls around the southern tip of Cibola Ridge, and ends at Devil's Kitchen, a point on the **Soldier Pass Trail.**

DIRECTIONS:
From the Y in Sedona Go:
   North on Highway on 89A (toward Flagstaff) for 0.3 miles *0.5 km* to Jordan Road, in the middle of uptown Sedona. Turn left (N) and take Jordan Road to its end, at 1.1 miles *1.8 km*. Turn left at the stop sign, onto Park Ridge Drive, a paved road, which goes through a subdivision and ends at 1.3 miles *2.1 km*. Keep going past the subdivision on the unpaved road, which has been improved since our last edition. At the 1.7 mile *2.7 km* point, you will come onto a bare redrock ledge at a curve. Park here. A new trailhead is under construction 0.25 miles *0.4 km* inside the gate.

TRAILHEAD: At the parking place, on the left side of the road.

DESCRIPTION: The Jordan Trail, new in 1999, is a delight in its own right and serves as a connector to other trails in the area, permitting hikers to make a number of interesting combinations.
   At first, the trail goes uphill along an old road until it reaches a power line. Then it turns west and follows the line. At 0.25 miles *0.4 km* you will look down on an electric power substation. At this point you are quite near the base of the southern edge of Cibola Ridge, and will enjoy looking at its redrock cliffs.
   At 0.33 miles *0.53 km* you will reach a high point from which you have nice views to the northeast into the Steamboat Rock area and southwest to **Sugarloaf.** You round the toe of the ridge and then turn north, still hugging the base of the ridge, but getting into more interesting, wilder country.

Cathedral Rock and Oak Creek

Soldier Pass

Coffee Pot Rock

Mitten Ridge Reflection

Jerome—Great Hiking and Views

Palatki Ruin

Encinoso Falls in the Springtime

Bell Rock

Sinagua Homestead

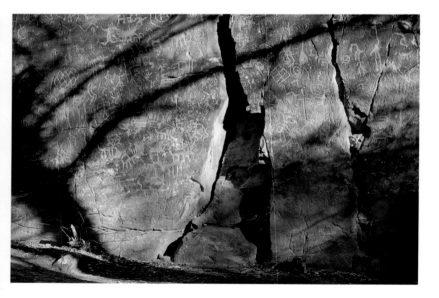

Petroglyphs, V Bar V Ranch

Storm over Red Canyon

You are hidden from the developed areas and have a nice feeling of being out in the country. There are some nice stands of Arizona cypress through which you move. We love these trees and enjoy the peaceful feeling we seem to get when we are in a grove of them.

From the 0.9 mile *1.4 km* point the Cibola Mittens come into view to the north. At the 1.1 mile *1.8 km* point the **Cibola Pass Trail** comes in from the right. Just beyond, the Jordan trail turns and moves west along the bank of a deep gulch. At 1.25 miles *2.0 km* you reach another trail junction. Go straight here, northwest, toward a redrock ledge. When you reach the ledge, you will walk along it until you come around a corner and find yourself on the brink of Devil's Kitchen, a natural sinkhole, and the place where you intersect the Soldier Pass Trail.

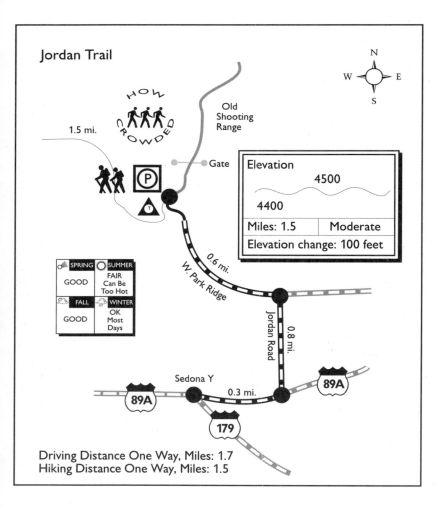

Kel Fox Trail

General Information
Location Map G3
Lake Montezuma USGS Map
Coconino Forest Service Map

Driving Distance One Way: 12.6 miles *20.2 km* (Time 30 minutes)
Access Road: Last 1.4 miles *2.2 km* need high clearance
Hiking Distance One Way: 2.0 miles *3.2 km* (Time 1 hour)
How Strenuous: Moderate
Features: Interesting mesas and peaked hills, Views

NUTSHELL: A sleeper—you would never know this fine hike is available in the rather drab landscape you see as you drive south on Highway 179. You follow an old cattle trail from a pond up to a pass from which you can see out over the Village of Oak Creek area, then descend on the other side of the pass into the Rancho Rojo Estates subdivision.

DIRECTIONS:
From the Sedona Y Go:

Southeast on Highway 179 (toward Phoenix) for 10.4 miles *16.6 km* (MP 303), to FR 120, the Beaverhead Flat Scenic Road, where you take a right turn onto the road (also marked Yavapai 78). Follow the road to the 11.2 mile *18.0 km* point, where you will see the pipeline road to your right, with gray gravel surfacing, a stop sign and a cattle guard. If you have a high clearance vehicle, you can drive all the way to Fuller Tank. If you are in a low slung car, drive as far as you are comfortable, then park and walk to the pond. It is an easy walk. Follow the pipeline markers to the tank and park.

TRAILHEAD: The trail starts on top of the high earth dam that forms the south end of Fuller Tank. Here you will find several upright steel poles marking the start of the trail, with a sign indicating the proper uses for it.

DESCRIPTION: Fuller Tank is a big tank with a broad catchment area, but we have never seen any appreciable amount of water in it.

Walk right up on top of the dam, where you will start the hike at the steel poles. We had the first part of this hike in earlier editions of this book as Deer Pass. In 2001, however, the gas company put a pipeline through the area and the Forest Service decided to build a trail along the pipeline easement. It worked beautifully. The trail now provides good footing and is easy to follow.

From the pond upward, this hike has a nice remote feeling. Pointy vol-

canic peaks surround you. There are a few places where some redrock ledges are exposed, adding a welcome touch of color.

As you near the top of the trail, at Deer Pass, you will see that you are heading toward a saddle. At the saddle you will look down on the tremendous development that has taken place in the last few years in the Village of Oak Creek area.

On the northern horizon some area landmarks are well displayed, such as Bell Rock, Courthouse Butte and Cathedral Rock. From here the trail descends and winds around the north toe of the big mesa to your right, which we think is called Castle Dome.

The trail ends at a neighborhood trailhead, on Arabian Drive in the Rancho Rojo Estates. Kel Fox was a rancher who had a winter range in the area of the trail and a summer range in Munds Park. The Foxboro Ranch School was named for his father.

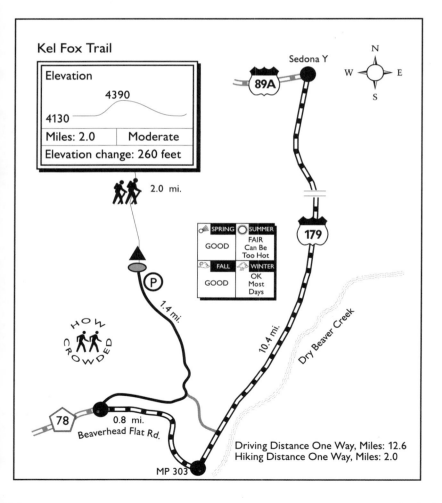

Lime Kiln Trail

General Information
Location Map F1
Clarkdale USGS Map
Coconino Forest Service Map

Driving Distance One Way: 22.4 miles *35.8 km* (Time 45 minutes)
Access Road*:* All cars, All paved
Hiking Distance One Way*:* 2.8 miles *4.5 km* (Time 1.5 hours)
(Eventually: 14.0 miles *22.4 km*, to Sedona)
How Strenuous*:* Moderate
Features*:* Easy to reach, Historic road

NUTSHELL: The Lime Kiln Trail starts inside the Dead Horse State Park in Cottonwood, meaning that one must pay an entrance fee. The trail passes the historic lime kiln for which it is named and then winds over ridgetops and plains.

DIRECTIONS:
From the Sedona Y Go:
   Southwest on Highway 89A for 18.6 miles *29.8 km*, to the first stoplight in Cottonwood. Go straight on Highway 89A to a second stoplight at 19.2 miles *30.7 km*. Go straight on Historic Highway 89A (Main Street). At 20.6 miles *33.0 km*, just past the cemetery, turn right on 10th Street. The entrance to the park is at 21.5 miles *34.4 km*. Pay your fee and then drive back on the main road 0.9 miles *1.4 km*, parking at the Lagoon parking lot.

TRAILHEAD: Walk down the main paved road for 0.1 miles *0.16 km*, over a bridge. On the other side, on your left, you will see the trailhead with a 2-panel trailhead sign.

DESCRIPTION: The Lime Kiln Trail starts at another place in the park. You will access it from the Lagoon Trail. Hike it for 0.2 miles *0.32 km* to intersect the Lime Kiln Trail, where you turn right. Almost immediately you will come to the site of the kiln. It doesn't look like much; just a small oven made of pink stones in a chalk-white cliff on the side of Rattlesnake Wash.
   Beyond the kiln the trail makes a steep climb up the Stairsteps to the top of a ridge. You will wonder how a loaded wagon could have negotiated this precipitous segment. Once on top of the ridge you will be able to see out over the Verde Valley and can spot Jerome nestled on the side of the Black Hills. We love old roads and marveled at the way the pioneers curved this road around ridgetops. In places it is very clear that you are on an old road

and in other patches erosion has made it seem that you are on a singletrack. In some places you can see other alignments of the road. In time the Lime Kiln Road quits ridge running and moves fairly straight across country.

At 1.8 miles *2.9 km* you will reach a major trail junction where a wide road goes off to your left. This detour runs about 0.25 miles *0.4 km* to the Rattlesnake Wash Overlook (we do not recommend this for most hikers— not interesting enough for the effort).

At 2.0 miles *3.2 k*m you will reach the Bill Ensign Trail, marked only by cairns, to your right. At 2.2 miles *3.5 km* is the junction with the Thumper Trail, left, marked by a lath reading "trail." Just beyond you come to a gate. From the gate the trail continues across flat land, meeting with FR 9538 at Last Chance Tank, where the trail ends for now at 2.8 miles *4.5 km*. There are plans to take the trail eventually all the way to the Red Rock State Park near Sedona, a distance of 14.0 miles *22.4 km*.

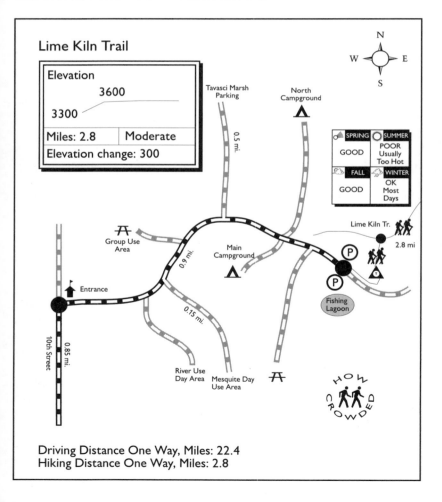

Lime Kiln Trail

Elevation

3600

3300

Miles: 2.8	Moderate
Elevation change: 300	

N
W—E
S

Tavasci Marsh Parking

North Campground

0.5 mi.

☀ SPRING	☀ SUMMER
GOOD	POOR Usually Too Hot
🍂 FALL	❄ WINTER
GOOD	OK Most Days

Lime Kiln Tr.

Group Use Area

Main Campground

0.9 mi.

Entrance

P

P

2.8 mi

Fishing Lagoon

0.15 mi.

10th Street

0.85 mi.

River Use Day Area

Mesquite Day Use Area

HOW CROWDED

Driving Distance One Way, Miles: 22.4
Hiking Distance One Way, Miles: 2.8

Little Horse Trail #61

General Information
Location Map E5
Munds Mountain and Sedona USGS Maps
Coconino Forest Service Map

Driving Distance One Way: 3.6 miles *5.8 km* (Time 10 minutes)
Access Road: All cars, All paved
Hiking Distance One Way: 2.2 miles *3.5 km* (Time 1 hour)
How Strenuous: Moderate
Features: Views, Redrocks

NUTSHELL: Located near downtown Sedona, this hike takes you across relatively flat land to the top of Chicken Point, a well-known landmark.

DIRECTIONS:
From the Sedona Y Go:
  South on Highway 179 (toward Phoenix) for a distance of 3.6 miles *5.8 km* (MP 309.8). You will see a large sign for the trailhead. Turn left into the trailhead parking lot. This is a major trailhead, with lots of parking and all facilities, including a toilet.

TRAILHEAD: At the parking lot, where you will find a map and signs.

DESCRIPTION: This trail is part of the Bell Rock Pathway system and is a very nice one, well posted, easy to follow and very scenic.
  You begin the hike by walking away from the highway, which is nice, and soon come up on top of a ridge. From here you can see the top of the Chapel of the Holy Cross in the distance. The trail moves you toward the Chapel and the beautiful redrock formation on which it is situated, Twin Buttes.
  The trail will bring you to the base of the redrocks of Twin Buttes, where you turn right. We love walking along here, so close to the majestic redrock. The erosion sculpting on the butte is quite fantastic. As you move along, you will come to a gate. This used to be a serious gate, closed at all times, but now it seems to be constantly open and neglected. Go through the gate. Just beyond the gate you will be at the foot of Chicken Point, which is at the top of the redrocks to your left. Chicken Point is a slickrock saddle between red buttes. The jeep tours drive there frequently, so don't be surprised if you hear people on top, towering above you.
  You will hike slightly past Chicken Point, and then the trail turns to the left, hooks back, and climbs to the top of the Chicken Point formation, mov-

ing up a nice natural ramp. Once up to the level of the point, you can walk over to the shelf where the jeeps park. The passengers always seem startled to see hikers come out of the canyon.

The trail is designed to connect with the **Broken Arrow Trail** at this point, but that would make for a very long hike if you were to go to the Broken Arrow trailhead. From there you would have to find some way to return to the Little Horse trailhead. Bikers can handle this distance, and you are likely to see them enjoying the trail.

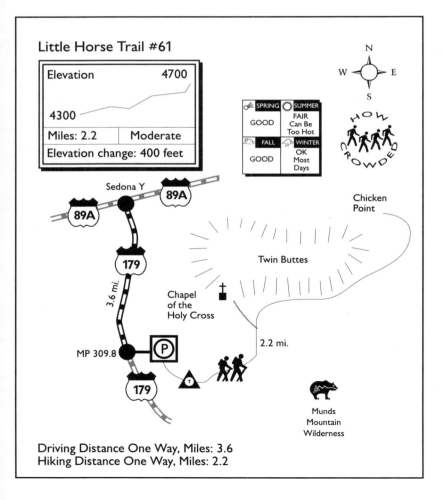

Little Horse Trail #61

Elevation 4700

4300

Miles: 2.2 Moderate

Elevation change: 400 feet

SPRING SUMMER
GOOD FAIR Can Be Too Hot
FALL WINTER
GOOD OK Most Days

N
W E
S

HOW CROWDED

Sedona Y 89A

89A

179

3.6 mi.

Chapel of the Holy Cross

Twin Buttes

Chicken Point

2.2 mi.

MP 309.8 P

179 T

Munds Mountain Wilderness

Driving Distance One Way, Miles: 3.6
Hiking Distance One Way, Miles: 2.2

Long Canyon Trail #63

General Information
Location Map G6
Casner Butte, Buckhorn Mtn. USGS Maps
Coconino Forest Service Map

Driving Distance One Way: 18.0 miles *28.8 km* (Time 30 minutes)
Access Road: All cars, Last 0.8 miles *1.3 km* good dirt road
Hiking Distance One Way: 2.5 miles *4.0 km* (Time 2 hours 30 minutes)
How Strenuous: Hard due to steep climb on first leg
Features: Views

NUTSHELL: Starting on the east bank of Wet Beaver Creek, this hike takes you along an old cattle trail, as you climb over one thousand feet.

DIRECTIONS:
From the Sedona Y Go:

South on Highway 179 (toward Phoenix) for 14.7 miles *23.5 km*, to the I-17 Interchange. Instead of going onto I-17, go underneath it and get onto the paved country road FR 618. You will pass the Beaver Creek Ranger Station and the bridge over Beaver Creek, where the paving ends. Just after the paving ends, you will reach a three-way fork at 17.4 miles *27.8 km*. Turn left here, where you see a sign for Southwest Academy. At 18.0 miles *28.8 km,* look to your right. You will see the trail sign uphill just beyond a fence. There is a parking area to your left.

TRAILHEAD: The trailhead is uphill to your right, where you will see a couple of vertical railroad ties used as fence supports. There is a wire gate with a hiker symbol on a fence post. On the other side is a sign that says, "Long Canyon Trail #63. Bell Trail #13—10 miles. Trail difficult to find after 2 miles." [We had no trouble finding the trail].

DESCRIPTION: This is an old cattle trail, like several others in the area, such as the **Bell Trail**. The Long Canyon Trail climbs steeply, rising 700 feet in the first 0.4 miles *0.6 km.*

As you rise, you begin to enjoy views. At first these views are of the nearby creek. You can see a ranch to the south and some of the buildings of the academy to the north of your starting point. Climbing even higher, you begin to see over the banks of Beaver Creek. The climb is steep, but the trail zigzags and is well maintained.

You climb to a ridge that is more level, and walk east along it. You can walk over to the rim of the ridge anywhere and have views of the Verde

Valley. You can also see some of the colored cliffs of the Sedona country. At the 1.0 miles *1.6 km* point you make another climb, but this one is not as steep or as long as the first climb.

When you finish the second climb, you emerge onto the top of a mesa, where it is fairly flat and the walking is easy—except for the fact that the ground is strewn with rocks everywhere, making for hard footing.

You will find the trail marked by wire-cage cairns. In spite of the warning sign at the trailhead, we had no trouble seeing the trail.

On top, we found the hike disappointing, as it passes through flat and uninteresting county. The trail moves east, parallel to the south side of Long Canyon. Maps indicate that the trail nears the edge of the canyon at about the 4.0 mile *6.4 km* point, and meets the Bell Trail, which skirts along the north side of Long Canyon, at the canyon's mouth. We stopped at the 2.5 mile point.

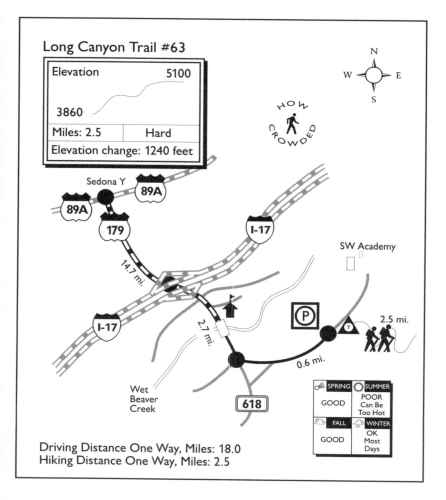

Long Canyon Trail #122

General Information
Location Map C3
Wilson Mt. USGS Map
Coconino Forest Service Map

Driving Distance One Way: 6.7 miles *10.7 km* (Time 15 minutes)
Access Road: All cars, All paved
Hiking Distance One Way: 3.0 miles *4.8 km* (Time 2 hours)
How Strenuous: Moderate
Features: Views, Great cliffs

NUTSHELL: Located 6.7 miles *10.7 km* northwest of uptown Sedona, this trail takes you right up against the base of gorgeous red cliffs. This is one of the best trails for viewing rock formations. **A personal favorite.**

DIRECTIONS:
From the Sedona Y Go:

Southwest on Highway 89A (toward Cottonwood) for a distance of 3.2 miles *5.1 km* (MP 371) to the Dry Creek Road. Turn right onto Dry Creek Road and follow it to the 6.1 mile *9.8 km* point, where there is a stop sign. The paved road to your right is the Long Canyon Road. Take it to the 6.7 miles *10.7 km* point, where you will see an unpaved road to your left. The entrance to the road is blocked with boulders. There is a parking area in front of the boulders. Park there.

TRAILHEAD: This is a marked and maintained trail. There is a rusty sign where you park reading, "Long Canyon #122."

DESCRIPTION: The trail begins as a wide jeep road. In fact, the Forest Service has moved several boulders across the road at its entrance to keep vehicles from using it.

At 0.3 miles *0.5 km* you will come to a 3-pronged fork. Take the left fork. At 0.6 miles *1.0 km* you will come to a gap in a fence. This marks the entrance to the Redrock-Secret Mt. Wilderness Area. Go through the gap. The trail is a footpath from this point. At 1.0 miles *1.6 km* you will reach another fork. Here one trail goes left parallel to a power line and the other trail goes right. Take the right fork. The left fork goes to Boynton Canyon.

For the first 1.5 miles *2.4 km* on this trail you will be walking in open country with almost no shade. This part of the trail isn't much fun in hot weather. After that you will enter a cypress forest where there is shade. By then you will have moved fairly close to Maroon Mountain which is to your

right (north). You will catch glimpses through the trees of the magnificent red and white sculptured cliffs of Maroon Mountain as you hike.

Beyond the 2.5 mile *4.0 km* point the vegetation becomes more alpine and less desert-like. Here you will encounter many oaks and huge alligator bark junipers. Some of the junipers are many centuries old.

At 3.0 miles *4.8 km* the trail, which has angled northwest parallel to the base of the mountain, turns straight north, climbing steeply. This is the stopping point for this hike. Here you will find genuine alpine conditions with pines and firs and a carpet of green on the forest floor. The canyon walls are nearer now and you have tremendous views.

The trail continues but becomes difficult. It plays out completely at 4.0 miles *6.4 km* in a side canyon, in a place that is one of the wildest in the Sedona area. It really feels remote. The path narrows there to a barely discernible game trail where you are totally out of sight of the works of man.

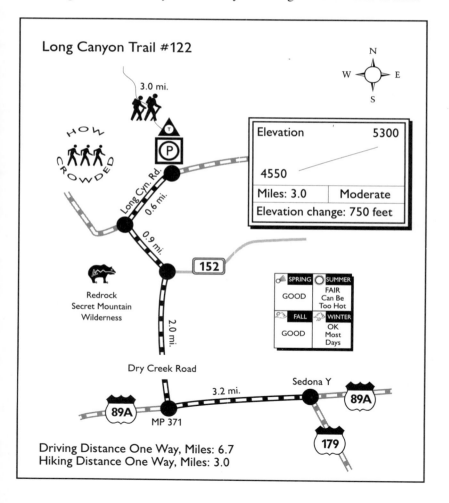

Lower Chimney Rock Trail

Driving Distance One Way: 4.3 miles *6.9 km* (Time 10 minutes)
Access Road: All cars, All paved
Hiking Distance, Complete Loop: 1.5 miles *2.4 km* (Time 45 minutes)
How Strenuous: Easy
Features: Close to town, easy all-weather access

NUTSHELL: Located 4.3 miles *6.9 km* west of downtown, this is a small hike that you can take when time is limited.

DIRECTIONS:
From the Sedona Y Go:
    Southwest on Highway 89A (toward Cottonwood) for 3.2 miles *5.1 km* (MP 371) to Dry Creek Road. Turn right on Dry Creek Road and proceed to the 3.7 mile *5.9 km* point. Turn right Thunder Mountain Road at the entrance to the Thunder Mountain subdivision. Drive to the 4.3 miles *6.9 km* point, then turn left into the trail parking lot.

TRAILHEAD: At the parking area. There is a sign with a map of the trails in the area, including this hike.

DESCRIPTION: Follow the main trail. At 0.1 miles *0.16 km* you will come to a trail junction marked by a signpost and a sign. The trail to the right is the **Thunder Mountain Trail**. Go straight ahead at this point.
    At 0.35 miles *0.56 km* you will reach a second signposted trail junction at the top of a little pass, where you can see down into the Dry Creek Road area, where there are many homes. This pass is a saddle between Little Sugarloaf, to your left, and Chimney Rock, to your right. The **Chimney Rock Loop Trail** takes off to the right at this junction, while the Lower Chimney Rock Trail goes straight ahead, down the north side of the ridge into the flat area below. A short distance beyond, the **Summit Route Trail** forks to the left.
    As you make the descent, the impressive Chimney Rock will come into view to your right. The big butte on your right has had several names: Thunder Mountain, Capitol Butte, Grey Mountain, and Shadow Mountain. You can see Lizard Head, a well-known landmark, in the white colored layers ahead and slightly to your right.

Down on the valley floor your views are restricted due to the fact that you are walking through a juniper forest. The Dry Creek Road is not far away, to your left, and the trail angles toward it. At 0.6 miles *1.0 km* you will come to a barbed wire fence around a housing area, where the trail turns left. At 0.75 miles *1.2 km* there is a confusing trail junction. A little stub to your right goes to a private drive off Dry Creek Road. Ignore it and take the left fork.

You will now proceed southeasterly around the west and south faces of Little Sugarloaf. At 1.25 miles *2.0 km* you pass through a rusty barbed wire fence and walk under a power line. At 1.5 miles *2.4 km* you return to the parking lot.

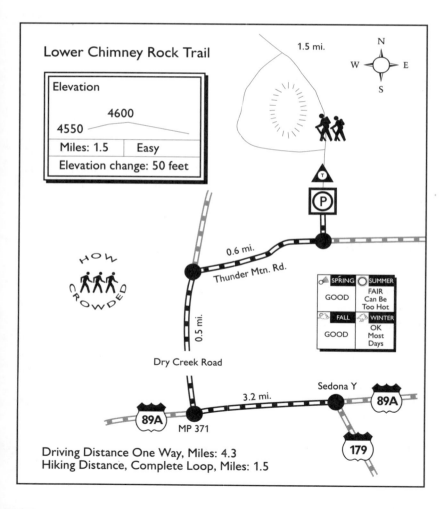

Loy Canyon Trail #5

General Information
Location Map C1
Loy Butte and Page Springs USGS Maps
Coconino Forest Service Map

Driving Distance One Way: 15.5 miles *24.8 km* (Time 40 minutes)
Access Road: All cars, Last 7.8 miles *12.5 km* good dirt road
Hiking Distance One Way: 4.0 miles *6.4 km* (Time 2.5 hours)
How Strenuous: Moderate
Features: Indian ruins, Scenic canyon, Views

NUTSHELL: Located 15.5 miles *24.8 km* northwest of Sedona, this trail takes you through a pleasant canyon to the base of the Mogollon Rim.

DIRECTIONS:
From The Y in Sedona Go:
Southwest on Highway 89A (toward Cottonwood) a distance of 3.2 miles *5.1 km,* to the Dry Creek Road. Turn right on the Dry Creek Road and drive this paved road to the stop sign at 6.1 miles *9.8 km.* Turn left on the paved road and drive to the 7.7 mile *12.3 km* point, where the road to Enchantment Resort forks right. Go left here, on the unpaved road FR 152C, to Boynton Pass. You will come to a road junction at 11.7 miles *18.7 km,* where you turn right on FR 525. Stay on FR 525 to the trailhead at the 15.5 mile point *24.8 km.* There is a parking lot large enough to hold several cars on the other side of the road.

TRAILHEAD: You will see a rusty sign marked, "Loy Canyon #5" on the right side of the road in front of a barbed wire fence.

DESCRIPTION: Since you are so close, drive on down the road another 0.7 miles *1.1 km* and visit **Honanki** if you haven't seen it, as it is the site of the Sedona area's finest Indian ruins.

The Loy Canyon trail was built as a cattle trail in the late 1890s. Like many other cattle trails now used for hiking, the purpose of this trail was to take cattle to the top of the Mogollon Rim. The cattle would be kept in the warm low country during the winter and then walked to the cool high country for the summer. The rim is over 1,000 feet high in most places, so it was hard to find spots where a trail could be built.

You start this hike by skirting the fence around a ranch for about half a mile, then begin to walk up the canyon bottom.

Look for a small Indian ruin set in a cave at 0.75 miles *1.2 km.* It is in a

cliff face to your left.

The trail rises gradually through a forest for 4.0 miles *6.4 km*, and meanders across a creekbed a few times, so you don't want to make the hike when water is running high. Because the trail gains in elevation the vegetation along the trail also changes. It is very desert-like at the beginning, with cactus and low shrubs, then changing as you progress to a pine forest.

At the end of 4.0 miles *6.4 km* you are at the base of the cliffs forming the rim, where we stop for an easy day hike. To go to the top requires some serious work. The trail becomes much steeper, requiring a strenuous climb of over one thousand feet in 1.0 miles *1.6 km.*

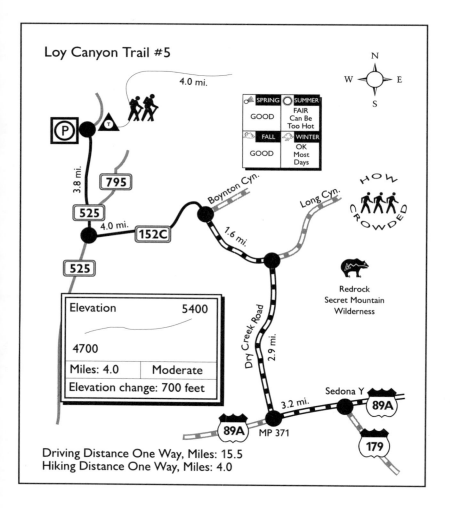

Marg's Draw Trail

General Information
Location Map E5
Sedona USGS Map
Coconino Forest Service Map

Driving Distance One Way: 0.9 miles *1.4 km* (Time 5 minutes)
Access Road: All cars, All paved
Hiking Distance One Way: 1.4/2.0 miles *2.2/3.2 km* (Time 1/1.5 hour)
How Strenuous: Moderate
Features: Views, Easy access

NUTSHELL: Marg's Draw is a beautiful area in Sedona's backyard, a bowl surrounded by the Crimson Cliffs, Munds Mountain, Lee Mountain and Twin Buttes. This trail is a means of traversing it from north to south.

DIRECTIONS:
From the Sedona Y Go:
   South on Highway 179 (toward Phoenix) for a distance of 0.7 miles *1.1 km* (MP 312.8) to Sombart Lane, which is at the Circle K store. Turn left on Sombart Lane and follow it to the 0.9 mile *1.4 km* point, where you will find a circular gravel parking lot lined with stones. Park there.

TRAILHEAD: At the parking lot. There is a nice big sign with a trail map and other information. (Alternate trailheads below).

DESCRIPTION: Something old, something new. For years Sedona hikers got onto the Marg's Draw trail at the Sombart Lane access point, but trouble developed about 1996 because of private property concerns. The Forest Service has worked out an arrangement with the property owner to restore this access. The trail itself, however, has been altered. In the past, we used to hike to the top, and then continue eastward on an old wagon road, toward the cliffs. The new alignment of the trail, however, keeps hikers at the portal of the bowl and runs north and south rather than east-west.
   The first leg of the trail is a brisk climb uphill, about 100 feet in 0.1 mile *0.16 km.* You then enter a relatively flat stretch. At 0.4 miles *0.6 km* you will come to a T trail junction. Here you have the option of going to the left (N), around the Crimson Cliffs to the Schnebly Hill Road. If you turn to the right (S), you will hike to the **Broken Arrow** trailhead.
   Both sections of the trail are interesting. Even though you are very close to the settled areas of Sedona on this trail, you are screened by vegetation, so that you have a nice backcountry feeling. The views of the cliffs sur-

rounding Marg's Draw are beautiful, whichever way you go.

From Sombart Lane you intersect the Margs trail at its midpoint. If you do either the north or south half of the trail, you will have a 2.8 mile *4.5 km* hike. If you start from either the south end at Broken Arrow trailhead or the north end off Schnebly Hill Road, you will have a 4.0 mile *6.4 km* hike.

To reach the south trailhead, follow the directions for the Broken Arrow hike. The trail goes north from the parking lot. It is signed, and is a clear track. To reach the north trailhead, drive up the Schnebly Hill Road for 1.0 miles *1.6 km* and park in the lot to the left and follow the trail signs.

Marg's Draw was named after a mule belonging to the first settler of Sedona, Abraham James. The mule, Marg, often hid in the area. It's ironic that a landmark should be named after his mule but that nothing in Sedona was named after James himself.

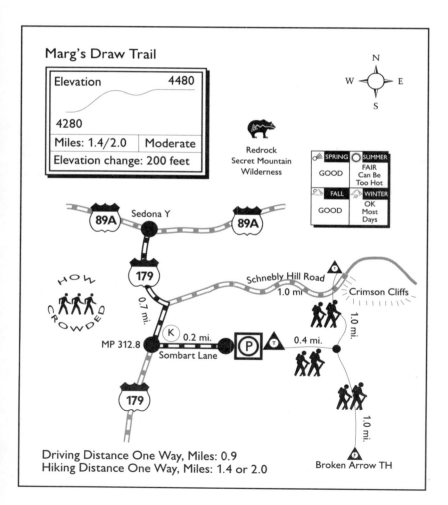

Mescal Mountain

General Information
Location Map C3
Wilson Mt. USGS Map
Coconino Forest Service Map

Driving Distance One Way: 6.7 miles *10.7 km* (Time 15 minutes)
Access Road: All cars, All paved
Hiking Distance One Way: 2.5 miles *4.0 km* (Time 90 minutes)
How Strenuous: Moderate
Features: Views, Indian ruins

NUTSHELL: Mescal Mountain is a small mesa at the mouth of Boynton Canyon 6.7 miles *10.7 km* northwest of Sedona. It takes a bit of scrambling to get to its top but the effort is worthwhile.

DIRECTIONS:
From the Sedona Y Go:
Southwest on Highway 89A (toward Cottonwood) for a distance of 3.2 miles *5.1 km* (MP 371) to the Dry Creek Road. Turn right onto Dry Creek Road and follow it to the 6.1 mile *9.8 km* point, where there is a stop sign, where you turn right on the paved Long Canyon Road. Take it to the 6.7 miles *10.7 km* point, where you will see an unpaved road to your left, where you pull in and park.

TRAILHEAD: You will begin this hike on the marked and maintained trail Long Canyon Trail #122, for which you will see a rusty sign at the parking area.

DESCRIPTION: Start the hike by taking the **Long Canyon Trail #122,** which begins as a wide jeep road. In fact, the Forest Service has moved several boulders across the road at its entrance to keep vehicles from using it.

At 0.3 miles *0.5 km* you will come to a 3-pronged fork. Take the leftmost fork. At 0.6 miles *1.0 km* you will come to a gap in the fence. This marks the entrance to the Redrock-Secret Mt. Wilderness Area. Instead of going through the gap, stay outside the fence and walk the old road that parallels it. At the 1.0 mile *1.6 km* point you will reach the foot of a butte, where the trail begins to climb sharply.

On the way up, you will see a cave to your right that looks large enough to contain an Indian ruin. It is large enough but there is no ruin due to a large crack in the cave roof that allows water to pour into the cave when it rains. A side trail goes to this cave and it is worth taking for the fun of exploring.

The main trail zigzags to a saddle on Mescal Mountain. Just below the saddle, in a red ledge, you will see a shallow cave containing a rudimentary Indian ruin.

On top of the saddle, you will see a distinct footpath marked with cairns going up to the left (S). A few yards along this trail there is the ruin of a pit house. Beyond it the trail winds right up to the face of the highest point on Mescal Mountain and then curves left, hugging the cliff at its base. It is fairly easy hiking, though steep, until you get to a point just below the top. There you will have to do some climbing if you want to go to the crest.

We don't do any rock climbing, as we are risk-averse and true rock climbing scares us. The small climb involved here is no worse than climbing a high ladder, though. Once you are on top, walk around the perimeter to enjoy the view. The distance to the top is 1.5 miles *2.4 km*. Fully exploring the top can add another mile to the hike.

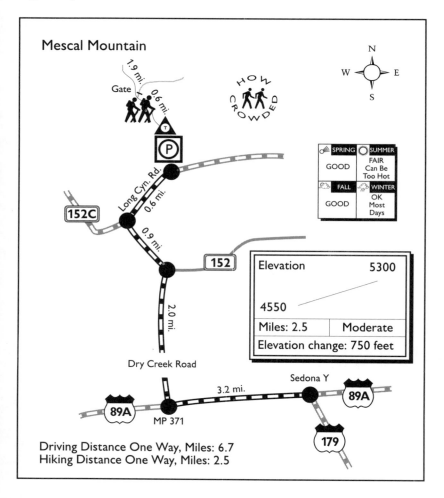

Mitten Ridge

VORTEX

General Information
Location Map E5
Munds Mt. and Munds Park USGS Maps
Coconino Forest Service Map

Driving Distance One Way: 3.8 miles *6.1 km* (Time 20 minutes)
Access Road: High clearance cars, Last 2.5 miles *4.0 km* rough dirt road
Hiking Distance One Way: 2.5 miles *4.0 km* (Time 2 hours)
How Strenuous: Moderate
Features: Views, Fascinating rock formations and sculptures, Vortex

NUTSHELL: Just 0.3 miles *0.5 km* from the Y, the Schnebly Hill Road is enjoyed by thousands of people. The hike takes you part way up the road, then across Bear Wallow Canyon to explore the redrock buttes on the west side of the canyon.

DIRECTIONS:
From the Sedona Y Go:
South on Highway 179 (toward Phoenix) for a distance of 0.3 miles *0.5 km* (MP 313.1) to the Schnebly Hill Road. It is just across the bridge past Tlaquepaque. Turn left onto the Schnebly Hill Road. It is paved for the first 1.0 mile *1.6 km* and then turns into a dirt road so rough that it is marked unsuitable for passenger cars. At the 3.8 mile *6.1 km* point, is a signed parking area; pull over and park.

TRAILHEAD: Follow the trail sign for the Cow Pies Trail.

DESCRIPTION: As you drive up Schnebly Hill Road you will become conscious of a deep streambed to your left. This is Bear Wallow Canyon. You will also be aware of a big butte between the road and Sedona. This is Mitten Ridge, one of the major Sedona landmarks, and it is your goal on this hike.

There is a parking place on the right-hand side of the road, and on the left you will see a small sign for the trail, which drops down from the road. It heads toward Mitten Ridge.

In about 200 yards you will come to a redrock shelf that was capped with a very thin layer of gray lava that has broken up into small stones. This place is one of the Sedona Vortex spots and believers often arrange some of these dark stones into a huge medicine wheel.

Thus far you are following the same trail that we have described for the **Cow Pies** hike. At 0.5 miles *0.8 km*, the paths split. You will go straight

instead of turning left as you would for the Cow Pies hike. You will walk toward ledges at the base of Mitten Ridge. Cairns usually mark the trail. It goes across several lower ledges to get up near the base of the cliffs. Once there you work your way west, at times ascending to a higher ledge. At first you will be walking through brush but at 1.5 miles *2.4 km* you will break out onto clear slickrock.

Here you will find an upper and lower trail. Try the lower one. You will soon see a saddle above you to the right. The saddle is a great viewpoint. You probably will not find a regular trail going to the saddle but it is easy and fun to walk up the sloping redrock face of the ridge to the saddle. The trail pinches out at the 2.5 miles *4.0 km* point.

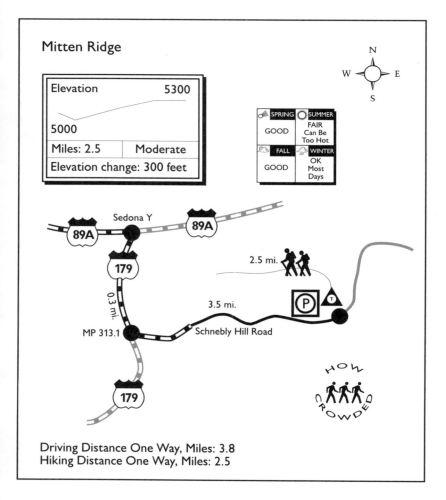

Mooney Trail #12

General Information
Location Map C1
Loy Butte USGS Map
Coconino Forest Service Map

Driving Distance One Way: 18.1 miles *29 km* (Time 30 minutes)
Access Road: All cars, Last 8.5 miles *13.6 km* good dirt road
Hiking Distance One Way: 3.75 miles *6.0 km* (Time 2.5 hours)
How Strenuous: Hard
Features: Views

NUTSHELL: This cattle trail starts at Black Tank 18.1 miles *29 km* southwest of Sedona and climbs to the base of the Mogollon Rim.

DIRECTIONS:
From the Sedona Y Go:
    Southwest on Highway 89A (toward Cottonwood) a distance of 9.6 miles *15.4 km* (MP 364.5) to the Red Canyon Road. Turn right on Red Canyon Road, also known as FR 525, and follow it to the 12.4 mile *19.8 km* point where FR 525C branches to the left. Sycamore Pass is your target. Turn left onto FR 525C. Follow it to the 18.1 mile *29 km* point, where FR 551 branches to the right. Pull in on FR 551 and park.

TRAILHEAD: This is a marked and maintained trail. You will see a rusty sign near the road reading, "Mooney Trail #12."

DESCRIPTION: You are near the trailhead when you see the red earth bank of a dam with fence posts on top on your right. This is Black Tank. Just as you curve around the tank there is a road to your right, FR 551. You will see the trail's rusty sign as you pull in.
    Park near the tank. If you have a high clearance vehicle you can drive about 1.0 miles *1.6 km* on FR 551, parking just before the road crosses a gully. The gully is Spring Creek.
    If you park at the tank, then walk through the fenced area toward the pumphouse, a small brick building. When you exit the gate at the other end of the tank area, turn right. You will see many trails because cattle are still run here and wherever they wander, they leave false trails. Follow the most heavily traveled jeep trail for 0.25 miles *0.4 km*, to a point where the road forks. Take the left fork marked FR 551A.
    The trail goes along foothills, gradually climbing to a ridge top. Then you walk along the top of the ridge. The ridge is javelina country and you

will see plenty of sign. It is hard to see these critters, as they are shy. Sometimes you may get a whiff of them. The javelina odor smells just like a cow barn. From the ridge top you get good distant views, particularly to the north, of the Mogollon Rim, but there isn't much to see close at hand. In fact, this is a rather drab trail.

You will reach another cattle tank called Sebra Tank. Beyond Sebra Tank you will come to the base of the Mogollon Rim, where the trail begins a steep ascent. There is an arch located in the cliff face here.

The trail to the top is hard. It is a severe climb and most of it is in the open, exposed to full sunlight. You wouldn't want to do this on a hot sunny day. At the top you will come out on a ridge at a place where the Mooney Trail, Taylor Cabin Trail and **Casner Mountain** trails all converge. If you turn left here, you will go to Casner Mountain; if you turn right, you will go to the top of the rim.

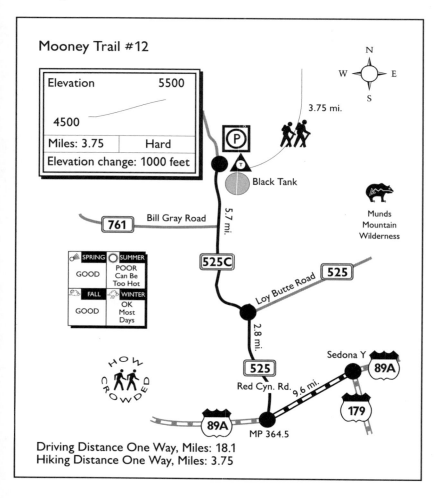

Mooney Trail #12

Elevation	5500
4500	
Miles: 3.75	Hard
Elevation change: 1000 feet	

Black Tank

761 — Bill Gray Road

Munds Mountain Wilderness

5.7 mi.

525C

Loy Butte Road — 525

	SPRING	SUMMER
GOOD		POOR Can Be Too Hot
	FALL	WINTER
GOOD		OK Most Days

2.8 mi.

525

Red Cyn. Rd. — 9.6 mi.

Sedona Y — 89A

179

HOW CROWDED

89A — MP 364.5

Driving Distance One Way, Miles: 18.1
Hiking Distance One Way, Miles: 3.75

Munds Mountain Trail #77

General Information
Location Map E5
Munds Mt. and Munds Park USGS Maps
Coconino Forest Service Map

Driving Distance One Way: 6.6 miles *10.6 km* (Time 30 minutes)
Access Road: High clearance cars, Last 5.3 miles *8.5 km* rough dirt road
Hiking Distance One Way: 2.9 miles *4.6 km* (Time 2.5 hours)
How Strenuous: Hard
Features: Views

NUTSHELL: This hike takes you to the top of the north end of Munds
Mountain, from where you have glorious views.

DIRECTIONS:
From the Sedona Y Go:

   South on Highway 179 (toward Phoenix) for 0.3 miles *0.5 km* (MP
313.1) to the Schnebly Hill Road, just across the bridge past Tlaquepaque.
Turn left on the Schnebly Hill Road, which is paved for the first 1.0 mile *1.6
km* and then turns into a dirt road so rough that it's marked unsuitable for
passenger cars. At 5.0 miles *8.0 km* you will see a gate made of very thick
steel pipes that closes the road in winter, about mid-November to mid-April.
(Call the Sedona Forest Service Ranger Station to find out whether it is
open.) Drive to the top, 6.6 miles *10.6 km* from the Y, where you will find
the Schnebly Hill Vista with a big parking area to your left. Park there.

TRAILHEAD: Your approach to the trailhead is over old jeep roads. From
the parking area walk up the main road about 100 paces, where you will see
a dirt road to your right (S). Take it. The route is the Old Schnebly Hill
Road, following the alignment it had from 1902 until the 1930s. If you have
a high clearance vehicle, you can drive a portion of it, though it has not been
maintained for years and is very rough. At 0.88 miles *1.4 km* on this road
you come to a fork. Go left (S) here. You will soon see a small microwave
tower. At 1.2 miles *1.9 km* you will come to a fork. Here the old road goes
right, to meet the **Schnebly Hill Trail.** Turn right and walk a short distance,
to the point where the road makes a hairpin curve to your right. At this point
you will see a footpath to the left (S) marked by a cairn. Take this path,
which is the second leg of the Schnebly Hill Trail.

   From here the trail follows the edge of the rim, with many excellent
viewpoints along the way. You will pass through two gates, the second
being located at Committee Tank. Soon after this the trail goes out on a thin

ridge connected to Munds Mt. At 2.4 miles *3.8 km* you will find the trailhead sign, "Munds Mt. Trail 77," just beyond the point where the **Jacks Canyon Trail** meets the ridge.

DESCRIPTION: At the trailhead the trail splits. Take the right fork, a sandy groove. The footing on this trail is poor, as it is covered with small white slippery rocks. The cairns are hard to see. The trail goes to the top by switchbacks, improving about halfway up. Beyond the midpoint, you will get thrilling glimpses into the Mitten Ridge area. At the top you emerge onto a rather bare park. Move around its edge for unsurpassed views.

In winter, when the Schnebly Hill is closed above the 5.0 mile *8.0 km* point, you can use the Schnebly Hill Trail as your approach and still make this hike. The top is above 6,000 feet, meaning there may be snow or mud, so keep this in mind.

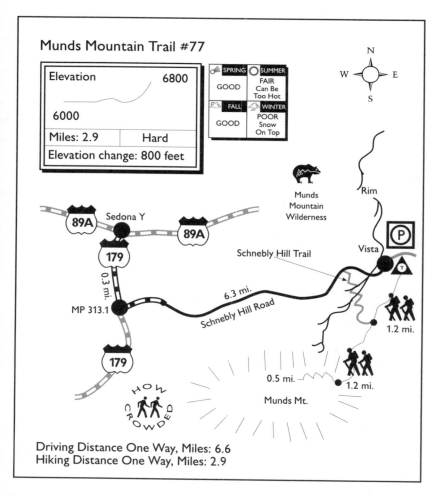

Munds Mountain Trail #77

Elevation	6800
6000	
Miles: 2.9	Hard
Elevation change: 800 feet	

SPRING	SUMMER
GOOD	FAIR Can Be Too Hot
FALL	WINTER
GOOD	POOR Snow On Top

N
W — E
S

89A
Sedona Y
89A

179

0.3 mi.

MP 313.1

179

Schnebly Hill Trail

6.3 mi.
Schnebly Hill Road

Munds Mountain Wilderness

Rim

Vista

P

T

1.2 mi.

0.5 mi.

1.2 mi.

Munds Mt.

HOW CROWDED

Driving Distance One Way, Miles: 6.6
Hiking Distance One Way, Miles: 2.9

Munds Wagon Trail

General Information
Location Map E5
Munds Mt. and Munds Park USGS Maps
Coconino Forest Service Map

Driving Distance One Way: 1.3 miles *2.1 km* (Time 10 minutes)
Access Road: All vehicles, All paved
Hiking Distance One Way: 4.5 miles *7.2 km* (Time 3 hours)
How Strenuous: Hard
Features: Historic road, Redrocks, Views

NUTSHELL: This hike takes you up Schnebly Hill the hard way, following portions of the old wagon road. It is very interesting and very scenic.

DIRECTIONS:
From the Sedona Y Go:
    South on Highway 179 (toward Phoenix) for a distance of 0.3 miles *0.5 km* (MP 313.1) to the Schnebly Hill Road. It is just across the bridge past Tlaquepaque. Turn left onto the Schnebly Hill Road. Drive to the 1.3 mile *2.1 km* point, where you will see a sign for the trailhead parking to your left. Pull in and park. This is a major trailhead with signs, maps, and a toilet.

TRAILHEAD: At the parking lot.

DESCRIPTION: The trail runs east from the parking lot, parallel to the modern road, and at times is very close to it. You cross the road, go above it for a time and then cross it again. At 0.8 miles *1.3 km* you reach an area where there is a small parking pad and the trail comes very close to the modern road. Up to here it has not been evident that you were on an old road, but for the next segment you can see that you are on it. It goes downhill and crosses the creek. You will find and lose the old road from time to time. You will reach a pair of concrete picnic tables at 1.25 miles *2.0 km*.
    We regard the trail from the picnic tables to the next road crossing as the middle part of the trail. We really enjoyed this part, with its immensely high, sheer white cliffs to the right and red cliffs on the left. The impact of the cliffs is much greater than when you see them while driving the present road. Near the end of this stretch the old road becomes very obvious. You are coming out of the canyon bottom, up steep switchbacks, when suddenly—right at eye level—there is a rock retaining wall, with the old road curving around and ahead.
    At 3.0 miles *4.8 km* you cross today's road and cross it again at 3.25

miles *5.2 km*—the final crossing. From here there is no question that you are on the old road, going straight up to the 4.0 mile *6.4 km* point, where it does a very interesting thing, winding halfway around the Merry-Go-Round, using a flat rock-free shelf of limestone as a natural roadway. This is a super part of the trail, great fun, with great views.

From here you follow the old road to the end of the trail, at 4.5 miles *7.2 km* where the trail meets the modern road. Across the road is the trailhead for the **Schnebly Hill Trail** going on up to the top of the rim.

The Munds ranching family had a ranch near Sedona and another close to Flagstaff, at Munds Park. They built a cattle trail to move their herds back and forth, to summer or winter range. In 1901 Sedona residents and Coconino County built a wagon road on the alignment of the cattle trail. It was called the Munds Wagon Road, but was later changed to the Schnebly Hill Road after Carl Schnebly, the man who led the effort to build it.

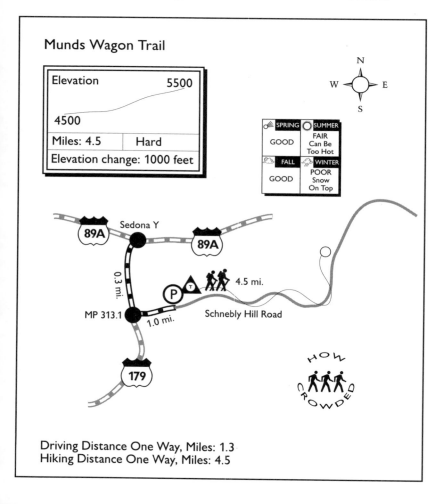

Mystic Trail

General Information
Location Map E5
Sedona USGS Map
Coconino Forest Service Map

Driving Distance One Way: 3.15 miles *5.0 km* (Time 10 minutes)
Access Road: All cars, All paved
Hiking Distance One Way: 1.0 miles *1.6 km* (Time 30 minutes)
How Strenuous: Easy
Features: Views, Easy to reach, All weather

NUTSHELL: This trail, new to the Sedona trail system in 1998, takes you from the road to the Chapel of the Holy Cross to the Sedona Cemetery.

DIRECTIONS:
From the Sedona Y Go:
    South on Highway 179 (toward Phoenix) for a distance of 2.8 miles *4.5 km* (MP 310.6) to Chapel Drive, which is the road to the world famous Chapel of the Holy Cross, one of the most important cultural landmarks of Sedona. Turn left (E) onto Chapel Drive and follow it until you are just east of Antelope Drive, the 3.15 mile *5.0 km* point, where you will see the trailhead to your left (N), at a gate in the fence. Park along the shoulder.

TRAILHEAD: At the gate.

DESCRIPTION: This path is part of the Bell Rock Pathway project, sponsored by the Sedona Kiwanis Club. Our thanks to Kiwanis for its participation in this worthwhile enterprise.
    This trail starts at the base of Twin Buttes, a lovely redrock formation, one of the largest buttes south of Sedona. The Chapel of the Holy Cross is built on the south face of this butte "around the corner" from the trailhead. (The Chapel is only 0.5 miles *0.8 km* from the trailhead—worth a side trip). We enjoy looking at the sheer cliffs of the buttes at the start of the hike, with a deep red base, and lighter colored cliffs and spires at the upper levels.
    This trail is much used by mountain bikers, so keep an eye out for them as you hike. From the markers encountered along the way, it seems that this trail follows a natural gas pipeline easement.
    From the starting point, the trail heads north, hugging the base of Twin Buttes. There are no major elevation changes, and the trail feels almost level, though it does slope downward from the south to the north end. As you hike, you soon emerge from a screen of trees and see many homes as well as

Highway 179. Airport Mesa is to your left (W). This is not a trail for someone seeking a wilderness experience, but it is just the ticket for someone who wants a nice little walk near town.

At the halfway point you come around the buttes to a point where you can see into Sedona and enjoy pleasant views to the north. Then you move more noticeably downhill, toward Battlement Mesa, finally ending at the north end of the trail, at a cul-de-sac in a little subdivision adjacent to the Sedona Cemetery.

It is possible to start the trail from the north end, but we hesitate to park our car there, because it feels as if we are parking in a homeowner's front yard. Directions: from the Y, drive south on Highway 179 for 1.6 miles *2.6 km*, turning left on Pine Drive, the road to the cemetery. In one block, turn right (S) on Pine Knolls and follow it to the 1.75 miles *2.8 km* point, where there is a parking circle.

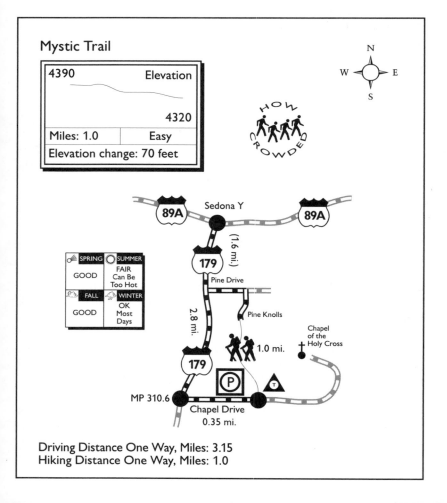

Mystic Trail

4390	Elevation
	4320
Miles: 1.0	Easy
Elevation change: 70 feet	

HOW CROWDED

N
W — E
S

Sedona Y

89A   89A

179   (1.6 mi.)

Pine Drive

SPRING	SUMMER
GOOD	FAIR Can Be Too Hot
FALL	WINTER
GOOD	OK Most Days

2.8 mi.

Pine Knolls

Chapel of the Holy Cross

1.0 mi.

179

MP 310.6

P   T

Chapel Drive
0.35 mi.

Driving Distance One Way, Miles: 3.15
Hiking Distance One Way, Miles: 1.0

Oak Creek-Verde River Confluence

General Information
Location Map G1
Cornville USGS Map
Coconino Forest Service Map

Driving Distance One Way: 22.4 miles *35.8 km* (Time 40 minutes)
Access Road: All cars, Last 1.1 miles *1.8 km* good dirt road
Hiking Distance One Way: 0.25 miles *0.4 km* (Time 15 minutes)
How Strenuous: Easy
Features: Indian ruins, River confluence

NUTSHELL: Located 22.4 miles *35.8 km* southwest of Sedona, this is more of a sightseeing experience than a hike, offering interesting exploration along a stream bank to see a river confluence and an Indian ruin.

DIRECTIONS:
From The Y in Sedona Go:
Southwest on Highway 89A (toward Cottonwood) for a distance of 17.0 miles *27.2 km* (MP 357), to the Cornville Road junction, where there is a stoplight. Turn left on the Cornville Road (Yavapai County Highway 30) and follow it 1.0 mile *1.6 km*, to the 18.0 mile *28.8 km* point. Go just past the golf course and turn right onto paved Tissaw Road. Follow Tissaw Road to the 21.3 mile *34.1 km* point, where the paving ends. Turn left on Thede Lane, which is marked with a Dead End sign (don't worry, the dead end will not affect you). Follow Thede Lane to the 22.0 mile *35.2 km* point, where an unmarked dirt road forks to the right. Take this road, which goes to the confluence in 0.4 miles *0.6 km*. You can drive right out to a point on the cliffs above the river, where there is a turnaround loop.

TRAILHEAD: None. You will see Indian ruins on a knob to your left. There is a social trail along the riverbank from the confluence overlook where you have parked over to the Indian ruin.

DESCRIPTION: The two streams, Oak Creek and the Verde River, meet at a V-shaped point overlooked by a high white bluff, on top of which you have parked. This bluff provides a natural perch, a place to sit and watch the meeting of the waters. As you sit on the point looking forward, Oak Creek is to your left and the Verde River is to your right. After a rain, Oak Creek runs red, while the Verde (true to its name, which means "green" in Spanish) runs green. It is fascinating to watch the waters mix. After enjoying this site, you can amble over to the Indian ruin.

The Indian ruin is a two-story structure located on a cliff above the river, a prime location. It is on private land and protected by a fence festooned with "No Trespassing" signs. You can get close enough for a good look without going onto the land. The ruin is the Atkeson Pueblo (formerly called Oak Creek Ruins), which contained 35 rooms in its prime, and was occupied from 1300-1425.

Look sharp as you are walking and you may find pottery shards and arrowheads along the river rim, as Indians inhabited this area for hundreds of years. Leave artifacts in place. Never remove them.

This is not a wilderness experience. Right across the river from the meeting of the waters is a big trailer and RV park and there are several ranches and homes in the area. Years ago before the trailer park was built, this was a magic place; but though the park has dimmed its luster, it is still an interesting place to visit.

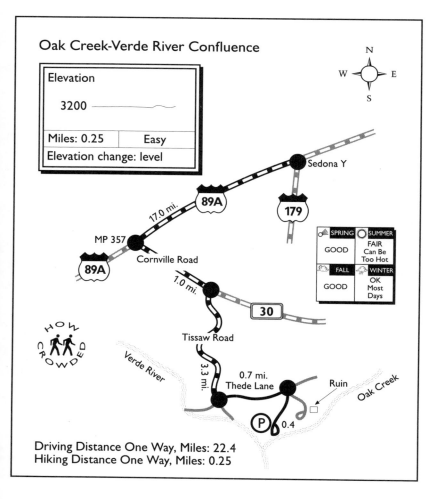

Oak Creek-Verde River Confluence

Elevation

3200

Miles: 0.25 — Easy

Elevation change: level

17.0 mi. — 89A — Sedona Y

MP 357 — 89A — Cornville Road — 179

1.0 mi. — 30

SPRING GOOD | SUMMER FAIR Can Be Too Hot
FALL GOOD | WINTER OK Most Days

HOW CROWDED

Tissaw Road

Verde River — 3.3 mi. — 0.7 mi. Thede Lane — Ruin — Oak Creek

P — 0.4

Driving Distance One Way, Miles: 22.4
Hiking Distance One Way, Miles: 0.25

Old Post Trail

General Information
Location Map E4
Sedona USGS Map
Coconino Forest Service Map

Driving Distance One Way: 6.2 miles *9.9 km* (Time 20 minutes)
Access Road*:* All cars, All paved
Hiking Distance One Way*:* 3.0 miles *4.8 km* (Time 1.5 hours)
How Strenuous*:* Moderate
Features*:* Easy to reach, Historic road, Views

NUTSHELL: Part of this trail is the historic road used for mail delivery in the old days. The trail itself winds around low hills west of Airport Mesa.

DIRECTIONS:
From the Sedona Y Go:
Southwest on Highway 89A (toward Cottonwood) a distance of 4.2 miles *6.8 km* (MP 368.9) to the Upper Red Rock Loop Road. Turn left and follow the Upper Red Rock Loop Road to the 6.0 mile *9.6 km* point, where you turn left, heading toward Crescent Moon Ranch Park on a paved road. At the 6.2 mile *9.9 km* point you will see a parking apron and 2-panel trailhead sign to your left. Park there.

TRAILHEAD: At the trail sign.

DESCRIPTION: You begin this hike by walking along an old road that has been converted into a hiking trail. At the 0.66 mile *1.1 k*m point you reach a V-fork where the **Herkenham Trail** branches off to the left. Keep going straight.

Shortly beyond this intersection the trail begins to climb its way up into the hills. At this point you can see that the trail/road was once an important one, because sections of it show a lot of work, with built-up rock supporting the sides of the road, etc. This road was important, as it was the mail route back in the horse-and-buggy days, used by the post office. This gives the trail its name, the Old Post Trail. There are some nice views from these high sections, and we found it to be the most interesting part of the trail. At 1.5 miles *2.4 km* you will meet the **Carroll Canyon Trail** coming in from your left. The Old Post and Carroll trails are blended together for the next 1.0 mile *1.6 km*, separating at the 2.5 mile *4.0 km* point, where the Carroll Canyon Trail forks to the right.

From this point, the Old Post Trail becomes a footpath taking off over a

rise, running behind a subdivision, to end at the Shelby Drive parking area at 3.0 miles *4.8 km*. This area is the trailhead for the **Bandit**, **Ridge**, and Carroll Canyon Trails in this book. This last half-mile is not very interesting, and we recommend that unless you have a second car at the Shelby Drive parking area, you turn back at the Carroll Canyon Trail junction and retrace your steps.

By looking at the map you can see how the Old Post Trail ties into other trails around Airport Mesa. It is easy and fun to hook into one of the other trails to make a loop instead of simply backtracking.

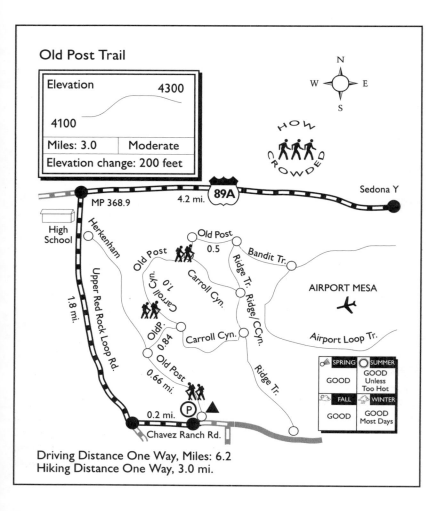

Overlook Point Trails #126

VORTEX

General Information
Location Map E4
Sedona USGS Map
Coconino Forest Service Map

Driving Distance One Way: 1.5 miles *2.4 km* (Time 10 minutes)
Access Road: All cars, All paved
Hiking Distance, Complete Loop: 0.7 miles *1.1 km* (Time 45 minutes)
How Strenuous: Easy to Hard
Features: Vortex Spot, Views

NUTSHELL: This is the easiest and most accessible Sedona Vortex spot.

DIRECTIONS:
From the Sedona Y Go:
    Southwest on Highway 89A for 1.0 mile *1.6 km,* to Airport Road. Turn left onto Airport Road and drive uphill half a mile, to the 1.5 miles *2.4 km* point. Here you will see a parking lot to the left big enough for 12 cars.

TRAILHEAD: At the cable fence on the east side of the parking lot.

DESCRIPTION: There are several trails here:
    Yavapai Route: Take one step through the cable fence and turn left on a narrow footpath. You will move north toward a bald red knob. In 0.1 mile *0.16 km* you will see a path going to your right. This is a connector that can be used as a shortcut.
    Coconino Loop: Keep going ahead from the place where the Yavapai Route meets the connector. As you reach the red knob, the trail turns to the right (E). You make a short climb to a gap and then go down to a red ledge at 0.3 miles *0.5 km.* You will probably find a medicine wheel here, for this is regarded as one of Sedona's vortex spots. You will see a path going off to the north here, but don't take it. It is not one of the loop trails. Instead head back south on a path that you will see well-worn into the redrocks. In 0.4 miles *0.6 km* you will meet the connector trail that you saw on the other side of the ridge. Keep going forward and in a few yards you will come to a place where the Overlook Trail goes uphill.
    Overlook Trail: This trail is very short, taking off from the Coconino Loop. It makes a steep climb to the top of a red knob, and is worth doing if you have the energy. It climbs 70 feet in 0.05 miles *0.08 km.* From the top, known as Overlook Point, you will enjoy the views. You can climb down the front face of the rock, but it is pretty scary for some people, as you must

scale down bare rock. Some people like to go back down the way they came up and take a path that is unnamed, parallel to the Yavapai Route but a few feet higher. It is well worn and takes you back to the top of the "stairs." If you do this, you will have hiked about 0.6 miles *1.0 km*. It's about another 0.1 mile *0.16 km* back down to the parking lot.

If you go down the front of Overlook Point, you come to a point at the top of the "stairs," a natural walkway up from the parking lot. Here you have a chance to take the last of the loop trail, to Courthouse Butte Vista.

Courthouse Butte Vista: This is a very short trail to the south, which climbs about 25 feet in less than 0.1 miles *0.16 km* to a viewpoint.

You will also see a distinct trail running SW along Airport Mesa. This is the **Airport Loop Trail,** which circumnavigates Airport Mesa.

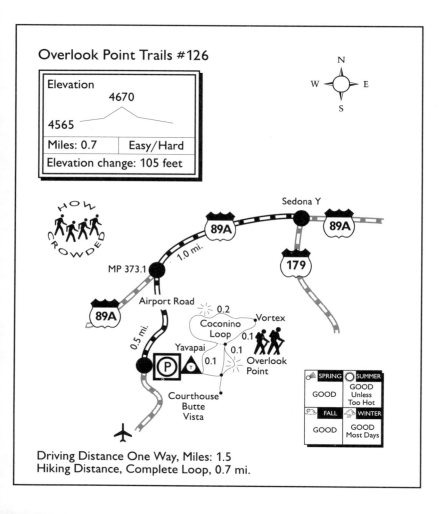

Page Springs Creekside Walk

General Information
Location Map F2
Page Springs USGS Map
Coconino Forest Service Map

Driving Distance One Way: 14.0 miles *22.4 km* (Time 30 minutes)
Access Road: All cars, All paved
Hiking Distance One Way: 0.75 miles *1.2 km* (Time 30 minutes)
How Strenuous: Easy
Features: Oak Creek, Beautiful old cottonwoods, Birding area

NUTSHELL: One of the few walks in the area that goes along the banks of Oak Creek. After an easy drive, you hike past the Fish Hatchery, ending at a place where an unusual rock outcrop furnishes a welcome touch of color.

DIRECTIONS:
From the Sedona Y Go:
Southwest on Highway 89A (toward Cottonwood) for a distance of 11.25 miles *18 km* to the Page Springs Road (Yavapai County Road 50). Turn left and follow the Page Springs Road to the 14.0 mile *22.4 km* point, the beginning of a bridge across Oak Creek. There are parking places along the right shoulder before you go over the bridge.

TRAILHEAD: There are no signs. You will see a trail going downhill to the creek on the south side, in the shadow of the bridge.

DESCRIPTION: This is a hiker-made trail, so there are no signs. When you get to creekside, move south, away from the trailer park. The trail is distinct here and easy to follow. In many places it runs along quite close to the water, always a refreshing treat in the Arizona desert.

Just past the bridge you will notice a cable strung across the creek, with a cage fastened to a tree. This is a gaging station. At times, a person will get into the cage and travel out over the middle of the creek to get a reading on the water depth and flow.

The banks of Oak Creek are lined with immense old cottonwood trees, giving abundant shade and making a habitat for many birds. It is a good birding area. We enjoyed the sight of half a dozen blue herons as we made our walk, plus many lesser birds.

You will soon see the Arizona Game and Fish Hatchery across the creek. (The Hatchery is 0.5 miles *0.8 km* from the bridge, and open to the public—visitors are welcome. Call 634-4805 for hours. Recommended.)

As you move past the Hatchery, the hike feels more "woodsy," away from homes and road noises. The path is less distinct, but it can be followed for the full distance unless high waters cut off part of it. At one point it moves toward the creek and cuts across an irrigation ditch. A log across the ditch makes an effective bridge.

After moving south, the creek and path make a bend to the east. You will see some interesting rock formations at water level on the other side of the creek. Not long after that, a hillside rises along the right edge of the trail. The shelf of land you are walking on eventually tapers to a point against this hillside, cutting off further travel. You will see a rocked-up irrigation ditch in this area. It is in this vicinity that the trail ends. You walk out onto strange rock outcrops here. The rock seems volcanic, but is an unusual burnt mauve laced with seams of a white quartz-like material. It is unusual and fascinating. This is a good place to sit, watch the birds, and listen to the stream.

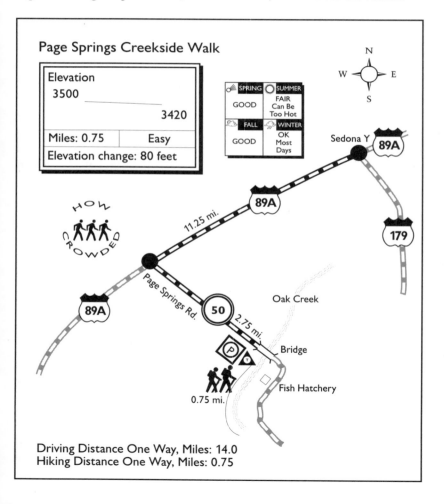

Page Springs Creekside Walk

Elevation	
3500	
	3420
Miles: 0.75	Easy
Elevation change: 80 feet	

SPRING	SUMMER
GOOD	FAIR Can Be Too Hot
FALL	WINTER
GOOD	OK Most Days

Sedona Y — 89A

89A

11.25 mi.

HOW CROWDED

89A

179

Page Springs Rd.

50

2.75 mi.

Oak Creek

P Y

Bridge

Fish Hatchery

0.75 mi.

Driving Distance One Way, Miles: 14.0
Hiking Distance One Way, Miles: 0.75

Palatki

General Information
Location Map C2
Loy Butte and Page Springs USGS Maps
Coconino Forest Service Map

Driving Distance One Way: 13.5 miles *21.6 km* (Time 25 minutes)
Access Road: All cars, Last 5.8 miles *9.3 km* good dirt road
Hiking Distance: Trail #1 is a 0.6 mile *1.0 km* loop; ***Trail #2*** is 0.3 miles *0.5 km* one way
How Strenuous: Both hikes are Easy
Features: Indian ruins, Pictographs, Caves

NUTSHELL: This adventure takes you to the Palatki Indian Ruins 13.5 miles *21.6 km* northwest of Sedona for a short jaunt to cliff dwellings and a meander along the base of Bear Mountain to see caves full of rock art.

DIRECTIONS:
From the Sedona Y Go:
    Southwest on Highway 89A (toward Cottonwood) a distance of 3.2 miles *5.1 km,* to the Dry Creek Road. Turn right on the Dry Creek Road and drive to the stop sign at 6.1 miles *9.8 km.* Turn left on the paved road and drive to the 7.7 mile *12.3 km* point, where the road to Enchantment Resort forks right. Go left here, on the unpaved road FR 152C, to Boynton Pass. You will come to a road junction at 11.7 miles *18.7 km,* where you turn right on FR 525. About 0.1 mile *0.16 km* from this junction, turn right on FR 795 and travel to the parking lot at 13.5 miles *21.6 km.*

TRAILHEAD: There are three trails signed at the parking area, though we think there are really only two hikes here, since the Palatki Vista Trail is only a connecting loop, at either end of which are the real hiking trails.

DESCRIPTION: Note: since mid-1997, this site is only open from 9:30 am to 4:30 pm, and a fee is charged; the money being used for the upkeep of the property. We think the delights of this site are well worth the money.
    Palatki Ruins Trail, 0.6 miles *1.0 km,* for the complete loop. This trail takes you to the Palatki ruins, and is the harder trail, requiring a climb. After 0.2 miles *0.3 km* of level walking you will make a short steep climb, requiring some rock-hopping, to the ruins. The ruins are in two shallow caves. The first ruin is the larger one, with a two story structure that contained eight rooms. The walls are well preserved—even to the juniper poles that support doors and windows. The second ruin is smaller and also contained eight

chambers, but its walls have collapsed and you cannot enter the area. Date of construction of both ruins is about 1200 A.D. The site housed about 100 people. Retrace your path to the bottom and finish the loop back to the parking lot.

Rock Art Trail, 0.3 miles *0.5 km*, one way. This trail zigzags up to the base of tall red cliffs to the left of and above the ranch house, taking you to a series of caves at the base of a butte. Behind (north of) the first cave you will find what appears to be a high-walled ancient ruin but is really a 1920s dwelling which was a temporary residence before the ranch house was built. The string of caves continues to the west. These caves contain the largest collection of rock art in the Verde Valley, ranging from art of the ancient Sinagua to the more modern Yavapais. They also contain inscriptions by Anglo pioneers—and modern vandals. This is also known as the Red Cliffs Trail.

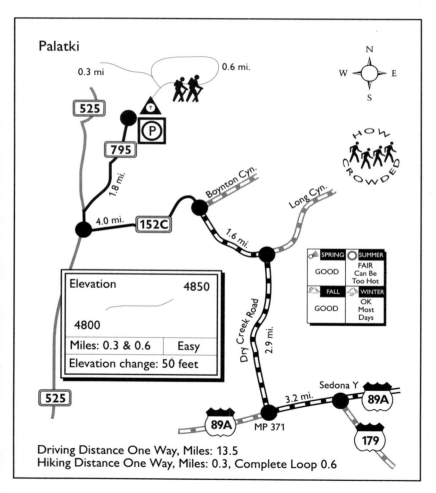

Palatki

Driving Distance One Way, Miles: 13.5
Hiking Distance One Way, Miles: 0.3, Complete Loop 0.6

Parsons Trail #65

General Information
Location Map F1
Clarkdale and Sycamore Basin USGS Maps
Coconino Forest Service Map

Driving Distance One Way: 34.3 miles *54.9 km* (Time 1 hour)
Access Road: All cars, Last 10.5 miles *16.8 km* good dirt road
Hiking Distance One Way: 4.0 miles *6.4 km* (Time 2 hours)
How Strenuous: Moderate
Features: Tremendous colorful canyon, Year around stream

NUTSHELL: This trail enters the south end of Sycamore Canyon, 34.3 miles *54.9 km* SW of Sedona. It is the easiest trail into the canyon.

DIRECTIONS:
From The Y in Sedona Go:
Southwest on Highway 89A a distance of 19.4 miles *31 km*, which will take you into the town of Cottonwood. Go straight through Cottonwood on Main Street and then on Broadway, headed toward Tuzigoot National Monument. At 23.4 miles *37.4 km* you will reach the road to Tuzigoot. Turn right onto it and follow it to the 23.8 mile *38.1 km* point, just over the bridge. Turn left on the first dirt road, FR 131. Stay on FR 131 to the 34.3 mile *54.9 km* point, a parking area at the top of Sycamore Canyon.

TRAILHEAD: The trail is well marked at the parking area. A rusty sign reads, "Parsons Trail #65."

DESCRIPTION: You hike into the south end of Sycamore Canyon, where the walls are not as tall as they are upstream. The walls display fascinating rock formations. The hue of the red stone is rosier than the rock in Sedona and is mixed with white rock and is very rough, grainy and chunky. Basalt is blended in, rather than being a cap as it is in Sedona.

The trail follows along Sycamore Creek, usually on the right bank, though it does cross the creek twice and it is fairly level. In all but extremely dry years, water runs year around up to Parsons Spring at 4.0 miles *6.4 km*, so you have the pleasant experience of walking beside running water. The vegetation is lush and cows often graze through the area.

The canyon for the first two miles seems wide and spacious. At 1.3 miles *2.1 km* you will reach Summers Spring which usually seeps water across the trail. Although the water looks clear and pure, the Forest Service advises not to drink it unless you treat it. Also be careful about eating the watercress

growing there: wherever there are cows, giardia is a threat.

Upstream from Summers Spring the trail gets rough. A heavy flood in 1980 tore out a lot of the trail and it has not been completely rebuilt. In spots you must scramble over boulders. Stay near the streambed and you will pick up the surviving parts of the trail every time you pass one of the washouts. There are large pools that hold fish.

Sycamore Canyon is in a mineralized zone and before it became a Wilderness Area some mining occurred there. You will pass the entrance to an agate mine at 2.7 miles *4.3 km*. It has been plugged but bits of hardware are still around.

The canyon narrows and the walls get steeper as you work your way upstream. You will reach Parsons Spring at 4.0 miles *6.4 km*. Above this point the stream is only intermittent. The spring is the place to stop for a day hike. The trail continues but becomes very difficult.

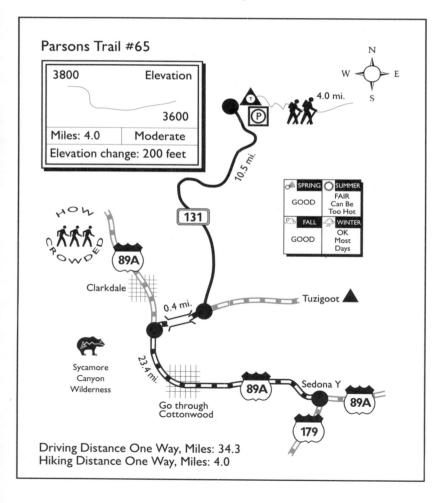

Purtymun Trail

General Information
Location Map B5
Munds Park and Wilson Mt. USGS Maps
Coconino Forest Service Map

Driving Distance One Way: 8.4 miles *13.4 km* (Time 20 minutes)
Access Road: All cars, All paved
Hiking Distance One Way: 1.0 miles *1.6 km* (Time 1 hour)
How Strenuous: Hard
Features: Views

NUTSHELL: This hard hike climbs the east wall of Oak Creek Canyon from a point directly across Highway 89A from the Junipine Resort in the upper canyon, 8.4 miles *13.4 km* north of Sedona. The trail is in poor condition.

DIRECTIONS:
From the Sedona Y Go:
    North on Highway 89A (toward Flagstaff) for a distance of 8.4 miles *13.4 km* (MP 382.6) to the entrance to the Junipine Resort, which is on your left (W). Parking is very limited. There is a place for one car to nose in just across from the entrance. A bit south of the entrance there is a wide spot on the shoulder on the west side.

TRAILHEAD: There are no markings for this trail. Go across the highway to the Fire Station. The trail starts there.

DESCRIPTION: The trailhead is not conspicuous. You will see a Fire Station across the highway from the resort. The trail starts at the south side of the Fire Station between the building and a yellow fire plug.
    This trail was built by the Purtymun family, which homesteaded the Junipine property in 1896. Like other families in the canyon they needed a way to get to the rim in order go to Flagstaff, so they built this trail. They did not have sophisticated equipment, just picks, shovels, crowbars and maybe a little dynamite, so the trail was crude. Their practice was to leave a wagon at the top. When they wanted to go to town they would walk a horse to the top, hitch it to the wagon and then drive to Flagstaff. In town they would load the wagon with goods, perhaps bartering some of the vegetables and fruits they had grown for flour and coffee. They would then drive the wagon back to Oak Creek Canyon and chain it to a tree at the top of the trail. After that they would carry the goods down in saddlebags. Such a trip could

take three or four days.

In spite of the hardships of using the trail, the alternative was worse. There was no convenient wagon road from Sedona to Flagstaff until the Schnebly Hill Road was built in 1902. Before that the only wagon road was the old **Beaverhead** route several miles farther south. Highway 89A did not come onto the scene until much later. It was built in phases starting in the early 1920s, and took a decade to complete.

This trail is so steep and so rough that we don't see how the Purtymuns could ever have gotten a horse up and down it. It is hard climbing for humans, who can grab onto trees for support. We rate this the worst kept and most difficult trail in the book. We do not recommend this hike but we include it as an historic trail.

If you want a good hike up the east rim of upper Oak Creek Canyon try **Cookstove**, **Harding Spring** or **Thomas Point**.

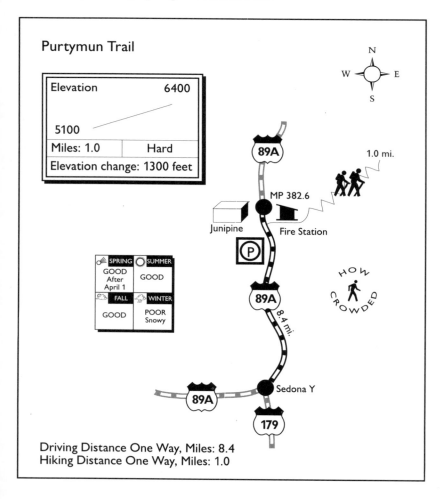

Purtymun Trail

Elevation 6400

5100

Miles: 1.0 | Hard
Elevation change: 1300 feet

1.0 mi.

89A

MP 382.6

Junipine | Fire Station

P

SPRING	SUMMER
GOOD After April 1	GOOD
FALL	WINTER
GOOD	POOR Snowy

89A

HOW CROWDED

89A

8.4 mi.

Sedona Y

89A

179

Driving Distance One Way, Miles: 8.4
Hiking Distance One Way, Miles: 1.0

Rabbit Ears

General Information
Location Map F5
Munds Mountain and Sedona USGS Maps
Coconino Forest Service Map

Driving Distance One Way: 9.4 miles *15.0 km* (Time 15 minutes)
Access Road: All cars, Last 0.1 mile *0.16 km* good dirt road
Hiking Distance One Way: 2.75 miles *4.4 km* (Time 1.5 hours)
How Strenuous: Moderate
Features: Views of Rabbit Ears rock formation

NUTSHELL: This trail follows an arc-shaped ridge. You hike northerly to the high point, where you look out at Rabbit Ears, then descend westerly to join the **Courthouse Butte Loop Trail.**

DIRECTIONS:
From the Sedona Y Go:
　　South on Highway 179 (toward Phoenix) for a distance of 7.2 miles *11.5 km* (MP 306.2) to Jack's Canyon Road (stoplight). Turn left (E) onto Jack's Canyon Road and follow it to the 9.3 miles *14.9 km* point, where you turn right onto an unpaved road into a corral area. Drive in and park at the 9.4 mile *15.0 km* point, next to a brown metal horse gate.

TRAILHEAD: You will see a pole gate and rusty sign reading, "Jack's Canyon #55." This is not really the trailhead for Rabbit Ears, but is the starting point.

DESCRIPTION: Do not go through the horse gate. Instead, walk back down to the paved road following the fence and staying outside it, along a primitive path. At the paved road, go through a horse gate, cross the paved road and go through the second horse gate on the other side. You are now on the Rabbit Ears path.
　　Soon after you begin, the trail crosses a wash. This is usually dry, but one spring, when there was a lot of runoff, this was carrying so much water that we had to abort the hike and wait a week.
　　You will make a gradual climb to the top of an L-shaped ridge. At 0.35 miles *0.6 km* you will see where the trail strayed over onto private land which has since been fenced. The trail makes a little detour to avoid the fence and then gets back on track. At 0.4 miles *0.6 km* you will reach the third and final horse gate. Here you look down to the left into a grassy bowl dotted with houses. The ridge on which this trail is located frames the east

and north sides of the bowl.

At 1.5 miles *2.4 km* you reach the highest point on the trail. This is a wonderful place, where you are far enough away from the developed areas so that they are out of sight. It feels remote and wild. You look out at Rabbit Ears to the NE, about 0.25 miles *0.4 km* away. This is a fine double fluted spire freestanding from the south face of Lee Mountain. To the west, you have fine views of Courthouse Butte. Between Lee Mountain and Courthouse Butte, in the distance, you can see Cathedral Rock.

From this high point, you descend the ridge to the west, hiking toward Courthouse Butte. At the bottom of the ridge, you will meet another horse trail. Turn right here and in a few yards you will emerge into a slickrock wash. The Courthouse Butte Loop Trail comes into this wash from the west. It is 1.5 miles *2.4 km* from here to its trailhead, or you can hike back the way you came.

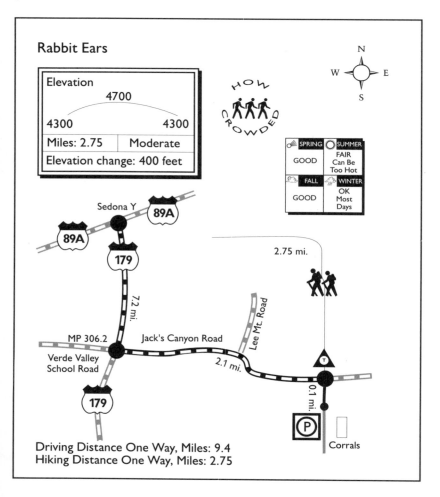

Rachel's Knoll

General Information
Location Map C3
Wilson Mt. USGS Map
Coconino Forest Service Map

Driving Distance One Way: 7.7 miles *12.3 km* (Time 20 minutes)
Access Road: All cars, Last 0.1 miles *0.16 km* good dirt road
Hiking Distance One Way: 0.5 miles *0.8 km* (Time 20 minutes)
How Strenuous: Easy
Features: Very simple, Very Sedona

NUTSHELL: This is an unusual trail, privately owned but open to the public. Its creator intends it as a monument to peace and has posted signs requesting that it be a quiet area for meditation. It is easy to reach, beautiful, and inspiring.

DIRECTIONS:
From the Sedona Y Go:
Southwest on Highway 89A (toward Cottonwood) for 3.2 miles *5.1 km* (MP 371); then turn right on the Dry Creek Road and follow it to the 6.1 mile *9.8 km* point, where there is a stop sign. Turn right on the paved Long Canyon Road and follow it to the end of the paving at 7.6 miles *12.2 km,* and keep going on the dirt road beyond the paving. There is a fork just beyond the end of the paving, where you go left. Soon afterwards you will come to the parking area with signs indicating where to park. You cannot drive up the hill, as the road is closed by a gate.

TRAILHEAD: Walk up the main road.

DESCRIPTION: About halfway up the hill, you will pass from private land to Forest Service land. At 0.2 miles *0.3 km* you will be at the top of the knoll, and re-enter private land, where you will find a sign giving the rules of the area, the "Hill Etiquette:" (1) Dedicated to Meditation & Prayer, (2) Honor the Silence, (3) Stay on the Trail, (4) Groups over 7 Require Permit. Go to the right here, still walking the road.
In a few yards you will reach a place where you may see some vehicles. Some of the jeep tours are permitted to come up here, but they can drive no farther. At 0.37 miles *0.6 km,* you will see a footpath veer off to the right. Stay on the road here and continue heading west. You are now entering the zone where beautiful views unfold. At 0.5 miles *0.8 km* you will be at the end of the road, where you have a choice of footpaths going down a few feet

to bare redrock ledges which are absolutely perfect for sitting, enjoying the unspoiled beauty of the cliffs to the north, and meditating.

The paths below the road are marked, and you can enjoy meandering around. You will probably find medicine wheels and other artifacts. As you curve back toward the way you came in, you will find a Peace Pillar. When we passed by, a group of six women were holding hands in a circle around it, and wished us well. You will also find a donation box at the top. Drop in a dollar or two and help support this inspired project.

People come to Sedona for many reasons. A substantial number believe that Sedona is a special place, endowed with cosmic powers. See the discussion on vortexes on page 255. We have been told that Rachel's Knoll is regarded as a vortex site, but we have not had this confirmed by any of the experts, so we do not include it on our list. However, there is no doubt that it is a place of sublime beauty and spiritual power.

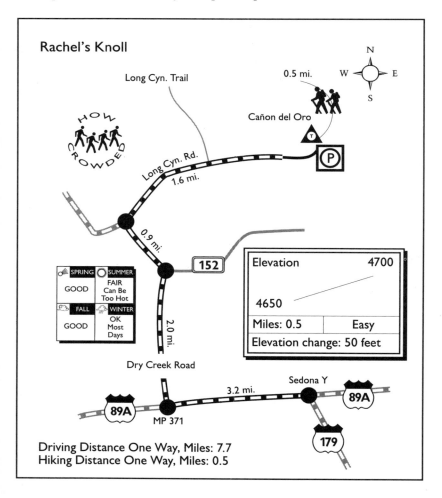

Rachel's Knoll

Long Cyn. Trail

0.5 mi.

Cañon del Oro

Long Cyn. Rd.

1.6 mi.

HOW CROWDED

0.9 mi.

152

	SPRING	SUMMER
	GOOD	FAIR Can Be Too Hot
	FALL	WINTER
	GOOD	OK Most Days

Elevation	4700
4650	
Miles: 0.5	Easy
Elevation change: 50 feet	

2.0 mi.

Dry Creek Road

Sedona Y

3.2 mi.

89A

89A

MP 371

179

Driving Distance One Way, Miles: 7.7
Hiking Distance One Way, Miles: 0.5

Raptor Hill Trail

General Information
Location Map F1
Clarkdale USGS Map
Coconino Forest Service Map

Driving Distance One Way: 21.5 miles *34.4 km* (Time 45 minutes)
Access Road: All cars, All paved
Hiking Distance One Way: 2.8 miles *4.5 km*
How Strenuous: Moderate
Features: Views of Verde Valley, Tuzigoot and Jerome

NUTSHELL: Originating in Dead Horse State Park at Cottonwood, this trail follows an old jeep road out of the park and up onto the flatlands high above.

DIRECTIONS:
From the Sedona Y Go:
Southwest on Highway 89A for 18.6 miles *29.8 km*, to the first stoplight in Cottonwood. Go straight on Highway 89A. You'll reach a second stoplight at 19.2 miles *30.7 km*. Go straight on Historic Highway 89A (Main Street). At 20.6 miles *33.0 km*, just past the cemetery, turn right on 10th Street, which is signed for the park. The entrance to the park is at 21.5 miles *34.4 km*, where you must pay a fee. Once inside the park follow the main road, taking the second turn to the left, which is marked "Tavasci Marsh." Drive to the end of the paved road, and park in the parking area there.

TRAILHEAD: The parking area is a joint trailhead for the Raptor Hill and **Tavasci Marsh** trails.

DESCRIPTIONS: From the parking area, go through the gate and walk up the wide dirt road. At 0.1 mile *0.16 km* the Raptor Hill Trail peels away from the Tavasci Marsh Trail, going to the right (E) uphill. Be sure to take this turn. There is a marker at the place.

You will now make a steep but brief climb, passing an old cabin on a knoll to your right. At 0.7 miles *1.1 km* you will pass through a gate in a fence that marks the boundary of Dead Horse State Park. From the gate, the trail follows an old jeep road for the rest of the way.

You continue to climb, although the climb is gradual, on a rather gentle pitch, and the higher you rise, the better views you have (behind you) of the Verde Valley. You look down on Tuzigoot National Monument from an aspect that is just right for photos. The terrain here is not dramatic. The area

up to the top looks like a pink and white layer cake but lacks the dramatic impact of some of the Sedona redrock hikes.

At 1.4 miles *2.2 km* you will pass through another fence. There is a high horse gate for riders and a stile for walkers. Another landmark is reached at 2.6 miles *4.2 km*, when you pass under a power line. The area here is quite flat and there is a veritable forest of chaparral. At 2.8 miles *4.5 km* you reach a multi-trail junction. There is a sign (which seems fragile and may not be there when you arrive) showing that the Thumper, **Lime Kiln** and Bill Ensign trails are to your right. The sign refers to the trail you have just completed as the South Raptor Hill trail. To the left, the sign shows the North Raptor Hill and Bones trails and Buckboard Road. Refer to the map to see the connections. Bikers can make a nice loop using the South Raptor-Thumper-Lime Kiln trails, but don't try this as a hiker unless you are really strong and have plenty of water.

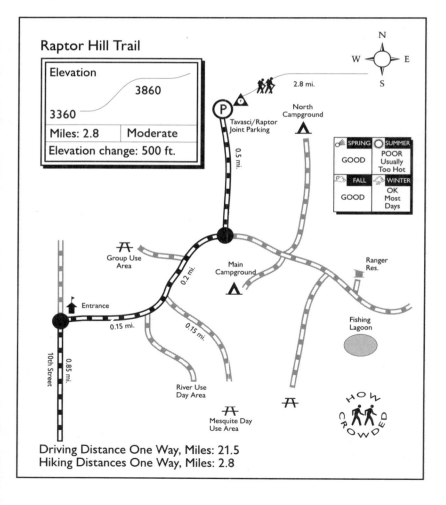

Raptor Hill Trail

Elevation	
3860	
3360	
Miles: 2.8	Moderate
Elevation change: 500 ft.	

	SPRING	SUMMER
	GOOD	POOR Usually Too Hot
	FALL	WINTER
	GOOD	OK Most Days

Driving Distance One Way, Miles: 21.5
Hiking Distances One Way, Miles: 2.8

Rattlesnake Canyon

General Information
Location Map G5
Munds Mt. USGS Map
Coconino Forest Service Map

Driving Distance One Way: 23.0 miles *36.8 km* (Time 45 minutes)
Access Road: All cars, Last 1.0 miles *1.6 km* medium gravel
Hiking Distance One Way: 0.75 miles *1.2 km* (Time 30 minutes)
How Strenuous: Moderate
Features: Remote scenic canyon

NUTSHELL: This trail takes you to the bottom of Rattlesnake Canyon, a little known beautiful spot.

DIRECTIONS:
From the Sedona Y Go:
    South on Highway 179 (toward Phoenix) for 14.7 miles *23.5 km*, to the I-17 Interchange. Turn north and head toward Flagstaff on I-17. At the 22.0 mile *35.2 km* spot you will see Exit 306 "Stoneman Lake" (MP 306.1). Make this exit. Go under I-17 into the lane marked south, to Phoenix, but look for a dirt road to your right (west), FR 647, just beyond the underpass. Turn off onto FR 647. For the first 0.75 miles *1.2 km* it is in good condition except for one gully. At the 22.75 mile *36.4 km* point you reach a T. Turn right here. The road becomes much worse, bare dirt with lots of ruts and rocks. Most cars should be able to make it to the 23.0 mile *36.8 km* point, beyond which the road is too rough. Pull off the road and park.

TRAILHEAD: There are no signs. You walk the road to the canyon rim and then hike down to the bottom.

DESCRIPTION: If you park at the 23.0 mile *36.8 km* point as we recommend, then you must walk about 0.25 miles *0.4 km* to the canyon.
    You won't have to ask *what* canyon. As you near the rim you can see it plainly. This is one of those hidden canyons that you don't see from anywhere unless you fly over it. But it is a deep and interesting canyon. The walls are quite sheer and are made of successive layers of columnar-jointed basalt. There are many such canyons in northern Arizona, but this one has more color and character than most.
    At the canyon rim you will see that the road goes down into the canyon but that no one drives it. Walk down the road. The road will disappear in about 0.1 miles *0.16 km*.

Beyond this point you will find a footpath in good condition. It is a real walking path, with erosion control and other improvements and you can see that a lot of work has been done on it. It is not a recreational trail, but is used to provide access to the gaging station that you will find at the bottom.

We think the rock walls you pass by are interesting and have some beautiful markings, including accents made by lichens and mosses.

At the bottom is a cable strung across the canyon and the gaging station, which is a sort of tall corrugated tube with a box on top. There is a depth gauge on the front of the tube showing depths as high as ten feet.

Beyond this there is a waterfall with a 30 foot drop. It seemed dangerous to climb. Other sources indicate that one can climb down it, but we do not recommend dangerous climbing. From this point, Rattlesnake Canyon joins **Woods Canyon** in about 2.25 miles *3.6 km.*

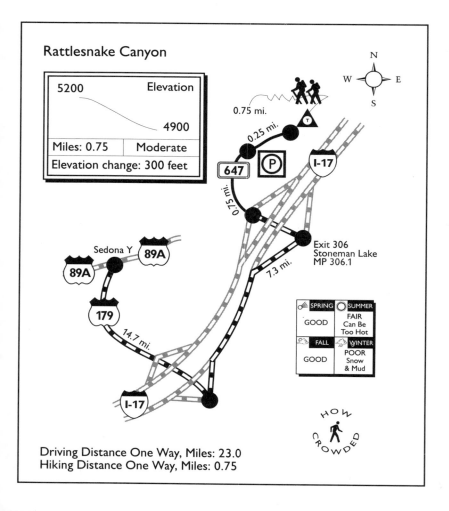

Red Rock Loop Trail #118

Driving Distance One Way: 5.9 miles *9.4 km* (Time 15 minutes)
Access Road: All vehicles, Last 0.1 mi. *0.16 km* good gravel road
Hiking Distance One Way: 1.8 miles *2.9 km* (Time 1.0 hours)
How Strenuous: Moderate
Features: Part of Arizona Pathways trails, Easy to reach, Views

NUTSHELL: Located a short, easy drive south of Sedona, this trail takes you around the toe of Scheurman Mountain, by the Sedona Red Rock High School, to end at the Upper Red Rock Loop Road.

DIRECTIONS:
From the Sedona Y Go:
   Southwest on Highway 89 (toward Cottonwood) for a distance of 5.5 miles *8.8 km* (MP 368.6) to the Lower Red Rock Loop Road. Turn left on the Lower Red Rock Loop Road and follow it to the 5.8 miles *9.3 km* point, where you turn left on a gravel road marked with an Arizona Pathways sign, also known as FR 9853. Drive in on this road to the 5.9 mile *9.4 km* point, where there is a parking lot.

TRAILHEAD: At the parking lot.

DESCRIPTION: The trail is very easy to follow. As you leave the parking lot, you will see that portions of the trail have been surfaced with a gray gravel, which makes it easy to see and identify.
   For the first part of the trail, you will climb onto the shoulder of Scheurman Mountain, and as you walk, you can see why the trail does this, because the Lower Red Rock Loop Road cuts in very close to the mountain, so that if hikers walked along at road level, they would almost be in traffic. This made things difficult for the trail builders, but it is a boon to the hiker, for it takes you up high enough to enjoy some splendid views. You also have the experience of being able to enjoy walking right on the redrocks. For about the first 0.5 miles *0.8 km* you walk along the base of beautiful high red cliffs, the best part of the trail. Benches have been thoughtfully placed at strategic intervals so that the hiker may pause and enjoy the scenery. There was a trail log at the second bench, indicating that the trail was first used in January 1997.

You round the toe of the mountain and then head toward Sedona. Here the views are not as good because you enter into an area covered with brush. The trail is also uncomfortably close to busy Highway 89. It is definitely not a remote wilderness experience. The red cliffs disappear here, as the red rock in this area is covered by volcanic rock and debris.

As you go farther, you walk adjacent to the playing fields of the Sedona Red Rock High School, and soon after this, will reach the end of the trail, where it meets the Upper Red Rock Loop Road.

This trail fills a need for many people, who don't have the time to get out into the country, or who face a situation where they want to hike but the weather has made the backcountry roads impassable. One should be able to make this hike almost any day of the year. We believe that short trails such as this fill a much-needed niche in the repertoire of Sedona trails.

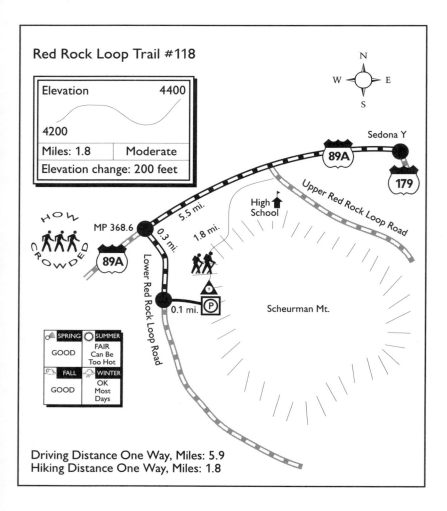

Red Rock State Park

General Information
Location Map F3
Sedona USGS Map
Coconino Forest Service Map

Drive Distance One Way: 8.8 miles *14.1 km* (Time 15 minutes)
Access Road: All cars, All paved
Hiking Distance: 8 hikes of various distances, see map
How Strenuous: Easy-Moderate, except Eagles' Nest, which is Hard
Features: Oak Creek, Red Rock State Park, Views

NUTSHELL: Eight trails located in Red Rock State Park 8.8 miles *14.1 km* SW of Sedona. They range from easy to hard and offer a variety of features. This is a good place to take the family.

DIRECTIONS:
From the Sedona Y Go:
    Southwest on Highway 89A (toward Cottonwood) for 5.5 miles *8.8 km* (MP 368.6) then turn left on the Lower Red Rock Loop Road and follow it to the 8.5 miles 13.6 *km* point, where you turn right into Red Rock State Park. An admission is charged at an information center. After paying the fee, drive to the Visitor Center and park, at 8.8 miles *14.1 km*.

TRAILHEAD: All hikes start at the Visitor Center.

DESCRIPTION: Go through the Visitor Center and turn right on the paved trail. At 0.08 miles *0.13 km* you will come to the first junction. (Note: our mileage includes connections to the trails.)
    (1) **Smoke Trail.** 0.4 miles *0.6 km*. Walk down to the water and turn right for a creekside stroll. Easy.
    (2) **Black Hawk Trail.** 0.6 mi. *1.0 km*. From the end of Smoke Trail, cross the creek to join the end of the Kisva Trail. Easy.
    (3) **Kisva Trail.** 1.0 miles *1.6 km*. Walk to Kingfisher Crossing bridge. Cross the creek and walk to the trail junction for the Apache Fire Trail and the Eagles' Nest Trail. Turn right. The Kisva Trail follows an old ranch road along the banks of the creek. Easy.
    (4) **Bunk House Trail.** 1.58 mi. *2.5 km* loop. Cross Kingfisher Bridge and turn right on Kisva. When you come to the bridge, turn right. Easy.
    (5) **Eagles' Nest Trail.** 3.23 miles *5.2 km* for a complete loop, requiring a 200 ft. climb. Take the Kisva Trail to its end, where you will see the Eagles' Nest Trail going uphill to the left. Make the steep climb to the top,

where you will enjoy great views. Then loop around to join the Kisva Trail at its midsection; though you could take the Coyote Ridge connector over to Apache Fire. Hard.

(6) **Apache Fire Trail.** 1.7 mi. *2.7 km* loop. Cross Kingfisher bridge. At the trail junction where the Kisva and Eagles' Nest trails go to the right, go left instead and walk to the base of the knoll on which the house is located. There you find the Apache Fire trail. Moderate.

(7) **Javelina Trail.** 2.0 mile *3.2 km* loop. Follow directions to the Apache Fire Trail and begin to hike it. Just before the Apache Fire trail begins climbing out of the creek bed, the Javelina Trail goes left. Moderate

(8) **Yavapai Trail.** 1.58 miles *2.5 km* loop. Walk across Kingfisher bridge to the Apache Fire Trail. Here you take the left fork, on the unpaved East Gate Road. Soon you will reach the Yavapai Trail, going to the left (N). The Javelina Trail joins the road here. Moderate.

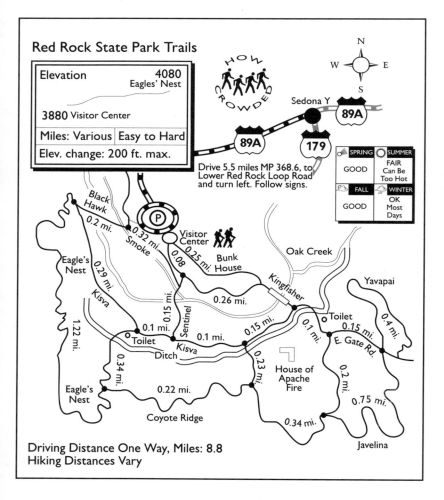

Ridge Trail

General Information
Location Map E4
Sedona USGS Map
Coconino Forest Service Map

Driving Distance One Way: 2.6 miles *4.2 km* (Time 10 minutes)
Access Road: All cars, All paved
Hiking Distance One Way: 2.3 miles *3.7 km* (Time 1.5 hours)
How Strenuous: Hard
Features: Nice views and variety, Connects to other trails

NUTSHELL: Part of the Airport Mesa trail system, this fine trail climbs up to the top of a ridge, then descends along the crest of a narrow spine on the other side of the mountain.

DIRECTIONS:
From the Sedona Y Go:
    Southwest on Highway 89A for 2.1 miles *3.4 km,* to a stoplight. Turn left on Shelby Drive. Continue on Shelby for 0.5 miles *0.8 km* (just past Stanley Steamer) and turn right into the parking lot of a building known as La Entrada, at 2155 Shelby Drive. At the back of the paved parking lot you will see three trailhead parking signs. Park at one of them.

TRAILHEAD: At the parking area.

DESCRIPTION: Take the footpath going into the trees from the parking area. Almost immediately you will see a sign for the **Old Post Trail**. Go past this; do not turn. Soon after this you will come to the junction for the **Bandit Trail**. Again, ignore the Bandit Trail and keep on going straight. You will curve along the base of Airport Mesa for a time.
    At 0.6 miles *1.0 km* you reach the trail junction where the **Carroll Canyon Trail** comes in from your right. Go straight, as the Carroll Canyon and Ridge Trails combine for a short segment. At 0.8 miles *1.3 km* the Carroll Canyon Trail splits off to the right. Go straight ahead here.
    You will now begin to climb. At first you will ascend the east side of Carroll Canyon, which becomes quite deep here, with impressive rock cliffs. In a short distance, however, as you continue to climb, you will begin moving away from the canyon. You climb to the toe of a ridge, the highest point on the trail, at 1.6 miles *2.6 km*. There are some very nice views from here. From this point you will see a trail going off to your left, which makes a steep climb uphill to join the **Table Top Trail** near the **Airport Loop Trail**.

Ignore this, as it is an illegal hiker-made trail that goes up to connect to the **Airport Loop Trail**. From this point, you will begin a steep descent. The trail was unmarked at this point when we last checked it, but it is the only trail going downhill, and frequent use makes it discernible.

The last segment of the trail goes down on the spine of a narrow ridge, with wonderful views, an exciting part of the trail. At 2.2 miles *3.5 km* you reach an old road, where there is a trail sign. Turn to the right and you will come to the lower access road at 2.3 miles *3.7 km*.

This is a good two-car hike. The end of the trail is reached by taking the Chavez Ranch Road off of the Upper Red Rock Loop (see **Old Post Trail**). At 0.4 miles *0.6 km* the paved road turns to the right. Drive straight, on the gray gravel road. At 0.9 miles *1.4 km* there is a dirt road to your left at a sharp angle, blocked by a dirt berm and boulder. This is the end of the trail. There is no parking space here. Go up the road a bit and find a place to park.

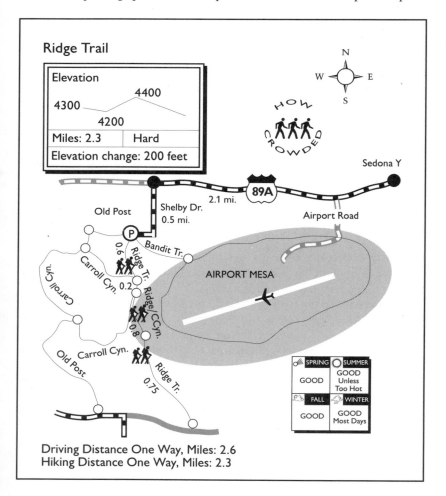

Robbers Roost

General Information
Location Map C1
Loy Butte and Page Springs USGS Maps
Coconino Forest Service Map

Driving Distance One Way: 19.2 miles *30.7 km* (Time 30 minutes)
Access Road: All cars, Last 9.6 miles *15.4 km* good dirt road
Hiking Distance One Way: 1.5 miles *2.4 km* (Time 45 minutes)
How Strenuous: Easy
Features: Fascinating cave with unique window

NUTSHELL: This is a short hike to an interesting cave in a red butte located 19.2 miles *30.7 km* northwest of Sedona.

DIRECTIONS:
From the Sedona Y Go:
    Southwest on Highway 89A (toward Cottonwood) a distance of 9.6 miles *15.4 km* (MP 364.5) to the Red Canyon Road. Turn right on Red Canyon Road, also known as FR 525, and follow it to the 12.4 mile *19.8 km* point where FR 525C branches to the left. Turn left on FR 525C and follow it to the 19.2 miles *30.7 km* point. There you will see a rough road branching to the right marked FR 9530. Take this but drive it only a short distance to the top of the hill, where you will park.

TRAILHEAD: You walk up the road, FR 9530, for 1.1 miles *1.8 km*. There you will see the trail going down into a ravine to your right. It is not signed.

DESCRIPTION: If you have a high clearance vehicle and tough tires you can drive right up to the trailhead and save a mile of walking, but don't try to make it in an ordinary passenger car.
    As you walk up the road you approach Casner Mountain. Your target is the muffin shaped red butte just in front of and on the right hand side of the mountain. Robbers Roost is located on the far side of that butte.
    At the trailhead you will see an area to your left where the vegetation is matted down because of cars parking there. Look for the trail to your right. Usually there are cairns marking the beginning of the trail. The trail goes straight downhill into the bottom of a ravine, then goes up the other side.
    The trail, after rising from the bottom of the ravine, curls around to the north side of the butte and climbs about two-thirds of the way to its top. At 0.35 miles *0.6 km* from the beginning of the trail, the trail forks. The right fork goes to the top. Ignore it for now and go left. This will require that you

walk out on the face of the butte on the slickrock (a misnomer, as the rock actually gives very good traction, like sandpaper). The two metal rods that used to stick vertically out of the rock face and acted as handholds were gone the last time we hiked here, but we had no trouble because of it.

After that you will see the cave. Rock walls have been built at the mouth of the cave to support dirt fill that was placed there to make the floor of the cave level. There are even steps to the "door" of the cave.

The cave looks out to the northeast, toward Bear Mountain and Maroon Mountain. Down below it there is a cattle tank.

There is a circular window in the cave that looks more to the south. This window is unique. There is nothing else like it in the Sedona area. The cave gets its name, Robbers Roost, from the fanciful notion that this would be a good hideout for robbers, who could use the window as a lookout. It was used by a moonshiner during Prohibition.

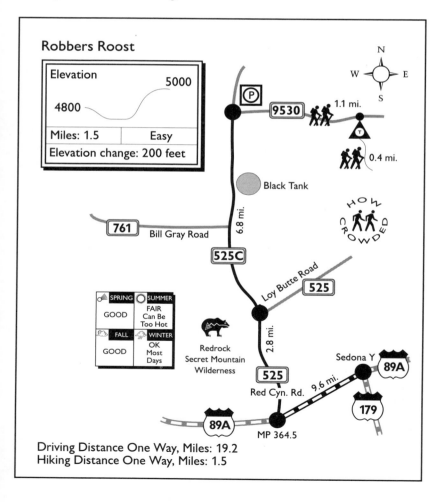

Robbers Roost

Elevation

5000

4800

Miles: 1.5 — Easy

Elevation change: 200 feet

9530 — 1.1 mi.

0.4 mi.

Black Tank

761 — Bill Gray Road

6.8 mi.

H O W C R O W D E D

525C

Loy Butte Road — 525

	SPRING	SUMMER
	GOOD	FAIR Can Be Too Hot
	FALL	WINTER
	GOOD	OK Most Days

Redrock Secret Mountain Wilderness

2.8 mi.

Sedona Y — 89A

525

Red Cyn. Rd. — 9.6 mi. — 179

89A — MP 364.5

Driving Distance One Way, Miles: 19.2
Hiking Distance One Way, Miles: 1.5

Rupp Trail

General Information
Location Map D3
Wilson Mountain USGS Map
Coconino Forest Service Map

Driving Distance One Way*:* 10.7 miles *17.1 km* (Time 20 minutes)
Access Road*:* All cars, Last 3.0 miles *4.8 km* good dirt roads
Hiking Distance One Way*:* 2.0 miles *3.2 km* (Time 1.0 hour)
How Strenuous*:* Moderate
Features*:* Views

NUTSHELL: This trail starts near Doe Mountain, proceeds southerly to the Cockscomb, then turns to follow the old Tree Farm fence until it meets a primitive jeep road. It then follows the jeep road to the canyon of Dry Creek, where it joins the **Girdner Trail**.

DIRECTIONS:
From the Sedona Y Go:
    Southwest on Highway 89A a distance of 3.2 miles *5.1 km* (MP 371) to Dry Creek Road and turn right onto Dry Creek Road. Follow it to the 6.1 mile *9.8 km* point, where it joins Long Canyon Road. Turn left here, staying on FR 152C. At the 7.7 mile *12.3 km* point, turn left on FR 152C, which becomes a dirt road. At the 9.7 mile *15.5 km* point, turn left on FR 9583 and follow it to the 10.7 mile *17.1 km* point, where you will find a locked gate. There is no real parking lot. Park on the shoulder of the road in such a way that you do not block access through the gate.

TRAILHEAD: The Rupp Trail is an orphan, with access from the Cockscomb Butte Route (the one we use here), the **Cockscomb Trail** or the **Girdner Trail**. At the gate you will see a sign marked "Public Trail," which is the trail to take to reach the Rupp trailhead.

DESCRIPTION: The Tree Farm, a Sedona institution for many years, has been sold to land developers. We understand that the trail we are using here has been protected by an agreement with the Forest Service, but by the time you use this, conditions on the land may have changed.
    The public trail follows the fence surrounding the Tree Farm property. At 0.5 miles *0.8 km* you reach a fence corner where you turn left, continuing to follow the fence line. You are at the base of the Cockscomb here. A gravel road inside the fence is only a few feet away from you at this point.
    At 0.75 miles *1.2 km* you reach a gate where an old jeep road went into

the farm. Don't take the jeep road; stay on the footpath, even though the fence will disappear from view for a while. At 1.0 miles *1.6 km* you start down a long downhill grade at the foot of which you meet the fence again where an old road went into the farm. Follow the trail along the fence until you come to an open gate blocked by boulders. Go inside and you will find the Rupp Trail marker on a signpost within at the 1.1 mile *1.8 km* point.

The Rupp Trail is a jeep road, easy to follow and easy to walk. It slopes downhill all the way and gives some good views out over many of the landmarks of the south area of Sedona. At 1.7 miles *2.7 km* you will find another Rupp Trail signpost where another jeep road comes in from the right. Turn left, going downhill. The trail ends at another signpost on the bank of Dry Creek where you join the Girdner Trail. The Rupp family owned the Tree Farm, giving the trail its name.

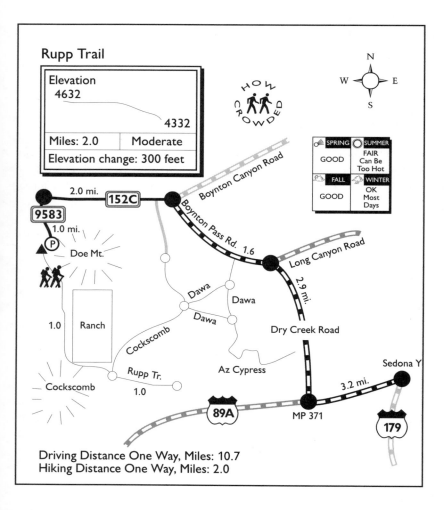

Sacred Mountain

General Information
Location Map G6
Casner Butte USGS Map
Coconino Forest Service Map

Driving Distance One Way: 18.1 miles *29.0 km* (Time 30 minutes)
Access Road: All cars, Last 0.8 miles *1.3 km* good dirt road
Hiking Distance One Way: 0.35 miles *0.6 km* (Time 30 minutes)
How Strenuous: Moderate
Features: Indian ruins, Views

NUTSHELL: Located 18.1 miles *29.0 km* southeast of Sedona, this special mountain takes moderate effort to climb. At the top are located some significant pueblo ruins and the views are fine.

DIRECTIONS:
From the Sedona Y Go:
    South on Highway 179 (toward Phoenix) for 14.7 miles *23.5 km*, to the I-17 Interchange. Instead of going onto I-17, go underneath it onto a paved road, FR 618. Stay on FR 618. The paving ends at the bridges at the Beaver Creek Campground. Half a mile beyond, at 17.9 miles *28.6 km*, as the road is curving right, you will see a dirt road, FR 9201A, to your left. Pull off on 9201A. You will see that it leads to a fence. Try to get as close to the fence as you can (it's about 0.2 miles *0.3 km*) and park.

TRAILHEAD: You will not see a trail sign. Go through the gate and turn right and walk parallel to the fence. The path is obvious.

DESCRIPTION: The mountains that fill the northern horizon as you drive through the Beaver Creek area are all part of the Mogollon Rim, a giant uplift that runs from Silver City, New Mexico to Ash Fork, Arizona. As you come around a curve in the road, Sacred Mountain appears. It is really more of a butte than a mountain in this country full of mountains, and it stands alone in front of the rim. It is set apart by its color—white—against the darker colors of the rim, which are gray, black and red.
    At times, when the low evening sun hits Sacred Mountain, the mountain seems to glow. We saw a beautiful example of this one March evening when we were at the nearby Montezuma's Well (worth a visit). From the top of the well we looked northwest and saw Sacred Mountain shining as if it were lit by a spotlight—magic. One can well understand why the ancient Indians thought that the mountain was sacred.

At the fence surrounding Sacred Mountain there is a small sign indicating that the ruins are protected by Federal law. Go through the gate and immediately turn right, walking along parallel to the fence. You will pick up the trail there and will see it going up the toe of the mountain that faces the road. The trail will take you to a sign with a visitors' register to which you may add your name. At the top of the mountain you will find extensive ruins. Unfortunately, these fine ruins were thoroughly pothunted before scientists could conduct a scientific excavation, greatly diminishing their archaeological value. Please do not disturb them.

The site has not been restored, just investigated. The remains of many walls have been uncovered so that you can see the outline of the pueblo. It was a fairly large site, perhaps one of great significance to the ancient people who dwelt there.

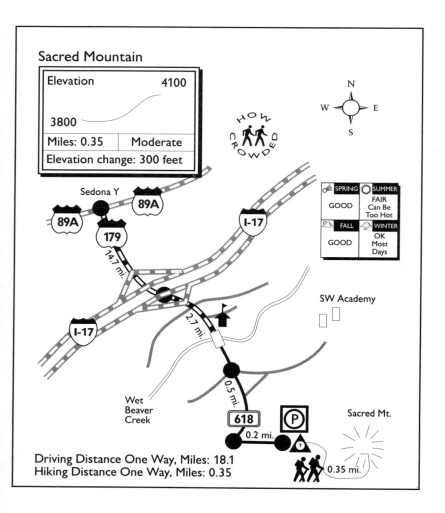

Scheurman Mountain Trail #56

General Information
Location Map E3
Sedona USGS Map
Coconino Forest Service Map

Driving Distance One Way: 4.5 miles *7.2 km* (Time 10 minutes)
Access Road: All cars, All paved
Hiking Distance One Way: 1.1 miles *1.8 km* (Time 1 hour)
How Strenuous: Moderate
Features: Views

NUTSHELL: This sprawling mountain southwest of Sedona is rather drab but is a platform for great views.

DIRECTIONS:
From the Sedona Y Go:
Southwest on Highway 89 (toward Cottonwood) for a distance of 4.2 miles *6.7 km* (MP 368.9) to the Upper Red Rock Loop Road, the road to the high school. Turn left on the Upper Red Rock Loop Road and follow it to the 4.45 miles *7.1 km* point, where you turn right on Scorpion Way. (You will pass Scorpion Drive first, then come to Scorpion Way.) You will see a sign for the trailhead at the turn. In another 0.05 miles *0.08 km*, turn left into the parking area, also signed. The parking place is just across from the high school's Building B, Administration Center.

TRAILHEAD: You will see a rusty trailhead sign on the south side of the parking lot, and the trail leading toward the mountain.

DESCRIPTION: In order to guide hikers onto the trail, the Forest Service has erected official cairns in wire cages. Look for them and you won't be misled. At 0.15 miles *0.24 km*, you will come to a gate. Beyond the gate the trail climbs up to a saddle. It is a good trail, winding its way uphill so that the climb is gradual. Almost immediately you are rewarded with good views. After a steep but short climb of 0.5 miles *0.8 km*, you will reach the top, a good place to catch your breath and enjoy the views.

At the top you will see that the trail has two branches. Each is worth exploring and is about 0.3 miles *0.5 km* long. The one we enjoy the most is the trail to the left. This goes out onto an overlook from where you will enjoy good views of Cathedral Rock and Oak Creek. The viewpoint is about 0.3 miles *0.5 km* from the fork. (About 30 paces from the beginning you will intersect a trail going to the right. It goes about 2.0 miles *3.2 km* SW to join

the Lower Red Rock Loop Road near the place where you park for the **Goosenecks** hike. We find this part of the trail to be colorless and not very interesting. Not recommended.)

After enjoying the views, return to the main trail junction and take the trail that goes westerly out into another lookout point. You have to pick your way out to the edge, but navigating is easy.

The mountain is named after Sedona pioneer Henry Schuerman, a German who spelled his name Schürman. The standard way to Americanize that spelling is to place an e after the u, making the correct spelling Schuerman, and this was the way Henry spelled his name. Map makers goofed and spelled it Scheurman. We regret this error, but go with the flow, using the incorrect but now-established spelling. Scheurman Mountain is an old shield volcano. Instead of exploding violently and forming a tall cone, shield volcanoes ooze up, making a low tapering shape.

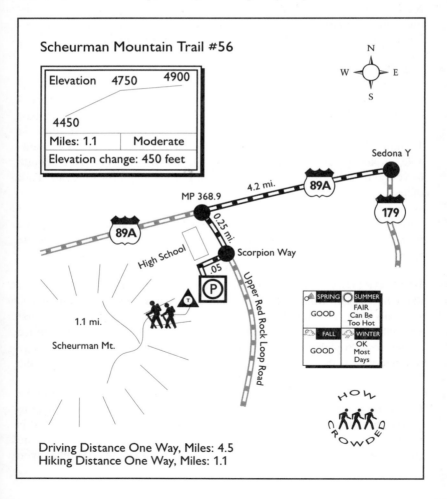

Scheurman Mountain Trail #56

Elevation 4750 4900 4450
Miles: 1.1 Moderate
Elevation change: 450 feet

Sedona Y

4.2 mi. 89A
MP 368.9
89A 179
0.25 mi.
High School Scorpion Way
.05
Upper Red Rock Loop Road
P
1.1 mi.
Scheurman Mt.

SPRING SUMMER
GOOD FAIR Can Be Too Hot
FALL WINTER
GOOD OK Most Days

HOW CROWDED

Driving Distance One Way, Miles: 4.5
Hiking Distance One Way, Miles: 1.1

Schnebly Hill Trail #158

General Information
Location Map E5
Munds Mt. and Munds Park USGS Maps
Coconino Forest Service Map

Driving Distance One Way: 5.5 miles *8.8 km* (Time 30 minutes)
Access Road: High clearance cars, Last 4.2 miles *6.7 km* rough dirt road
Hiking Distance One Way: 2.4 miles *3.8 km* (Time 1.5 hours)
How Strenuous: Hard
Features: Historic road, Views

NUTSHELL: This trail starts where the **Munds Wagon Trail** ends, climbing to the top of Schnebly Hill, on an old road, then swinging south and following the edge of the rim to join the **Munds Mountain Trail**.

DIRECTIONS:
From the Sedona Y Go:
    South on Highway 179 (toward Phoenix) for a distance of 0.3 miles *0.5 km* (MP 313.1) to the Schnebly Hill Road. It is just across the bridge past Tlaquepaque. Turn left onto the Schnebly Hill Road. It is paved for the first 1.0 miles *1.6 km* and then turns into a dirt road so rough it is marked unsuitable for passenger cars. At 5.5 miles *8.8 km*, you will see a low redrock butte to your left with a parking area in front of it big enough for four cars. Park there.

TRAILHEAD: Walk down the road about twenty yards from the place where you have parked. You will see the trailhead marker to your left, on the uphill side of the road.

DESCRIPTION: The first half of the trail is the original 1902 alignment of the Schnebly Hill Road, (originally called the **Munds Wagon Trail**) and as you walk along it, you will have fascinating and ever- changing views. First you will look down into the Bear Wallow-Mitten Ridge area. As you move farther south (uphill) you will begin to see around the south end of the ridge into Sedona. At the top you can see right through a natural corridor into the Verde Valley. There are many superb vista points.
    At the 1.2 miles *1.9 km* point look to your right just as you come to the top of the grade, at a hairpin curve. Here you will see a footpath going to your right (S), into the trees. Follow it. This is the new leg of the trail. It is marked by cairns and takes you south along the rim. In some places you are right on the rim and have choice views into colorful country. At others you

go inland a bit. You will pass through two gates. The second gate is at Committee Tank, located to your left (E), a favorite spot for wildlife.

Soon after, the trail reaches a thin ridge connecting to Munds Mountain. This ridge is a wonderful and unusual land feature. From the ridge you can see to the north into the Schnebly Hill area and south into Jacks Canyon, a great double-header. You are high enough to have sweeping views out over the landscape on top of the Mogollon Rim. The San Francisco Peaks stand out and are very attractive from here. The ridge then dips down to join the **Munds Mountain Trail** at the 2.4 miles *3.8 km* point, a place marked by a super cairn. The **Jacks Canyon Trail** terminates here, coming up from the bottom of Jacks Canyon.

The Munds Mountain Trail is steep, climbing 500 feet in half a mile *0.8 km* to the top.

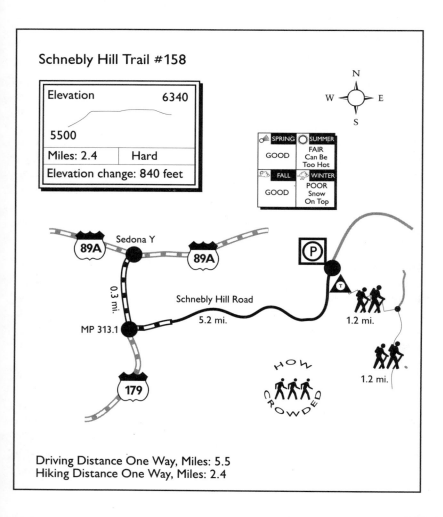

Schnebly Hill Trail #158

Elevation	6340
5500	
Miles: 2.4	Hard
Elevation change: 840 feet	

SPRING	SUMMER
GOOD	FAIR Can Be Too Hot
FALL	WINTER
GOOD	POOR Snow On Top

89A — Sedona Y — 89A

Schnebly Hill Road — 5.2 mi.

0.3 mi.

MP 313.1

179

1.2 mi.

1.2 mi.

HOW CROWDED

Driving Distance One Way, Miles: 5.5
Hiking Distance One Way, Miles: 2.4

Secret Canyon Trail #121

General Information
Location Map C4
Loy Butte and Wilson Mt. USGS Maps
Coconino Forest Service Map

Driving Distance One Way: 8.6 miles *13.8 km* (Time 30 minutes)
Access Road: Most cars, Last 3.4 miles *5.4 km* rough dirt road
Hiking Distance One Way: 5.5 miles *8.8 km* (Time 3 hours)
How Strenuous: Hard
Features: Views, Remote canyon

NUTSHELL: This beautiful canyon, 8.6 miles *13.8 km* northwest of uptown Sedona, provides a delightful hike along a streambed through the redrocks. **A personal favorite.**

DIRECTIONS:
From the Sedona Y Go:
Southwest on Highway 89A (toward Cottonwood) for 3.2 miles *5.1 km* (MP 371) to Dry Creek Road. Turn right on Dry Creek Road and proceed to the 5.2 mile *8.3 km* point, where you turn right on FR 152, the Vultee Arch Road, and follow it to the 8.6 mile *13.8 km* point. You will see a road sign pointing to the trail turnoff. Make a sharp turn to your left into the parking area.

TRAILHEAD: There is a signboard with map, and bronze plaque in memory of David Miller.

DESCRIPTION: The access road to this hike, FR 152, is rough. We frequently see people in ordinary passenger cars driving this road, but be on the lookout for washouts and rocks.

Watch carefully for the turnoff to the Secret Canyon trailhead. The road in this area is lined with a screen of brush and trees and the entry is a brief opening in this screen. A large sign has been installed, making this trailhead easier to find.

The driveway into the parking space is rough. The area holds only about five cars.

From the parking area the trail goes immediately to Dry Creek and then turns right (N) and runs along the bottom of Dry Creek, going up (NW) toward its headwater. If water is running in Dry Creek you may not be able to make this hike, as the trail winds back and forth across the creek several times.

The trail takes you through some beautiful back country, passing through impressive redrocks. At 0.6 miles *1.0 km* you will see the **H S Canyon** trail taking off to the left.

We like the first part of the Secret Canyon hike the best, where you are going through the redrocks. There are several side canyons that are fun to explore, and are recommended.

At about 2.0 miles *3.2 km* you come up out of the canyon bottom and walk along the side of the canyon, right on the redrocks. At 2.1 miles *3.4 km* you will meet the **Dave Miller Trail**, which branches to the right.

Just beyond this trail junction the Secret Canyon Trail enters a pine forest. For the purposes of this book, which features day hikes, we recommend that you stop in the cool pines at 2.5 miles *4.0 km*, in which case this is a moderate hike. The trail goes 3.0 miles *4.8 km* farther, following the course of the canyon as it winds its way to the base of the rim.

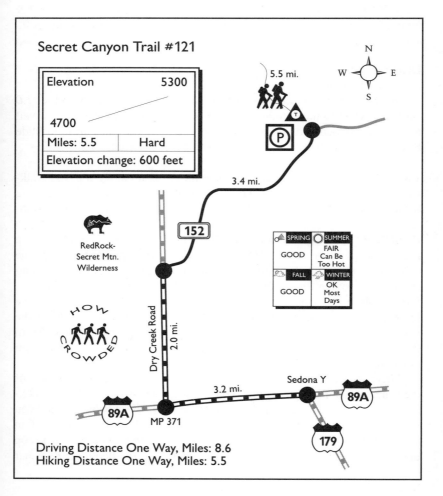

Secret Canyon Trail #121

Elevation 5300
4700
Miles: 5.5 | Hard
Elevation change: 600 feet

5.5 mi.

N
W ←◇→ E
S

3.4 mi.

152

RedRock-
Secret Mtn.
Wilderness

SPRING / SUMMER
GOOD | FAIR Can Be Too Hot
FALL / WINTER
GOOD | OK Most Days

HOW CROWDED

Dry Creek Road
2.0 mi.

Sedona Y

3.2 mi.

89A

89A
MP 371

179

Driving Distance One Way, Miles: 8.6
Hiking Distance One Way, Miles: 5.5

Slide Rock

General Information
Location Map C5
Wilson Mt. USGS Map
Coconino Forest Service Map

Driving Distance One Way: 6.9 miles *11.0 km* (Time 15 minutes)
Access Road: All cars, All paved
Hiking Distance One Way: 0.5 miles *0.8 km* (Time 30 minutes)
How Strenuous: Easy
Features: Slide Rock State Park

NUTSHELL: You enjoy two hiking trails in Slide Rock State Park 6.9 miles *11.0 km* north of Sedona, one at water's edge and the other on the cliffs above Oak Creek.

DIRECTIONS:
From The Y in Sedona Go:
   North on Highway 89A (toward Flagstaff) a distance of 6.9 miles *11.0 km* (MP 381.1) to the entrance to Slide Rock State Park. The park is well marked and signed and you will have no trouble finding it. Pull in to Slide Rock State Park (there is an entry fee) and park on the large lot.

TRAILHEAD: From the parking lot, walk upstream along a paved walkway, the Pendley Homestead Trail. When you get to the Apple Packing Shed, you will be at the place where the Cliff Top and Creekside trails start.

DESCRIPTION: (1) **Creekside Trail**: At the Packing Shed you will see a flight of steps going down to Oak Creek. Take the steps. You will emerge onto a long redrock ledge going upstream. It is easy and fun to walk along the ledge, enjoying the water and the redrock cliffs on either side. This is a favorite place for visitors and is likely to be crowded. You will see a place in the creek where the water has cut a channel into the bedrock. This is the *slide* of Slide Rock and you will probably see people using it, as they sit in the water at the beginning of the channel and let the current sweep them down to its end in a deep pool.
   There are well-worn trails at the base of the cliffs and also at the edge of the water. When the water is low, you can walk across the creek on a duckboard bridge, but we think the best sights are on the west bank, the side you start on. The trails end at an interesting old shed built of rock in front of an irrigation flume at about 0.5 miles *0.8 km*. From there you can rock hop upstream for a considerable distance depending on the depth of the water

and your desire to explore.

(2) **Clifftop Trail**: Now go back to the top of the stairs. There you will see a sign for the Cliff Top Trail. The trail runs along the top of the cliffs parallel to the creek, providing several places where you can step off the trail and go over to the cliff tops to look down on Slide Rock. The Cliff Top Trail ends at about 0.1 mile *0.16 km* at the ruins of a concrete gatehouse that controlled the flow of water in the irrigation ditch. You can go a few paces beyond this for a view of the irrigation flume winding its way around the face of cliffs, but can go no farther due to a *No Trespassing* sign.

Slide Rock has been a popular spot for years, but its use soared when the state bought it and improved the access and parking. In the height of the tourist season, it can be so crowded as to be annoying. We like to visit it in the off season in order to avoid the throngs.

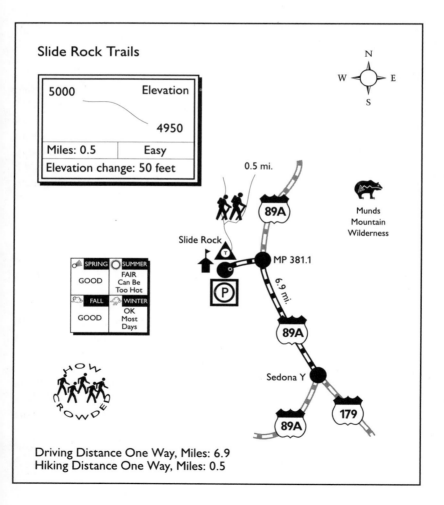

Slide Rock Trails

5000	Elevation
	4950
Miles: 0.5	Easy
Elevation change: 50 feet	

0.5 mi.

89A

Munds Mountain Wilderness

Slide Rock

MP 381.1

6.9 mi.

SPRING	SUMMER
GOOD	FAIR Can Be Too Hot
FALL	WINTER
GOOD	OK Most Days

89A

Sedona Y

179

89A

Driving Distance One Way, Miles: 6.9
Hiking Distance One Way, Miles: 0.5

Soldier Pass Arches

General Information
Location Map D4
Sedona and Wilson Mt. USGS Maps
Coconino Forest Service Map

Driving Distance One Way: 3.0 miles *4.8 km* (Time 10 minutes)
Access Road: All cars, All paved
Hiking Distance One Way: 1.5 miles *2.4 km* (Time 60 minutes)
How Strenuous: Moderate
Features: Views, Arches

NUTSHELL: Located off of Soldier Pass Road, the trailhead for this hike is only 3.0 miles *4.8 km* from the Y. The hike follows the **Soldier Pass Trail** most of its way, then veers off to reach a trio of interesting arches.

DIRECTIONS:
From the Sedona Y Go:
   Southwest on Highway 89A (toward Cottonwood) for a distance of 1.25 miles *2.0 km* (MP 372.8) to Soldier Pass Road. Turn right onto Soldier Pass Road and follow it to the 2.75 mile *4.4 km* point, where it intersects Rim Shadows Drive, where you turn right. The roads and road signs turn funky here. Disregard the street names and go straight ahead to the 3.0 miles *4.8 km* point. Take the paved road to your left there and park in the parking area. This is well defined and spacious.

TRAILHEAD: You will see a rusty sign at the parking area reading "Soldier Pass Trail #66."

DESCRIPTION: In 1996 a new trail was constructed here so that hikers no longer have to dodge jeeps on the road. A locked gate controls access, open from 8 am—6 pm. Drive out before 6 so you won't be locked in.
   The first leg of the trail takes you to Devil's Kitchen, the area's biggest sinkhole, in 0.15 miles *0.2 km*. Look for white diamond markers from this point onward. They will lead you around the rim of the sinkhole and onto the main part of the trail.
   At the 0.55 mile *0.9 km* point you will come out onto a bare redrock where the Seven Sacred Pools are located in a little canyon to your left. These natural scoops, though small, hold water even in dry periods and are important to birds and animals.
   From here, you will hike to the 1.25 mile *2.0 km* point, the end of the marked trail, at the Wilderness Boundary. The path forks at this point. A

broad trail goes straight ahead, uphill, and is the path to the Soldier Pass Arches. A minor path to the left, blocked in 2002, is the continuation of the Soldier Pass Trail.

You will climb out of the wash onto a large red slickrock ledge, which provides good views in all directions. You are in a box canyon at this point, with interesting and colorful cliffs on all sides except south (toward Sedona). Walk up to the left edge of the ledge. If you look up at the cliffs to your left from this spot you will see one arch.

From there the trail is narrow and steep (180 feet) up to the arch, but it is a short climb (0.2 miles *0.3 km*). When you arrive you will see two arches. You can walk under the first one. It is fun to explore, as it forms a sort of cave. There is a third arch that you can't see. You can reach it by walking along the cliff face on a faint trail. The third arch is the smallest and least interesting. Just above you on top of the rim is the **Brins Mesa Trail**.

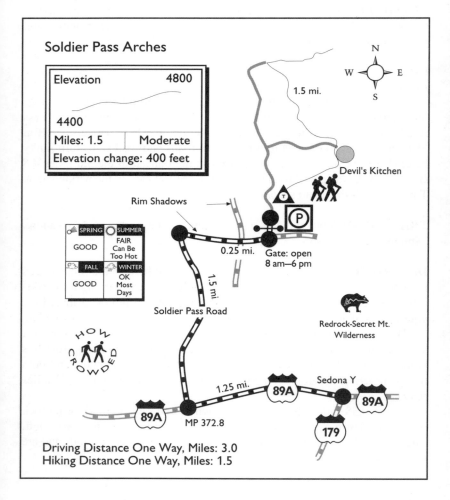

Soldier Pass Arches

Elevation 4800

4400

Miles: 1.5	Moderate
Elevation change: 400 feet	

1.5 mi.

N
W E
S

Devil's Kitchen

Rim Shadows

0.25 mi.

Gate: open
8 am—6 pm

SPRING	SUMMER
GOOD	FAIR Can Be Too Hot
FALL	WINTER
GOOD	OK Most Days

1.5 mi.

Soldier Pass Road

Redrock-Secret Mt. Wilderness

HOW CROWDED

1.25 mi.

89A

Sedona Y

89A

89A

MP 372.8

179

Driving Distance One Way, Miles: 3.0
Hiking Distance One Way, Miles: 1.5

Soldier Pass Trail #66

General Information
Location Map D4
Sedona and Wilson Mt. USGS Maps
Coconino Forest Service Map

Driving Distance One Way: 3.0 miles *4.8 km* (Time 10 minutes)
Access Road: All cars, All paved
Hiking Distance One Way: 2.2 miles *3.5 km* (Time 1 hour)
How Strenuous: Moderate
Features: Views

NUTSHELL: Located off Soldier Pass Road, the trailhead for this hike is easily reached. The trail takes you through colorful redrock country, and climbs to the top of Brins Mesa, a Sedona landmark.

DIRECTIONS:
From the Sedona Y Go:
   Southwest on Highway 89A (toward Cottonwood) for a distance of 1.25 miles *2.0 km* (MP 372.8) to Soldier Pass Road. Turn right onto Soldier Pass Road and follow it to the 2.75 mile *4.4 km* point, where it intersects Rim Shadows Drive, where you turn right. The roads and road signs turn funky here. Disregard the street names and go straight ahead to the 3.0 miles *4.8 km* point. Take the paved road to your left there and park in the parking area. This is well defined and spacious.

TRAILHEAD: You will see a rusty sign at the parking area reading, "Soldier Pass Trail #66."

DESCRIPTION: In 1996 a new trail was created here so that hikers need not dodge jeeps while hiking on the road. Access to the parking lot is controlled by a gate that is unlocked only from 8 am—6 pm. You must time your hike so that you are out of the lot before 6 pm or you will be locked in.
   The first leg of the trail takes you to Devil's Kitchen, the area's biggest sinkhole, in 0.15 miles *0.2 km*. Look for white diamond markers from this point onward. They will lead you around the rim of the sinkhole and onto the main part of the trail. You pass the **Teacup Trail** junction at 0.3 miles *0.5 km*.
   At the 0.55 mile *0.9 km* point you will come out onto a bare redrock where the Seven Sacred Pools are located in a little canyon to your left. These natural scoops, though small, hold water even in dry periods and are important to birds and animals.

From here, you will hike to the 1.25 mile *2.0 km* point, the end of the marked trail, at the Wilderness Boundary. The path forks at this point. A broad trail goes straight ahead, uphill, and is the path to the **Soldier Pass Arches**, where we found an informal sign.

A trail to your left along the canyon bottom is the Soldier Pass Trail. The trail moves along a streambed and then climbs 370 feet in 0.4 miles *0.6 km*, following along the crest of a ridge that rises gently to the top of Brins Mesa. As it climbs, the trail lifts out of the bottom and affords some great views.

The trail tops out on a redrock shelf at 2.2 miles *3.5 km*. To the right is a little connector going 0.25 miles *0.4 km* to link up with the **Brins Mesa Trail**. The final leg of the Soldier Pass Trail going downhill to join the Vultee Arch Road at the Brins Mesa Trailhead is now blocked, so the trail ends here.

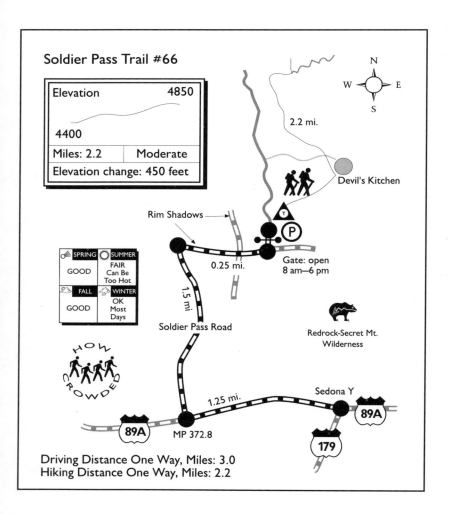

Soldier Pass Trail #66

Elevation 4850

4400

Miles: 2.2 | Moderate

Elevation change: 450 feet

2.2 mi.

Devil's Kitchen

Rim Shadows

P

Gate: open
8 am—6 pm

0.25 mi.

SPRING | SUMMER
GOOD | FAIR Can Be Too Hot
FALL | WINTER
GOOD | OK Most Days

1.5 mi.

Soldier Pass Road

Redrock-Secret Mt. Wilderness

HOW CROWDED

Sedona Y

89A

1.25 mi.

89A | MP 372.8

179

Driving Distance One Way, Miles: 3.0
Hiking Distance One Way, Miles: 2.2

Sterling Pass Trail #46

General Information
Location Map C5
Munds Park and Wilson Mt. USGS Maps
Coconino Forest Service Map

Driving Distance One Way: 6.2 miles *9.9 km* (Time 10 minutes)
Access Road: All cars, All paved
Hiking Distance One Way: 1.65 miles *2.6 km* (Time 60 minutes)
How Strenuous: Hard
Features: Views, Great rock formations

NUTSHELL: Located 6.2 miles *9.9 km* north of Sedona, just above the north end of Manzanita Campground, and just below the Canyon Wren Lodge, this steep but beautiful hike climbs through a heavy forest to a mountain pass, with scenic views along the way.

DIRECTIONS:
From the Sedona Y Go:
  North on Highway 89A (toward Flagstaff) for a distance of 6.2 miles *9.9 km* (MP 380.4). Park anywhere you can along the roadside in this area.

TRAILHEAD: There is a rusty sign in a little alcove marking this maintained trail. The sign reads, "Sterling Pass #46."

DESCRIPTION: There is very little parking at the roadside near the trailhead. You have to pick out a wide spot on the shoulder and do your best.
  This trail rises steeply, climbing all the way. For the first portion you parallel a little side canyon, which may contain running water during spring thaw. When it does, it creates a charming waterfall near the highway. The trail wanders back and forth over the streambed four times.
  For those who think of the Oak Creek area as sun swept expanses of redrock dotted with cactus, this trail will be an eye-opener. It goes through a cool pine forest. While you will cross over a bit of red slickrock at the beginning and will see some gorgeous red cliffs and buttes as you progress, the soil underfoot will be a rich brown loam. The forest is heavy. In addition to the familiar ponderosa pine you will see some Douglas fir and a few spruces. After about the first 0.25 miles *0.4 km* you are far enough away from the road so that you can no longer hear its sounds and can see no signs of human activity. The area feels primeval and is truly delightful.
  Because the forest is so heavy, you can't see much until you have gone about 1.25 miles *2.0 km*. Until then you get glimpses of giant white cliffs

ahead of you (W) and red cliffs on your right and left. Then you rise above the trees for great views across Oak Creek Canyon and nearby. The cliffs here are a treat to the eye, highly sculptured, with many interesting lines and angles. You will find a viewpoint at a bend of the trail where you can look over into an adjacent canyon to your left for views of soaring white cliffs.

The crest is at about 1.65 miles *2.6 km*, where you come onto a saddle. There is a heavy stand of trees here with oaks on the east side and oaks and maples on the west wide. Because of these trees the views are not as good at the top as they are just below the top. This is a true mountain pass, there being a decided gap in the cliffs here.

The trail continues down the other side, another 0.75 miles *1.2 km*, to intersect the **Vultee Arch Trail.** If you do go down the west side you might as well go on to Vultee Arch, which is only 0.2 miles *0.3 km* from the trail junction. Many hikers will stop at the saddle.

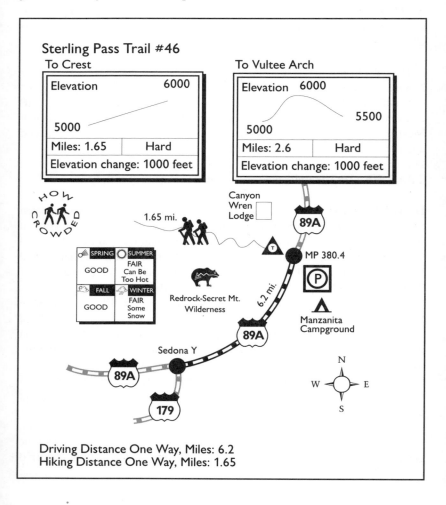

Sterling Pass Trail #46

To Crest

Elevation	6000
5000	
Miles: 1.65	Hard
Elevation change: 1000 feet	

To Vultee Arch

Elevation	6000
5000	5500
Miles: 2.6	Hard
Elevation change: 1000 feet	

HOW CROWDED

1.65 mi.

Canyon Wren Lodge

89A

MP 380.4

SPRING	SUMMER
GOOD	FAIR Can Be Too Hot
FALL	WINTER
GOOD	FAIR Some Snow

Redrock-Secret Mt. Wilderness

6.2 mi.

P

Manzanita Campground

89A

Sedona Y

89A

179

N W E S

Driving Distance One Way, Miles: 6.2
Hiking Distance One Way, Miles: 1.65

Submarine Rock Trail

General Information
Location Map E5
Sedona USGS Map
Coconino Forest Service Map

Driving Distance One Way: 2.1 miles *3.4 km* (Time 10 minutes)
Access Road: All cars, Last 0.1 mile *0.16 km* good dirt road
Hiking Distance One Way: 1.0 miles *1.6 km* (Time 30 minutes)
How Strenuous: Easy
Features: Interesting rock formation, Views

NUTSHELL: Located only a couple of miles southeast of uptown Sedona, this interesting rock formation is fun to climb and pretend that you are Captain Nemo.

DIRECTIONS:
From the Sedona Y Go:
    South on Highway 179 (toward Phoenix) for 1.4 miles *2.2 km* (MP 312.1) to Morgan Road in the Broken Arrow Subdivision. Turn left (east) on Morgan Road and follow it to its end, at 2.0 miles *3.2 km*, then proceed another 0.1 mile *0.16 km* to the parking lot.

TRAILHEAD: The trailhead for the **Broken Arrow Trail.**

DESCRIPTION: There is a nice parking lot at the trailhead, although you may find it full on weekends. The main purpose in creating the Broken Arrow Trail, it seems, was to avoid the problem that used to exist here and was becoming steadily worse: jeep tours use the road and it was harder and harder for hikers and bikers to have a quality experience. The Broken Arrow Trail provides a footpath so you can now avoid the jeeps.
    The Broken Arrow Trail is well marked and you will have no trouble finding and following it. At first it takes you close to Battlement Mesa, where you will enjoy looking at the red cliffs. The trail climbs so that you will also have enjoyable views out over the area to your left, including the town of Sedona.
    At 0.5 miles *0.8 km* you will come downhill to a hole enclosed by a barbed wire fence. This is the Devil's Dining Room, a natural sinkhole that is considered a local landmark. We used to include the hike to this point as a separate excursion but now it is just a waypoint on the Broken Arrow Trail.
    At 0.75 miles *1.2 km* you will come to a trail junction. The trail to the right goes to Chicken Point. You want to take the left fork, going downhill

to Submarine Rock. The trail crosses the road and then works its way to the north end of the rock. We found no distinct trail going up to the top of the rock, but that is not a problem because it is easy to pick a way up. Once you are on top of it you can have great fun walking around it, getting the views from the top of the "conning tower." The jeep tours come in on the other (lower) end of the rock.

Submarine Rock is located at the south end of **Marg's Draw**, a scenic bowl. This is a beautiful natural area and the home of several good hikes. Marg's Draw is remarkable, being unspoiled and yet close to developed parts of Sedona. Land barons would love to get their hands on it and subdivide it but—fortunately for outdoor lovers—part of it is protected by being included in the Munds Mt. Wilderness Area.

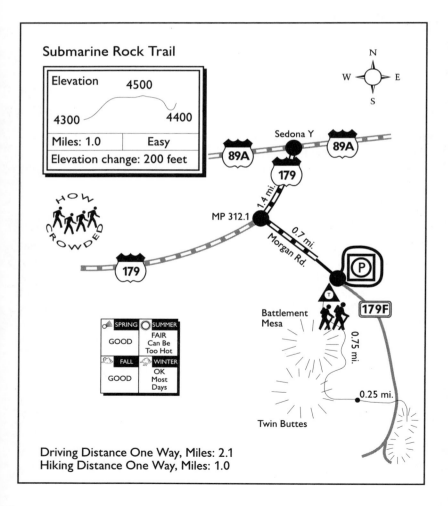

Submarine Rock Trail

Elevation: 4300 — 4500 — 4400
Miles: 1.0 | Easy
Elevation change: 200 feet

HOW CROWDED

	SPRING	SUMMER
	GOOD	FAIR Can Be Too Hot
	FALL	WINTER
	GOOD	OK Most Days

Sedona Y
89A
179
1.4 mi.
MP 312.1
0.7 mi.
Morgan Rd.
179
P
179F
Battlement Mesa
0.75 mi.
0.25 mi.
Twin Buttes

Driving Distance One Way, Miles: 2.1
Hiking Distance One Way, Miles: 1.0

Sugarloaf Loop Trail

General Information
Location Map D4
Sedona and Wilson Mountain USGS Maps
Coconino Forest Service Map

Driving Distance One Way: 2.85 miles *4.6 km* (Time 10 minutes)
Access Road: All cars, All paved
Hiking Distance One Way: 1.0 mile *1.6 km* (Time: 30 minutes)
How Strenuous: Moderate
Features: Easy access, Gorgeous views

NUTSHELL: You climb up the back of a ramp-shaped butte to enjoy wonderful views from its top.

DIRECTIONS:
From the Sedona Y Go:
    Southwest on Highway 89A (toward Cottonwood) for a distance of 1.9 miles *3.0 km* (MP 372.7 to Coffee Pot Drive (at stoplight by Basha's Shopping Center). Turn right onto Coffee Pot Drive. Follow it to the 2.5 mile *4.0 km* point where you turn left on Sanborn and proceed west to the 2.65 mile *4.2 km* point, where you turn right on Little Elf Drive. At the end of Little Elf, the 2.85 mile *4.6 km* point, turn right and drive a few yards, then turn left into an unmarked parking lot.

TRAILHEAD: At the parking area. There is a signboard with maps.

DESCRIPTION: From the parking area, you walk north. The trail immediately splits and you take the right fork. Even though there are some signs, there are so many official and unofficial trails running through the area that you may easily be confused. Just keep moving north and heading toward Sugarloaf. You will reach a power line at 0.3 miles *0.5 km* and go just beyond it to a T intersection, where there is a signpost, indicating that the **Thunder Mountain Trail** goes left and the **Teacup Trail** goes right. Turn right.
    At the 0.5 mile *0.8 km,* point, you will find another posted trail junction. The sign points straight ahead for the Teacup Trail and to the right for the Sugarloaf Loop. Turn right. The trail leads up the ramp-like back side of Sugarloaf. It is easy to follow until you get to the 0.6 mile *1.0 km* point. Here is another trail junction, but when we hiked it, the junction was not marked and had no sign. We call it Uphill Junction, as you are well up the slope when you reach it. You must turn right here to get to the top.

As you rise above the tree line, you begin to enjoy the views. At first these are to the north, into the Capitol Butte (Thunder Mountain) area. When you reach the top, you will find that you are on a perfect viewing platform. There are no trees to block your view and you are able to see out in all directions. There are some nice natural places to sit and just enjoy the sights. This is a great place to come in the evening to watch the sunset.

On the way down, when you come to Uphill Junction, you have a decision to make. The Forest Service has designed the trail to turn to the right and come down an arc to rejoin the Teacup Trail. We tried this and found the trail hard to locate. We recommend that you turn left at this junction and return to the trailhead the way you came.

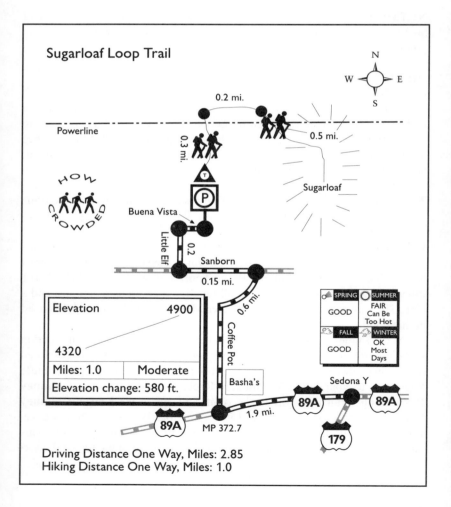

Summit Route Trail

General Information
Location Map D4
Sedona USGS Map
Coconino Forest Service Map

Driving Distance One Way: 4.3 miles *6.9 km* (Time 10 minutes)
Access Road: All cars, All paved
Hiking Distance One Way: 0.66 miles *1.05 km* (Time 40 minutes)
How Strenuous: Moderate
Features: Close to town, easy all-weather access, Views

NUTSHELL: Located 4.3 miles *6.9 km* west of downtown, this is a small hike that you can make in a hurry, but it will give you a good workout and you will enjoy sweeping panoramic views.

DIRECTIONS:
From the Sedona Y Go:
   Southwest on Highway 89A (toward Cottonwood) for 3.2 miles *5.1 km* (MP 371) to Dry Creek Road. Turn right on Dry Creek Road and proceed to the 3.7 mile *5.9 km* point. Turn right Thunder Mountain Road at the entrance to the Thunder Mountain subdivision. Drive to the 4.3 miles *6.9 km* point, then turn left into the trail parking lot.

TRAILHEAD: At the parking area. There is a sign with a map of the trails in the area, but this hike is not on it.

DESCRIPTION: (Note: we called this the Little Sugarloaf Trail in an earlier edition, when it was a social trail. Now it is a system trail, but the Forest Service has named it the Summit Route Trail). Follow the main trail. At 0.1 miles *0.16 km* you will come to a trail junction marked by a signpost and a sign. The trail to the right is the Thunder Mountain Trail. Go straight ahead at this point.
   At 0.35 miles *0.56 km* you will reach a second signposted trail junction at the top of a little pass, where you can see down into the Dry Creek Road area, where there are many homes. This pass is a saddle between Little Sugarloaf, to your left, and Chimney Rock, to your right. The **Chimney Rock Loop Trail** takes off to the right here, while the **Lower Chimney Rock Trail** goes straight ahead. Little Sugarloaf is shaped like a wedge, with a high cliff face on the south, tapering down toward the north. This tapering creates a ramp and makes it possible to climb to the top of the formation.

Walk straight ahead just a few feet. At 0.5 miles *0.8 km,* just as the trail begins to go downhill, turn left (S). There is a small sign here. There is a six-foot tall juniper stump—looking like a fencepost—at the place where you turn.

Almost immediately you will approach Little Sugarloaf and begin to climb its north face. There are several trails going up, and it doesn't much matter which you take, as there is only one route, and all trails will eventually combine. Take the most-used one. At the top, you emerge onto bare slickrock with unobstructed views, very fine for enjoying the Sedona landscape.

By calling this a "route" hikers are alerted to the fact that there is no developed trail to the top and that some pathfinding may be required. Don't be daunted by this, as it is easy and rather fun, to pick your way up the butte.

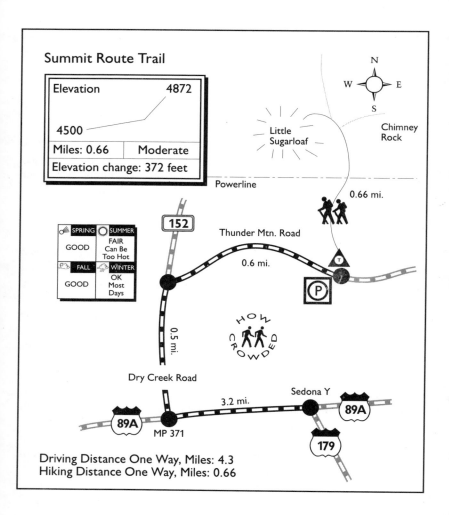

Sunrise Trail

General Information
Location Map D4
Sedona and Wilson Mt. USGS Maps
Coconino Forest Service Map

Driving Distance One Way: 1.5 miles *2.4 km* (Time 5 minutes)
Access Road: All cars, All paved
Hiking Distance One Way: 1.2 miles *1.9 km* (Time 45 minutes)
How Strenuous: Easy
Features: Convenience, all-weather surface, nature trail features, connections to other trails

NUTSHELL: This urban trail is the perfect place to walk the dog in the evening or just stretch your legs after a day at the office. It's easy to reach and pleasant.

DIRECTIONS:
From the Sedona Y Go:
   Southwest on Highway 89A (toward Cottonwood) for a distance of 1.25 miles *2.0 km* (MP 372.8) to Soldier Pass Road. Turn right onto Soldier Pass Road and follow it to the 1.5 mile *2.4 km* point, just beyond Calle Contenta. On the left side of the road you will see the Sunrise Trail joining the Soldier Pass Road, where there is a parking apron. Park on the apron.

TRAILHEAD: At the parking apron.

DESCRIPTION: The Sunrise Trail is designed as part of the Sedona urban trail system, so you are not going to have a wilderness experience when you make this hike. Instead, you will enjoy what the planners intended, a nice, well-maintained trail that is accessible and easy to use.
   The trail runs along in a generally northward direction parallel to the Soldier Pass Road. It is wide and well surfaced and marked with trail signs. In addition, it serves as a modest nature trail, as there are little signs identifying some of the plants that grow along the side of the trail.
   At the 0.15 mile *0.24 km* point, you will find a side trail to your left with a sign for the upper level. We recommend that you take this little detour, as you get away from the Soldier Pass Road and have better views. You will climb about 50 feet to the top of a hill. Turn right (NE) at the top and walk past an elevated open stage. Keep going until you meet the paved Carruth Road at the 0.5 mile *0.8 km* point. Across the street you will see the **Carruth Trail**, another part of this trail system.

Turn right at Carruth Road (E) and walk downhill. You will rejoin the Sunrise Trail at Soldier Pass Road at the 0.6 mile *1.0 km* point. Turn left (NNE), walk across Carruth Road, and pick up the Sunrise Trail again on the other side.

At the 1.1 mile *1.8 km* point you will find the Carruth Trail joining the Sunrise Trail to your left, creating a loop possibility if you leave the Sunrise Trail and take the Carruth Trail at this point. At the 1.2 mile *1.9 km* point the Sunrise Trail ends, bumping into the Soldier Pass Road.

The trail planners in the Sedona area are trying to provide trails for all possible users. This one was obviously designed for those who wouldn't dream of taking one of the strenuous hikes, but do enjoy getting out and walking.

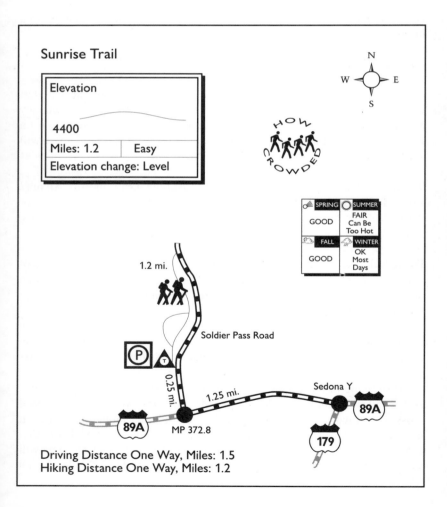

Table Top Trail

General Information
Location Map E4
Sedona USGS Map
Coconino Forest Service Map

Driving Distance One Way: 2.6 miles *4.2 km* (Time 10 minutes)
Access Road: All cars, All paved
Hiking Distance One Way: 1.9 miles *3.0 km* (Time 1.25 hours)
How Strenuous: Moderate
Features: 360-degree views, Vortex site

NUTSHELL: This trail takes you up onto the Airport Mesa, then out to a knob.

DIRECTIONS:
From the Sedona Y Go:
   Southwest on Highway 89A for 2.1 miles *3.4 km,* to a stoplight. Turn left on Shelby Drive. Continue on Shelby for 0.5 miles *0.8 km* (just past Stanley Steamer) and turn right into the parking lot of a building known as La Entrada, at 2155 Shelby Drive. At the back of the paved parking lot you will see three trailhead parking signs. Park at one of them.

TRAILHEAD: Orphan. Access is via the **Bandit Trail** and the **Airport Loop Trail**. Aside from the parking signs there are no trailhead signs or markers at the starting place. Look for a small footpath going into the trees. This is the path to take.

DESCRIPTION: Start walking on the trail. Almost immediately you will come to the junction with the **Old Post Trail**. Pass by this junction. Soon after this you will reach the junction where the Bandit Trail starts, where you turn to the left. Take the Bandit Trail.
   The Bandit Trail skirts the boundary of private properties, bringing you up very close to the fence that surrounds a storage yard. Then you begin to climb, making a steep ascent up the shoulder of Airport Mesa. At 0.6 miles *1.0 km* you will intersect the Airport Loop Trail.
   Turn to the right, still climbing, on the joint Airport Loop-Bandit trails. At 0.9 miles *1.4 km* to your left at the side of the trail you will find a metal cross with a nameplate reading "Bandit" and a small mound of stones. It isn't explained, but it would seem that Bandit was a well-loved pet. You keep climbing the side of the mesa, topping out at 1.2 miles *1.9 km*. You will walk a bit farther, going around the toe of the mesa until at 1.4 miles *2.2 km*

the trail ends where it meets the junction with the Table Top Trail. The Airport Loop Trail continues.

From here it is a short easy walk out to the top of the knob, from which there are wonderful views. Some psychics regard the knob as a vortex site. As you begin to walk out to the knob you will see another trail veering off to the left, descending steeply. This is an illegally constructed social trail that goes down to join the **Ridge Trail**. Bypass it and make the easy walk out to the tippy top of the knob at the end of the Table Top Trail. We like the sensation of being able to stand on the very pinnacle of a formation, which is possible on this knob. We found a few New Age rock arrangements out on the knob, evidence of the claim we have seen that it is considered to be a Vortex site.

Airport Mesa is officially called Table Top Mesa on the Sedona 7.5 topo map, and the trail takes its name from this designation.

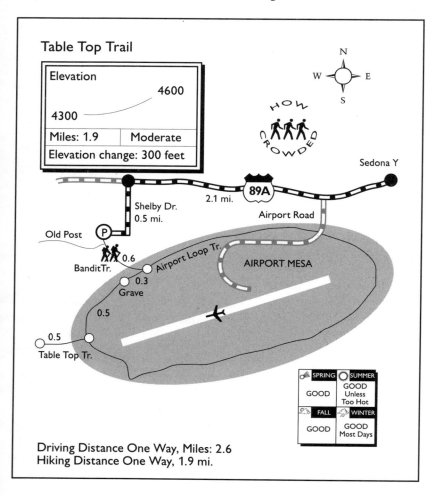

Table Top Trail

Elevation
4600
4300
Miles: 1.9 | Moderate
Elevation change: 300 feet

Sedona Y

89A

2.1 mi.

Shelby Dr.
0.5 mi.

Airport Road

Old Post

P

BanditTr.   0.6

Airport Loop Tr.

AIRPORT MESA

0.3
Grave

0.5

0.5
Table Top Tr.

SPRING	SUMMER
GOOD	GOOD Unless Too Hot
FALL	WINTER
GOOD	GOOD Most Days

Driving Distance One Way, Miles: 2.6
Hiking Distance One Way, 1.9 mi.

Teacup Trail

General Information
Location Map D4
Sedona and Wilson Mt. USGS Maps
Coconino Forest Service Map

Driving Distance One Way: 3.0 miles *4.8 km* (Time 10 minutes)
Access Road: All cars, All paved
Hiking Distance One Way: 1.6 miles *2.6 km* (Time 1 hour)
How Strenuous: Moderate
Features: Views, Connects to other system trails, Easy to reach

NUTSHELL: Starting at the Soldier Pass Trailhead, this trail moves west, passes under the lip of Coffeepot Rock, for some fine views, and then drops south to join the Thunder Mountain Trail behind Sugarloaf. A good trail when you don't have much time to drive out into the country.

DIRECTIONS:
From the Sedona Y Go:
Southwest on Highway 89A (toward Cottonwood) for a distance of 1.25 miles *2.0 km* (MP 372.8) to Soldier Pass Road. Turn right onto Soldier Pass Road and follow it to the 2.75 mile *4.4 km* point, where it intersects Rim Shadows Drive, where you turn right. You will see trailhead signs. Drive to the 3.0 miles *4.8 km* point. Take the paved road to your left there and park in the parking area. Caution: entry is controlled by a gate, which is closed from 6 pm to 8 am. Be sure to drive away before the gate closes.

TRAILHEAD: You will see a rusty sign at the parking area reading, "Soldier Pass Trail #66."

DESCRIPTION: From the trailhead, follow the Soldier Pass Trail to Devil's Kitchen, a big sinkhole, about 0.2 mile *0.32 km* away. From here, go west, taking the jeep road downhill until you get to the main road, at the 0.4 mile *0.64 km* point. Turn to the right and walk up the road a few feet, to a point where you will see a sign for the Teacup Trail to your left. Follow the trail sign.
From this point you will walk westerly toward Coffee Pot Rock, a well-known landmark that has been seen by millions of people in Sedona photographs. You walk uphill through an Arizona cypress forest, though the climb is not great, about 125 feet. At the 0.8 mile *1.3 km* point the forest thins and you find yourself looking down onto an area of extensively developed homesites, which is still jarring to us, as we remember when this area

was entirely undeveloped not so many years ago.

From this point to the end of the hike, you will enjoy looking at the massive cliffs of which Coffeepot Rock is the tip. The trail skirts along the base of these cliffs, undulating a bit, though there are no great changes in grade. Once you move a bit west of Coffeepot Rock, you will notice a prominent spire on the skyline. The top of this spire has been undercut so that it is tulip-shaped. This top is the teacup which gives the trail its name. Why is it a teacup instead of a coffee cup? Ah, the vagaries of nomenclature!

Once around the base of Coffeepot Rock, you come to a point where you cannot see the housing developments and you feel as it you are out in the country again, and the trail begins to move southerly, toward **Sugarloaf**, another Sedona landmark. At the 1.6 mile *2.6 km* point, the Teacup Trail joins the **Thunder Mountain Trail** just north of Sugarloaf. From this junction you can go east or west on the Thunder Mountain trail.

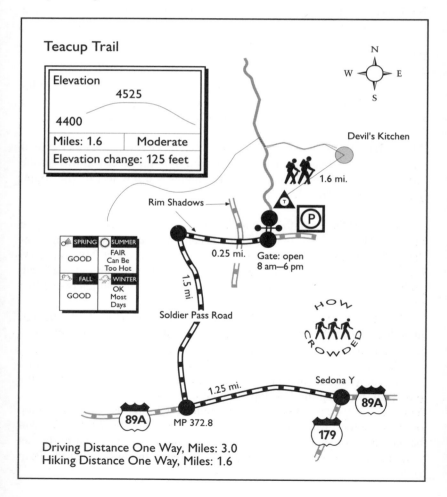

Teacup Trail

Elevation
4525
4400

Miles: 1.6	Moderate
Elevation change: 125 feet	

SPRING	SUMMER
GOOD	FAIR Can Be Too Hot
FALL	WINTER
GOOD	OK Most Days

N
W — E
S

Devil's Kitchen

1.6 mi.

Rim Shadows

T

P

0.25 mi.   Gate: open 8 am–6 pm

1.5 mi.

Soldier Pass Road

HOW CROWDED

Sedona Y

1.25 mi.

89A

MP 372.8

89A

179

Driving Distance One Way, Miles: 3.0
Hiking Distance One Way, Miles: 1.6

Telephone Trail #72

General Information
Location Map B5
Munds Park USGS Map
Coconino Forest Service Map

Driving Distance One Way: 10.9 miles *17.4 km* (Time 20 minutes)
Access Road: All cars, All paved
Hiking Distance One Way: 1.25 miles *2.0 km* (Time 2.0 Hours)
How Strenuous: Hard (Very steep)
Features: Interesting rock formations, Views

NUTSHELL: This is a marked and posted trail in upper Oak Creek. It climbs northerly to a ridge top and then turns east to reach the rim.

DIRECTIONS:
From the Sedona Y Go:
   North on Highway 89A (toward Flagstaff) for a distance of 10.9 miles *17.4 km* (MP 385.1). Here you will see a wide apron on the right side of the highway under a twenty foot high cliff. Park here.

TRAILHEAD: From the parking place, walk up Highway 89A on the right shoulder for about one hundred yards. Uphill from the road, you will see the typical rusty metal trailhead sign off the highway a few feet to your right. The sign reads, "Trail 72, Telephone."

DESCRIPTION: From the sign look sharp and you will see cairns marking the trail. The trail itself is hard to see because it is covered with pine needles. The trail runs along parallel to the highway for about 0.05 mile *0.08 km*, then swings to the right, where you will walk along an old road bed, probably a construction road that was created while the old telephone line was being installed.
   At 0.1 miles *0.16 km* you will walk under the new phone line. The trail up to here is obvious and easy to follow. From this point on, the trail is difficult to find, and is *for experienced hikers only.*
   The next leg of the hike takes you sharply uphill, to your left (N). You will zigzag your way up to the top of a finger ridge that runs west from the East Rim, reaching the first top at about 0.5 miles *0.8 km*. Turn right (E). You are in a zone of white sandstone studded with fossils. You stay on top of the ridge for a while and then dip below it. At 0.6 miles *1.0 km*, you will be on top again, and will come to a fascinating little reef about thirty feet long and twelve feet high that contains several windows, called the Peep Holes.

There is a rough spot beyond this, where the trail dips again and gets difficult. There are several confusing game trails. Be sure to follow the flags and cairns. You will find one of the old phone pole stubs, with guy wire and support sleeve where the trail turns back to the top. Hard scrambling in here.

When you get back to the ridge top, the trail becomes more obvious. At about 0.75 miles *1.2 km*, you move along another intermediate top. Soon after that, you begin the very steep climb to the top of the rim. This is in a beautiful fir forest, which lasts all the way to the tip top. Along the way here you will see the remains of several old phone poles.

The trail ends at the top at 1.25 miles *2.0 km*, at a large cairn. You can walk out to the rim in several places here for wonderful views out toward the cliffs of West Fork.

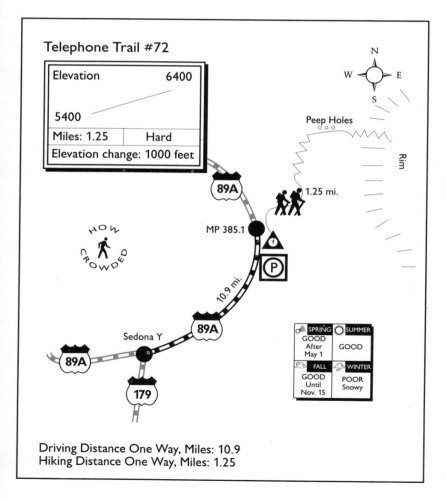

Driving Distance One Way, Miles: 10.9
Hiking Distance One Way, Miles: 1.25

Templeton Trail

General Information
Location Map F4
Munds Mountain and Sedona USGS Maps
Coconino Forest Service Map

Driving Distance One Way: 4.7 miles *7.5 km* (Time 10 minutes)
Access Road: All cars, All paved
Hiking Distance One Way: 3.5 miles *5.6 km* (Time 2 hours)
How Strenuous: Moderate
Features: Views, Redrocks, Creekside, Variety

NUTSHELL: This hike leaves the Bell Rock Pathway, crosses under Highway 179, works its way to Cathedral Rock, rounds it on a high redrock shelf, and then drops down to Oak Creek on the other side, offering along the way almost all of the scenery for which visitors come to Sedona.

DIRECTIONS: (Note: these are our shortcut directions, not the official starting point)
From the Sedona Y Go:
   South on Highway 179 (toward Phoenix) for a distance of 4.7 miles *7.5 km* MP 308.7, where you turn right onto a wide paved parking apron and park. There are no signs but it is legal to park here, with lots of room.

TRAILHEAD: There is no official trailhead. Start the hike from the parking place.

DESCRIPTION: From the parking area walk down into the arroyo on the south side. Here you will see a sign marked "Trail" with arrows to the left and right. (If you went left you would go through a tunnel to the place where the trail joins the Bell Rock Pathway in 0.1 miles *0.16 km*). Turn right, following the trail as it crosses the arroyo and comes out on the other bank in a few feet.
   You will next hike a relatively level area, with a few mild ups and downs. You move away from the highway and get into some nice remote-feeling areas, where you have good views of Twin Buttes, Cathedral Rock and other splendid sights.
   At 1.0 miles *1.6 k*m you will meet the **H. T. Trail**, coming in from your right. From this point you will make a beeline toward Cathedral Rock. As you near its base, the trail undulates, and at about 1.7 miles *2.7 km* you will see some old metal roofing, all that remains of a couple of shacks that were once here. Then you climb up onto a redrock ledge, which makes a natural

pathway. We love this part of the hike—very redrock without requiring any strenuous or risky climbing.

At 2.5 miles *4.0 km* the **Cathedral Rock Trail** comes up from your right from the trailhead at Back O' Beyond. Continue hiking along the ledge. At the 3.0 miles *4.8 km* point, when you are rounding the north tip of the formation, the trail starts down, winding its way to creek level at 3.25 miles *5.2 km*. There is a heavy screen of trees which blocks your view of Oak Creek, though you can hear the waters running. There is a break in the screen of trees on the banks of Oak Creek after you have hiked a few yards, and you can see the water and go down to creekside to sit on boulders and meditate—one of the nicest parts of the trail.

All too soon the trail moves away from the stream though you can still hear it. The trail ends at the 3.5 mile *5.6 km* point where it joins the **Baldwin Trail**.

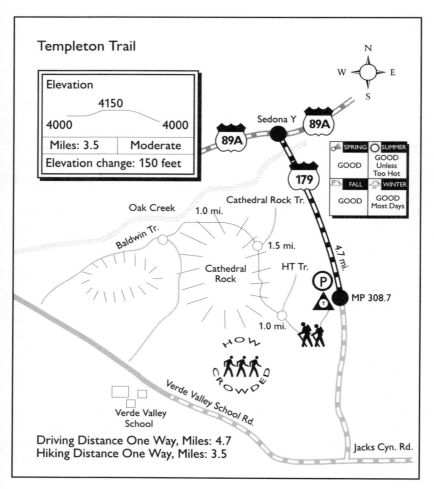

Thomas Point Trail #142

General Information
Location Map B5
Munds Park USGS Map
Coconino Forest Service Map

Driving Distance One Way: 10.5 miles *16.8 km* (Time 20 minutes)
Access Road: All cars, All paved
Hiking Distance One Way: 1.0 miles *1.6 km* (Time 60 minutes)
How Strenuous: Hard
Features: Views

NUTSHELL: This is a marked and posted trail that climbs the east wall of upper Oak Creek Canyon 10.5 miles *16.8 km* north of Sedona.

DIRECTIONS:
From the Sedona Y Go:
   North on Highway 89A (toward Flagstaff) for a distance of 10.5 miles *16.8 km* (MP 384.7) You will see a road sign for the West Fork parking area, which requires a sharp turn to your left (W).

TRAILHEAD: There is a fee for parking in the lot. The driveway forms a loop, and you want to park at the farthest point, the south end of the loop. Walk the trail you will see heading south, parallel to the highway and not very far from it. The trail will fork soon. Take the left (SE) fork and walk to Highway 89A. Cross over the paving, turn right (S) and walk along the east shoulder of Highway 89A about 100 yards. You will find the trailhead to your left, uphill a bit from the road.

DESCRIPTION: The start of the trail looks like a groove worn into the soil bank with the trailhead sign at the beginning of the groove. Look sharp, for the sign is hard to see.
   Like the other trails that climb the east wall of the canyon, this trail goes nearly straight up, with little artfulness. You start the hike in a pine and spruce forest. The trail zigzags in such a way that it isn't a killer trail like the **Purtymun Trail** or Thompson's Ladder.
   After hiking a short distance you are high enough for good views of the sheer white cliffs of the West Fork and East Pocket areas across the canyon, and can see the path of Oak Creek and glimpse bits of the highway.
   At about the half-mile point the trail winds around onto an unshaded south face of the canyon wall. Here the pines disappear and you enter the chaparral and juniper life zone. These plants are small compared to the pines

so you have better views along this part of the trail. Near the top you come back into the pine and spruce forest.

At the top, pine needles may cover the trail and make it indistinct, so look for cairns. They mark an extension of the trail to a viewpoint to the left (N), where Thomas Point is located. Thomas Point is well named, for it is a peninsula or tongue pointing west. Standing at the tip of the point you will have good views north, west and south. Particularly good are the views of the San Francisco Peaks and the head of Oak Creek Canyon. Since you are on top of the rim, you might enjoy walking along it in both directions to find different viewpoints and places of interest.

The point was named after J. L. V. "Dad" Thomas, who bought the West Fork Ranch in 1888 and built this trail in 1890. Before 1914, when the road through the canyon was finished, Flagstaff people who wanted to visit Oak Creek used the Thomas Point Trail.

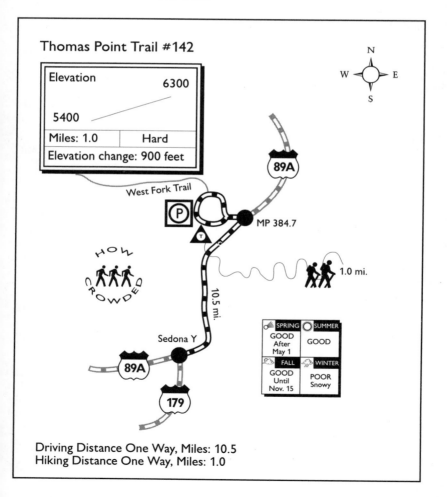

Thomas Point Trail #142

Elevation	6300
5400	
Miles: 1.0	Hard
Elevation change: 900 feet	

West Fork Trail

MP 384.7

1.0 mi.

HOW CROWDED

10.5 mi.

Sedona Y

89A

179

SPRING	SUMMER
GOOD After May 1	GOOD
FALL	WINTER
GOOD Until Nov. 15	POOR Snowy

Driving Distance One Way, Miles: 10.5
Hiking Distance One Way, Miles: 1.0

Thunder Mountain Trail

General Information
Location Map D4
Sedona and Wilson Mountain USGS Maps
Coconino Forest Service Map

Driving Distance One Way: 4.3 miles *6.9 km* (Time 15 minutes)
Access Road: All cars, All paved
Hiking Distance One Way: 2.0 miles *3.2 km* (Time 1 hour)
How Strenuous: Easy
Features: Rock formations, Views

NUTSHELL: This trail is easy to reach, a short drive from town, and provides a nice little easy hike, as well as being a connector to other good trails.

DIRECTIONS:
From the Sedona Y Go:
  Southwest on Highway 89A (toward Cottonwood) for 3.2 miles *5.1 km* (MP 371) to Dry Creek Road. Turn right on Dry Creek Road and proceed to the 3.7 mile *5.9 km* point. Turn right Thunder Mountain Road at the entrance to the Thunder Mountain subdivision. Drive to the 4.3 miles *6.9 km* point, then turn left into the trail parking lot.

TRAILHEAD: At the parking area. There is a sign with a map of the trails in the area.

DESCRIPTION: The Thunder Mountain Trail is part of the Red Rock Pathways system of interlinking trails around Sedona. It is interesting in its own right and also serves as a connector to other trails.
  From the parking area, you walk north, toward the redrock buttes. At 0.2 miles *0.32 km* you reach a trail junction with a sign. There is a trail going straight ahead of you, but it is for the Chimney Rock trails. Turn right here. You are now at the beginning of the Thunder Mountain Trail. The trail moves easily to the east, holding to one contour with only a few dips and rises.
  At 0.65 miles *1.04 km* you reach another trail junction. The trail to the right goes downhill to a big green water tank. Go straight ahead here. At 0.75 miles *1.2 km* you come to another trail junction. The trail to the left goes up to **Chimney Rock**. Keep going straight.
  As you continue east from this trail junction you will see a large number of social or hiker-created trails. Many of these come up from the subdi-

vision to your right so you are not likely to go off in the wrong direction on them. Others are not so easy to distinguish. So keep your eyes open.

You are very close to habitation to your right as you walk along this trail, but there is enough of a screen between you and the subdivisions to create a feeling of being out in the country. The views to your left are wonderful, as you see the interesting sculptures of Thunder Mountain, also called Capitol Butte, Grey Mountain and Shadow Mountain.

At 2.0 miles *3.2 km* you are under a powerline at a wash, where you find another trail junction. To your right is a connection coming north from the parking lot off of Little Elf (see Sugarloaf). It looks as if the Thunder Mountain Trail continues to the east here, but in fact, it ends and the **Teacup Trail** begins at this trail junction.

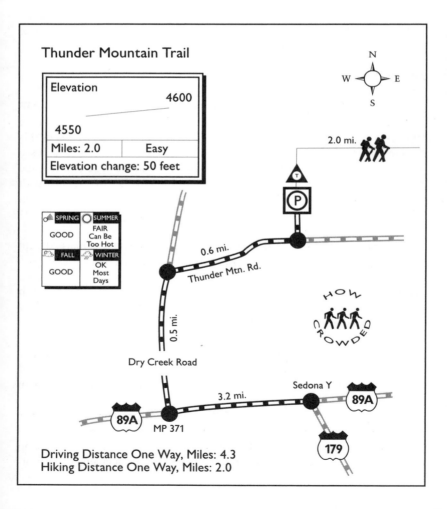

Thunder Mountain Trail

Elevation		
4550	4600	
Miles: 2.0	Easy	
Elevation change: 50 feet		

SPRING	SUMMER
GOOD	FAIR Can Be Too Hot
FALL	WINTER
GOOD	OK Most Days

2.0 mi.

0.6 mi.

Thunder Mtn. Rd.

0.5 mi.

Dry Creek Road

HOW CROWDED

Sedona Y

89A

89A   MP 371

3.2 mi.

179

Driving Distance One Way, Miles: 4.3
Hiking Distance One Way, Miles: 2.0

Turkey Creek Trail #92

General Information
Location Map F3
Sedona USGS Map
Coconino Forest Service Map

Driving Distance One Way: 11.9 miles *19.0 km* (Time 30 minutes)
Access Road: All cars, Last 1.7 miles *2.7 km* good dirt roads
Hiking Distance One Way: 3.5 miles *5.6 km* (Time 2.0 hours)
How Strenuous: Hard
Features: Rock formations, Views

NUTSHELL: Located 11.9 miles *19.0 km* southwest of Sedona, behind the Verde Valley School, this hard hike has you climb 1,000 feet in about a mile through interesting redrocks to the top of House Mountain.

DIRECTIONS:
From the Sedona Y Go:

South on Highway 179 (toward Phoenix) for 7.2 miles *11.5 km* (MP 306.1), to the Verde Valley School Road, where there is a stoplight. Turn right (W) onto Verde Valley School Road. The first 3.0 miles *4.8 km* of this road are paved. Follow it to the 11.3 mile *18.1 km* point where you will see a sign marking the **Turkey Creek Trail**. Just beyond the sign you will see FR 9216B, a dirt road to your left. Turn onto FR 9216B. Any vehicle with medium clearance can handle the road. At 11.9 miles *19.0 km* you will reach a V fork. Turn left here and park on the shoulder of the little loop.

TRAILHEAD: The trailhead is at Turkey Creek Tank and is marked with a rusty sign, but you have to walk 1.5 miles *2.4 km* to get there.

DESCRIPTION: At the parking place, you will see an old road to the south that is closed by a barrier of stones. Walk down this road for 0.25 miles *0.4 km*, where you will find a V junction. The fork to your right (SW) is the trail to Turkey Creek. The fork to the left (SE) goes to **Twin Pillars**.

You will soon see a faint unmarked trail coming on to the road from your right, which is the alternate trail that goes to the gate at the rear entrance of Redrock State Park and then skirts around it. Continue walking the main road south.

When you get near Turkey Creek Tank you will recognize its presence because it is encircled by cottonwood trees. It is a pleasant oasis, though it goes dry in summer. The hiking trail starts at its farthest edge and goes along a former jeep road, winding through some fine redrocks. It changes to a foot-

path in about half a mile *0.8 km.*

Soon after this you begin to climb House Mountain. The path is fairly steep but the footing is good. The path is an old stock trail. It zigzags to a saddle on the top, where you crest out on the rim of an extinct volcanic crater, a rather flat and shallow one. From that point you can take the trail down into the bowl of the crater, though there isn't much to see there. We prefer to bushwhack along the rim to the north for the fine views of Sedona, which are magnificent from there. The mountain's high point is to the north, a basalt tower worth scaling.

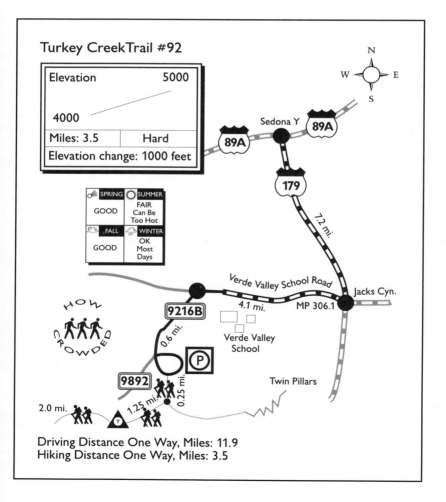

Twin Pillars

General Information
Location Map F4
Sedona USGS Map
Coconino Forest Service Map

Driving Distance One Way: 11.9 miles *19.0 km* (Time 30 minutes)
Access Road: All cars, Last 1.7 miles *2.7 km* good dirt roads
Hiking Distance One Way: 1.0 miles *1.6 km* (Time 45 minutes)
How Strenuous: Moderate
Features: Rock formations, Views

NUTSHELL: Located 11.9 miles *19.0 km* southwest of Sedona, behind the Verde Valley School, this moderate hike has you climb through interesting redrocks to the top of a ridge overlooking the school.

DIRECTIONS:
From the Sedona Y Go:
 South on Highway 179 (toward Phoenix) for 7.2 miles *11.5 km* (MP 306.1), to the Verde Valley School Road, where there is a stoplight. Turn right (W) onto Verde Valley School Road. The first 3.0 miles *4.8 km* of this road are paved. Follow it to the 11.3 mile *18.1 km* point where you will see a sign marking the **Turkey Creek Trail**. Just beyond the sign you will see FR 9216B, a dirt road to your left. Turn onto FR 9216B. Any vehicle with medium clearance can handle the road. At 11.9 miles *19.0 km* you will reach a V fork. Turn left here and park on the shoulder of the little loop.

TRAILHEAD: Not marked. The trail begins where you park.

DESCRIPTION: The access road for this hike is the same up to a point as that for the **Turkey Creek Trail**, which is a recommended hike.
 At the parking place, you will see an old road to the south that is closed by a barrier of stones. Walk down this road for 0.25 miles *0.4 km*, where you will find a V junction. The fork to your right (SW) is the trail to Turkey Creek. You want to take the fork to the left (SE).
 You will continue to walk down a closed road that takes you ever closer to a redrock butte. The road ends at the foot of the butte, 0.5 miles *0.8 km* from the parking place, against a red wall, where you will see a foot trail going uphill.
 There are always hoof prints on this trail and we would guess that the trail was created as a horse path for the students at Verde Valley School, which is on the other (E) side of the butte. It makes a good hiking trail.

Though the trail was not marked, we had no trouble following it. The path winds around in such a fashion that it makes good use of the terrain to climb the butte gradually. It is not very steep, rising 200 feet in 0.35 miles *0.6 km*. As you climb you rise high enough to get good views of some pretty country.

At the top you come onto the saddle. The Twin Pillars for which we named the hike are to your right (S). We could find no name for this place on any map, so we christened it after these prominent redrock pillars. From the saddle you look down onto the school, white buildings with red roofs in a beautiful setting.

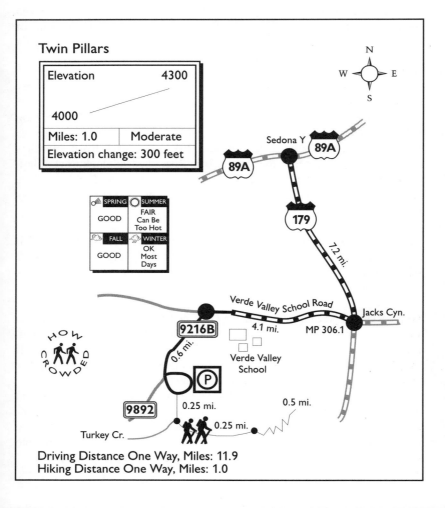

Twin Pillars

Elevation 4300

4000

| Miles: 1.0 | Moderate |

Elevation change: 300 feet

SPRING	SUMMER
GOOD	FAIR Can Be Too Hot
FALL	WINTER
GOOD	OK Most Days

HOW CROWDED

Sedona Y

89A

89A

179

7.2 mi.

Verde Valley School Road

Jacks Cyn.

9216B

4.1 mi.

MP 306.1

Verde Valley School

0.6 mi.

P

9892

0.25 mi.

0.5 mi.

0.25 mi.

Turkey Cr.

Driving Distance One Way, Miles: 11.9
Hiking Distance One Way, Miles: 1.0

Two Fences Trail

General Information
Location Map D3
Loy Butte and Wilson Mt. USGS Maps
Coconino Forest Service Map

Driving Distance One Way: 5.2 miles *8.3 km* (Time 15 minutes)
Access Road: All cars, All paved
Hiking Distance One Way: 2.1 miles *3.4 km* (Time 1 hour and 15 minutes)
How Strenuous: Easy
Features: Easy little diversion close to town and easy to reach.

NUTSHELL: Located 5.2 miles *8.3 km* west of Sedona on good paved roads, this seems designed to give access to the backcountry to residents of subdivisions along the Dry Creek Road. It's not a major trail but is pleasant and adds something new to the system.

DIRECTIONS:
From the Sedona Y Go:
Southwest on Highway 89A (toward Cottonwood) for 3.2 miles *5.1 km* (MP 371) to Dry Creek Road. Turn right on Dry Creek Road and proceed to the 5.2 mile *8.3 km* point, where FR 152, the Vultee Arch Road, branches off to the right. Don't take the Vultee Arch Road. Instead, look to your left, below the road, and you will see a small trail sign on a post. Park at the side of the road as near to this sign as you can get. There is no designated parking.

TRAILHEAD: Orphan. Access is via the **Girdner Trail**. Start at the trail sign mentioned above. It marks the Girdner Trail. Trying to start the hike where the trail joins the Dry Creek Road is possible but is too difficult unless signs are added.

DESCRIPTION: Start by hiking the Girdner Trail. At 1.1 miles *1.8 km* you will reach the trailhead for the Two Fences Trail. From this starting point, the Two Fences Trail moves easterly along the bank of an unnamed wash. It runs parallel to the Girdner Trail at first but you can't see the Girdner because of the vegetation. Soon it veers away from the Girdner.

At 1.5 miles *2.4 km* you will see how the trail got its name, when you reach the two fences. The barbed wire fence on your right marks the boundary of private property, an upscale subdivision in which there are huge homes. The fence on your left marks public land. There is a lane between the two fences about ten feet wide (3 meters), and this trail uses that lane.

Quite a bit of trail work has been done on this path. It is a fully developed trail. From the point where you enter the lane between the two fences you can see that you are aimed at Chimney Rock. It is clear as you hike that the trail is going to meet the Dry Creek Road. As you get very close to the road, the trail's end becomes ambiguous. It has been very easy to follow up to this point. No matter. We suggest that you end it by turning around when you are close to the paving and retracing your footsteps back to your car, although you could turn left and walk down the road instead.

There are no exciting views on this trail, and it is clearly suburban rather than wilderness, but it is a nice little trail in its own right.

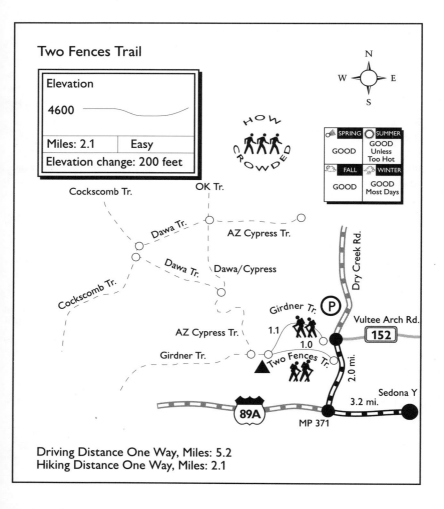

Two Fences Trail

Elevation

4600

Miles: 2.1	Easy
Elevation change: 200 feet	

HOW CROWDED

SPRING	SUMMER
GOOD	GOOD Unless Too Hot
FALL	WINTER
GOOD	GOOD Most Days

N
W ← → E
S

Cockscomb Tr.

OK Tr.

Dawa Tr.

AZ Cypress Tr.

Dawa Tr.

Dawa/Cypress

Cockscomb Tr.

Girdner Tr. P

Dry Creek Rd.

Vultee Arch Rd.

AZ Cypress Tr.   1.1   152

1.0

Girdner Tr.   Two Fences Tr.

2.0 mi.

Sedona Y
3.2 mi.

89A

MP 371

Driving Distance One Way, Miles: 5.2
Hiking Distance One Way, Miles: 2.1

Van Deren Cabin

General Information
Location Map C4
Wilson Mt. USGS Map
Coconino Forest Service Map

Driving Distance One Way: 7.6 miles *12.2 km* (Time 30 minutes)
Access Road: Most cars, Last 2.4 miles *3.8 km* medium dirt road
Hiking Distance One Way: 0.3 miles *0.5 km* (Time 15 minutes)
How Strenuous: Easy
Features: Historic cabin, Views

NUTSHELL: This is a short easy hike to a historic cabin located off the road to Vultee Arch, 7.6 miles *12.2 km* northwest of Sedona.

DIRECTIONS:
From the Sedona Y Go:
 Southwest on Highway 89A (toward Cottonwood) for a distance of 3.2 miles *5.1 km* (MP 371) to the Dry Creek Road. Turn right on Dry Creek Road, and follow it to the 5.2 mile *8.3 km* point, where FR 152 branches to the right. Take FR 152. You will see a sign for Vultee Arch on this road. Follow the road to the 7.6 miles *12.2 km* point, where you will see an unmarked road to your left, a narrow opening in the brush. Turn left on this road and park as soon as you can.

TRAILHEAD: There are no trail signs. Walk the road, which is FR 9917.

DESCRIPTION: Jeep tours regularly come here and drive FR 9917 all the way to the cabin. However, we recommend that you park just off the main road and walk to the cabin because the road is uneven and rough and this is a book of hikes.
 At 0.16 miles *0.3 km* you will come to the place where the road fords Dry Creek. If the water is high you might want to wait for another day. Upstream to your right there is a broad redrock ledge cut by the action of the creek into charming sculptures. It is well worth a short detour to walk along it and enjoy the shapes.
 When you cross the creek the road goes to the top of the bank on the other side. The road forks there. Take the left fork and follow it to its end. From there you will see the cabin. The old homestead was composed of several acres, but the Forest Service purchased the cabin site only, and has devoted it to public use. The remainder of the old ranch is private property. This private land has been enclosed by a fence that is garlanded with No

Trespassing signs. Don't worry about these, because access to the cabin site is open to the public, But please give the cabin the respect shown to any ruin and cause no harm to it.

The cabin was built by pioneer Earl Van Deren in the 1890s. The oldest part is nearest to the new fence. After he built the cabin, Earl fell in love but his fiancee refused to marry him until he expanded the place. He added a second unit and connected the two units with a roof, forming a breezeway. This expansion satisfied his fiancee, and they married.

Earl ranched and made a bit of money as a movie extra. In the 1940s he bought acreage in what turned out later to be uptown Sedona, where there is today a Van Deren Road honoring him. At the back of the cabin site, you can see the remains of Earl's root cellar. Legend says that the cellar was used by a bootlegger after Earl moved to town and that the bootlegger was murdered there, a crime that was never solved.

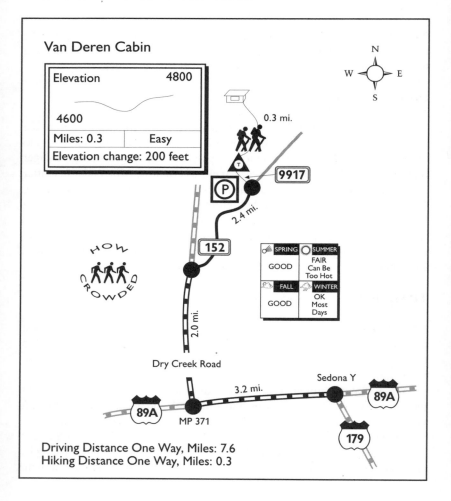

Van Deren Cabin

Elevation	4800
4600	
Miles: 0.3	Easy
Elevation change: 200 feet	

0.3 mi.

9917

2.4 mi.

152

HOW CROWDED

SPRING	SUMMER
GOOD	FAIR Can Be Too Hot
FALL	WINTER
GOOD	OK Most Days

2.0 mi.

Dry Creek Road

Sedona Y

3.2 mi.

89A   89A

89A   MP 371

179

Driving Distance One Way, Miles: 7.6
Hiking Distance One Way, Miles: 0.3

V-Bar-V Petroglyphs

General Information
Location Map G6
Casner Butte USGS Map
Coconino Forest Service Map

Driving Distance One Way: 17.4 miles *27.8 km* (Time 25 minutes)
Access Road: All cars, Short segment of good dirt road
Hiking Distance One Way: 0.5 miles *0.8 km* (Time 15 minutes)
How Strenuous: Easy
Features: One of the area's finest collections of prehistoric rock art; Near the banks of Wet Beaver Creek, a perennial stream.

NUTSHELL: Located in the Wet Beaver Creek country, this easy hike takes you along an old ranch road to a wonderful protected rock art site. On the way back you can enjoy the waters of Wet Beaver Creek.

DIRECTIONS:
From the Sedona Y Go:
    South on Highway 179 (toward Phoenix) for 14.7 miles *23.5 km*, to the I-17 Interchange. Instead of going onto I-17, go underneath it and get onto the paved county road 618. You will pass the old Beaver Creek Ranger Station and the bridge over Beaver Creek, where the paving ends. Just after the paving ends, you will reach a three-way fork at 17.4 miles *27.8 km,* where you will see a sign. Go through the gate and proceed to the parking lot. NOTICE: This site is gated and the hours of visitation are controlled. As we write this, it is open from 9:30 am to 3:30 pm, Friday to Monday. An entry fee is charged, of $3 per adult, although the sign says also that Red Rock passes are honored. Children under 17 are admitted free.

TRAILHEAD: At the parking lot.

DESCRIPTION: Follow the signs. The trail runs in a generally southwest direction parallel to Wet Beaver Creek, but you never get right down next to the creek. The correct path does not move away from the road and go down to the ranch house.
    You will pass through a series of fields that were formerly farmed. Near the end of the road it narrows down to a footpath and ahead of you to the left you will see a bank of thirty-foot high red cliffs. This is your destination.
    At the 0.5 mile *0.8 km* point the trail comes up to a small area against the cliffs that is enclosed by an eight-foot high chain link fence. The petroglyphs are inside the fence. You cannot get up to the figures but must look at them

from outside the protective fence. This is not a problem as you are close enough to the rock art to see and photograph the figures easily.

There are two major panels of rock art, and both of them are very fine. This is one of the major rock art sites in the Sedona area, with many figures. We noted several depictions of herons, evidence that these graceful birds have inhabited the area for centuries. Other recognizable animals are depicted. In addition to these animal figures, there are abstract designs.

On the way back, you might want to walk down to the creek and enjoy a streamside experience. There is no particular trail that takes you there, but there are several spots where you can see that you can easily get to the creek.

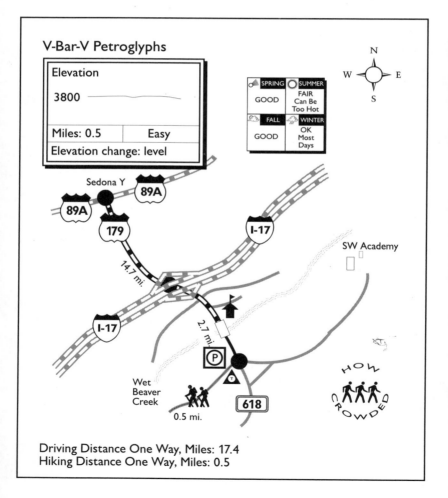

Vultee Arch Trail #22

General Information
Location Map C4
Loy Butte and Wilson Mt. USGS Maps
Coconino Forest Service Map

Driving Distance One Way: 9.6 miles *15.4 km* (Time 45 minutes)
Access Road: Last 4.4 miles *7.0 km* rocky, bumpy, but OK for most cars
Hiking Distance One Way: 1.6 miles *2.6 km* (Time 1 hour)
How Strenuous: Moderate
Features: Arch, Historic marker, Scenic canyon

NUTSHELL: Located 9.6 miles *15.4 km* north of Sedona, this hike takes you to a natural arch and a commemorative plaque in a beautiful box canyon. **A personal favorite**.

DIRECTIONS:
From the Sedona Y Go:

Southwest on Highway 89A (toward Cottonwood) for 3.2 miles *5.1 km* (MP 371) to Dry Creek Road. Turn right on Dry Creek Road and proceed to the 5.2 mile *8.3 km* point. Turn right on FR 152, the Vultee Arch Road, and follow it to the 9.6 mile *15.4 km* point. Here there is a parking loop, with the **Vultee Arch** Trailhead at the tip. Parking is provided at the trailhead.

TRAILHEAD: This is a marked and maintained trail. You will see a rusty sign at the parking place reading, "Vultee Arch #22."

DESCRIPTION: Even though we see many passenger cars on FR 152, it can be a very rough road. It receives maintenance from time to time, but in between times, the road can be a real challenge to a car with low clearance and thin tires.

The hiking trail is sandy and gives nice soft footing. The trail climbs as it progresses, passing through several life zones, which causes interesting changes in the vegetation surrounding the trail. When you begin the trail you are in a forest of Arizona cypress. After that you will go through oak and pine and finally you will find Douglas fir. The route is shaded the entire way, which makes it a good trail in hot weather.

The trail crosses a creekbed several times, so don't try to hike it when a lot of water is running in the creek. The creek is dry except for a few weeks in the spring, generally in March and April or after a hard summer rain.

At 1.4 miles *2.2 km* you will reach the junction of this trail and the **Sterling Pass Trail**, which forks to the right.

At the end of the trail you will break out into a clearing in a box canyon and the trail will climb onto redrock ledges. You will see Vultee Arch against a far wall (N) of the box canyon. There is a trail leading to it that you can easily pick up. It is possible to walk right up to the arch and even to climb on top of it.

The historical plaque is cast in bronze and fastened to the face of a redrock ledge, the second ledge above you as you enter the box canyon. The plaque commemorates the airplane crash that killed Gerald Vultee, an aviation pioneer, and his wife in 1938. They did not crash here, but on nearby East Pocket, when they were caught in a storm at night. Had Vultee been flying one of today's planes with modern instruments, he probably would have brought it in safely.

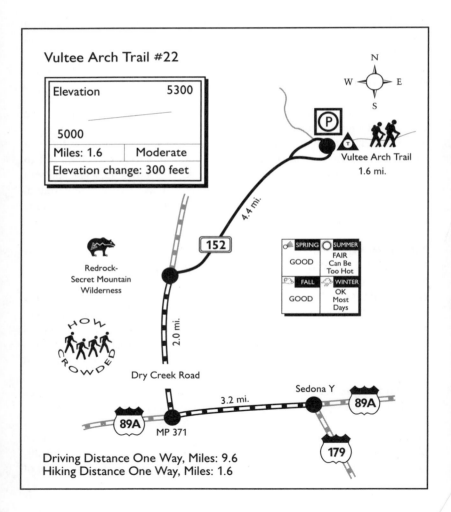

Vultee Arch Trail #22

Elevation	5300
5000	
Miles: 1.6	Moderate
Elevation change: 300 feet	

Vultee Arch Trail
1.6 mi.

4.4 mi.

152

Redrock-
Secret Mountain
Wilderness

SPRING	SUMMER
GOOD	FAIR Can Be Too Hot
FALL	WINTER
GOOD	OK Most Days

HOW CROWDED

2.0 mi.

Dry Creek Road

Sedona Y

3.2 mi.

89A

89A   MP 371

179

Driving Distance One Way, Miles: 9.6
Hiking Distance One Way, Miles: 1.6

West Clear Creek Trail #17

General Information
Location Map G6
Buckhorn Mtn., Walker Mtn. USGS Maps
Coconino Forest Service Map

Driving Distance One Way: 29.5 miles *47.2 km* (Time 1 hour)
Access Road: All cars, Last 12.3 miles *19.7 km* good dirt road
Hiking Distance One Way: 1.0 miles *1.6 km* (Time 30 minutes)
How Strenuous: Easy
Features: Historic ranch, Permanent creek, Wide easy trail, Views

NUTSHELL: This easy trail starts from the West Clear Creek Campground 29.5 miles *47.2 km* south of Sedona and takes you through an interesting old ranch to a lovely creek in a deep scenic canyon.

DIRECTIONS:
From the Sedona Y Go:
South on Highway 179 (toward Phoenix) for 14.7 miles *23.5 km*, to the I-17 Interchange. Instead of going onto I-17, go underneath it onto paved road FR 618. The paving ends at the Beaver Creek bridge. Follow FR 618. At the 24.5 mile *39.2 km* point, you will see a dirt road branching left to Cedar Flat. Keep going south on FR 618. At 26.5 miles *42.4 km* you will come to a road to the left (FR 215) to the West Clear Creek Campground. Turn left on FR 215 and go to the 29.5 mile *47.2 km* point, all the way to the end of the road. Parking for the trail is located there and signed.

TRAILHEAD: At the parking area you will see trail signs for the West Clear Creek Trail #17, and the Blodgett Basin Trail.

DESCRIPTION: This trail takes you across the old Bull Pen Ranch, which is now public property. (This trail is also called the Bull Pen Trail.) Go through the gate and walk the bygone ranch road The first part of the road is lovely, as it is quite close to the creek and passes through a lush riparian forest. Farther on it moves away from Clear Creek and opens up into typical scrub and cactus habitat.
At 0.66 miles *1.1 km* you will come out into an open field, where you see a sight that sticks in the mind of every visitor to this place, a rock house with cactus growing on its roof. When you inspect this small structure, which is about 20 x 12 feet, you will see that the builders heaped dirt on the roof, an old trick in the Southwest. Prickly pears and agave got established in this dirt and have grown there for years. Behind the rock house, on the north side of

the canyon, there is a ledge of exposed red sandstone adding a welcome touch of color to the landscape. The ranch site is truly beautiful.

You will continue along the road to the 1.0 mile *1.6 km* point where the fields end and the road dips down to the creek. There you will find some slickrock ledges just above the water that seem to have been placed there by nature as places to sit and take the sun and watch the creek gurgle by.

When the water is low enough, you can wade across the creek here and hike upstream on the opposite bank for another mile with relative ease. Beyond that point the hike gets pretty tough. There is a place at about 3.0 miles *4.8 km* where the trail lifts out of the canyon on the north wall, requiring a strenuous 2,000 foot climb to a point on FR 214 about 1.2 miles *1.9 km* above the Blodgett Basin trail terminus.

For an easy and satisfying day hike we recommend stopping at the 1.0 mile *1.6 km* point.

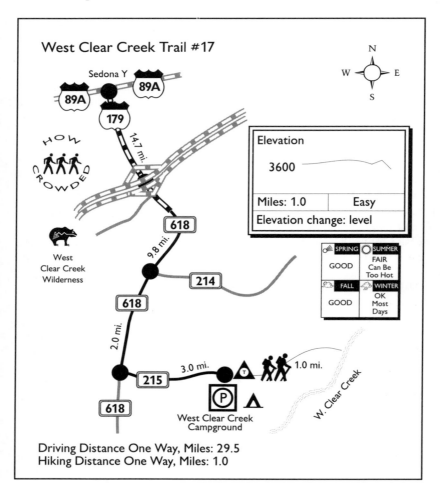

West Clear Creek Trail #17

Sedona Y

89A   89A

179

14.7 mi.

HOW CROWDED

West Clear Creek Wilderness

618

9.8 mi.

618   214

2.0 mi.

Elevation	
3600	
Miles: 1.0	Easy
Elevation change: level	

SPRING	SUMMER
GOOD	FAIR Can Be Too Hot
FALL	WINTER
GOOD	OK Most Days

215   3.0 mi.   1.0 mi.

618

West Clear Creek Campground

W. Clear Creek

N
W — E
S

Driving Distance One Way, Miles: 29.5
Hiking Distance One Way, Miles: 1.0

West Fork Trail #108

General Information
Location Map B5
Dutton Hill and Munds Park USGS Maps
Coconino Forest Service Map

Driving Distance One Way: 10.5 miles *16.8 km* (Time 20 minutes)
Access Road: All cars, All paved
Hiking Distance One Way: 3.0 miles *4.8 km* (Time 90 minutes)
How Strenuous: Moderate
Features: Gorgeous canyon with stream

NUTSHELL: One of the best, most popular hikes in Arizona. The trailhead is located 10.5 miles *16.8 km* north of Sedona. **A personal favorite**.

DIRECTIONS:
From the Sedona Y Go:
   North on Highway 89A (toward Flagstaff) for a distance of 10.5 miles *16.8 km* (MP 384.7.) You will see a road sign for the parking area, which requires a sharp turn to your left (W). An entry fee is required.

TRAILHEAD: On the west side of the parking area loop, you will see a sign board. This marks the trailhead.

DESCRIPTION: This hike is so popular that a parking area was created for it, complete with toilets. There is a signboard with a map, and you can get information at the ticket booth. This wonderful hike has been made much easier by the construction of a footbridge over Oak Creek. Once over the creek, you climb up the opposite bank and turn left (S) on a wide sandy track. The clearing you will find there is the site of the old Lolomai Lodge. Soon you will draw abreast of houses across the creek. Just beyond the last house, you will walk through the ruins of Mayhews Lodge, where a few brick structures still stand. This point is 0.3 miles *0.5 km* from the beginning.
   The Dad Thomas family (**Thomas Point** was named for them) built a home here, which was remodeled as a hunting and fishing lodge in the early 1900s. Carl Mayhew bought and enlarged it in 1925. Zane Grey used the location as the setting for his novel *The Call of the Canyon*. The owners tried to raise as much of their own food as they could for guests, and you can see areas where they had orchards and vegetable gardens, and you will even see the remains of their chicken coop set into a shallow cave. The Forest Service bought the lodge in 1969 only to have it burn in 1980.
   As you enter the West Fork canyon you are immediately aware of its

charm, with the gentle stream flowing through a lush habitat framed by tremendously high and colorful canyon walls. It is a magic place.

The path follows along the streambed, crossing back and forth over the water. At the crossings you will usually find stepping stones that allow you to get across without getting wet, but these are not foolproof. You should count on getting your feet wet. Some hikers prefer to wear old tennies or Tevas and wade. You will find distance markers placed at every half mile along the hiking path.

The canyon is narrow, so you are often right next to the cliffs. The stream has undercut them in many places, creating interesting overhangs. You feel the majesty of the canyon on this hike, for the cliffs absolutely dwarf you.

The canyon is 12.0 miles *19.2 km* long. We have you stop at 3.0 miles, a distance that allows you to see some of the finest parts. Don't try to make the full hike without special preparations.

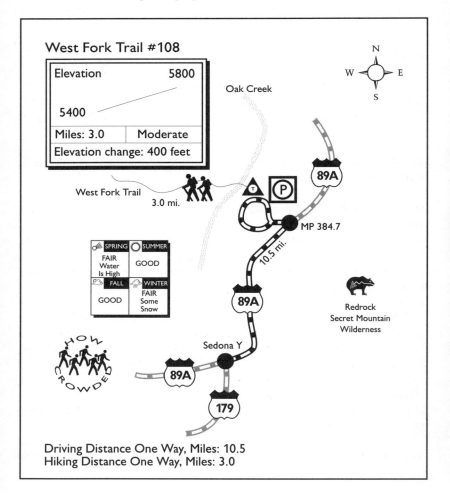

West Fork Trail #108

Elevation	5800
5400	
Miles: 3.0	Moderate
Elevation change: 400 feet	

Oak Creek

N
W — E
S

89A

West Fork Trail
3.0 mi.

T P

MP 384.7

10.5 mi.

SPRING	SUMMER
FAIR Water Is High	GOOD
FALL	WINTER
GOOD	FAIR Some Snow

89A

Redrock
Secret Mountain
Wilderness

HOW CROWDED

Sedona Y

89A

179

Driving Distance One Way, Miles: 10.5
Hiking Distance One Way, Miles: 3.0

White Mesa Trail #86

General Information
Location Map G6
Casner Butte USGS Map
Coconino Forest Service Map

Driving Distance One Way: 17.2 miles *27.6 km* (Time 30 minutes)
Access Road: All cars, Last 0.3 miles *0.5 km* gravel, in good condition
Hiking Distance One Way: 2.2 miles *3.5 km* (Time 1.25 hours)
How Strenuous: Hard
Features: Permanent Stream, Rock Art, Views

NUTSHELL: This trail follows the Bell Trail along the banks of Wet Beaver Creek and then branches off to climb to the top of a mesa.

DIRECTIONS:
From the Sedona Y Go:
   South on Highway 179 (toward Phoenix) for 14.7 miles *23.5 km* (MP 298.9), to the I-17 intersection. Go straight here rather than getting on I-17. Follow paved road FR 618 until you see a sign for the trailheads at 16.9 miles *27.1 km*. Turn left. Parking is at 17.2 miles *27.6 km*.

TRAILHEAD: Several hiking trails here share a common trailhead that is well marked with signs at the parking area.

DESCRIPTION: From the trailhead, the **Bell Trail** goes up canyon along Wet Beaver Creek. The trail is an old road, broad and easy to walk. It was built by cattle rancher Charles Bell in 1932, as a means for taking his cattle to the top of the Mogollon Rim in the spring.
   At about 0.6 miles *1.0 km*, look for a large boulder on the left side of the trail. On the side that faces away from you are a number of interesting petroglyphs.
   The White Mesa Trail is 1.5 miles *2.4 km* from the trailhead. There is a good sign at the trail junction where you leave the Bell Trail and get onto the White Mesa Trail. There is also a guest register to sign. Comments in the register indicate that hikers find this to be a difficult trail.
   The trail goes up the south wall of Casner Canyon in a straight line, not zigzagging as many trails do. It is not terribly strenuous, though it does climb 1,000 feet in 0.70 miles *1.2 km*. Along the way you are treated to some good views and some shows of colorful redrock.
   The top of the mesa is covered by a hundred foot thick layer of lava, which is typical of all the mesas in this area. In most places—as here—there

are sheer cliffs at these mesa rims. This trail takes advantage of a gap in the caprock and emerges at the top without requiring any rock climbing. On the top, the trail ends abruptly at a cairn at a point 2.2 miles *3.5 km* from the beginning.

We suggest that you turn left and walk to the edge of the mesa overlooking Beaver Creek (about 0.20 miles *0.32 km*) for some excellent views of the creek and the Verde Valley. Hikers along the Bell Trail will wonder how you got there.

The Casner family was very active in the livestock business and left its name in several locations. You will find the **Casner Mountain South** and **Casner Canyon** hikes in this book.

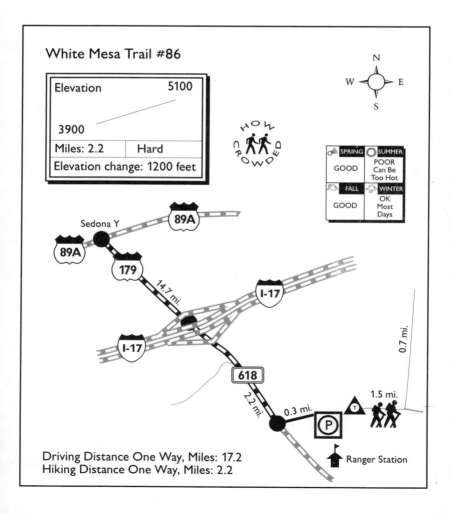

White Mesa Trail #86

Elevation	5100
3900	
Miles: 2.2	Hard
Elevation change: 1200 feet	

HOW CROWDED

SPRING	SUMMER
GOOD	POOR Can Be Too Hot
FALL	WINTER
GOOD	OK Most Days

Sedona Y

89A

89A

179

14.7 mi.

I-17

I-17

0.7 mi.

618

2.2 mi.

0.3 mi.

T

1.5 mi.

P

Ranger Station

Driving Distance One Way, Miles: 17.2
Hiking Distance One Way, Miles: 2.2

Wilson Canyon Trail #49

General Information
Location Map D5
Munds Park USGS Map
Coconino Forest Service Map

Driving Distance One Way: 1.1 miles *1.8 km* (Time 5 minutes)
Access Road: All cars, All paved
Hiking Distance One Way: 1.5 miles *2.4 km* (Time 1 hour)
How Strenuous: Moderate
Features: Views

NUTSHELL: Just 1.1 miles *1.8 km* north of Sedona, Wilson Canyon is spanned by Midgley Bridge. You can take a short easy stroll along the rim of the canyon or a longer hike up the canyon.

DIRECTIONS:
From the Sedona Y Go:
   North on Highway 89A (toward Flagstaff) for a distance of 1.1 miles *1.8 km* (MP 375.9). Go just across Midgley Bridge and turn left into the parking area.

TRAILHEAD: You will see a rusty sign at the parking lot. It reads, "Wilson Canyon #49."

DESCRIPTION: You will see the parking area just across the bridge. This is a very popular spot and you may not find a parking place open. If not, go up the road a bit. There are several wide shoulders for parking.
   The trailhead is easy to locate. Just walk toward the picnic tables at the end of the parking lot. There you will find the Wilson Monument, a bronze plaque set in stone, and two rusty signs. The sign to the left marks Wilson Canyon #49 and is the one you want for this hike. The other sign marks an uphill trail, Wilson Mountain #10, which we call **Wilson Mountain South**.
   The Wilson Canyon hike is little more than a leisurely stroll for the first 0.25 miles *0.4 km*. This may be as much of a hike as some readers want.
   Up to the 0.25 mile *0.4 km* point, the trail is as broad and flat as a roadway. It was a road. Turn around and look at Midgley Bridge and imagine what the road would have been without it. Drivers had to make a sharp turn and go up the canyon to a point where it narrowed and a bridge could readily be installed, cross over the canyon, then go back out and make another sharp turn. Old-timers tell us that the sharp unexpected turns were very dangerous. You will see the old bridge placements at the head of Wilson

Canyon. This is the place to stop for the short hike.

For the longer hike, you keep walking up the canyon, which is sometimes wet. The trail meanders from bank to bank There are many intersecting paths, but it is easy to stay on course if you keep paralleling the canyon. At about 0.5 miles *0.8 km* you will see a footpath going uphill to your left. This is part of the **Jim Thompson Road**. A few yards beyond that you will see an alternate branch of the Old Jim Thompson Road coming down to intersect your path.

The trail is a gradual uphill climb, quite gentle. In a few places the trail will seem to scramble up a steep bank and go to the top. Ignore these side trails and keep following the canyon bottom.

The canyon encloses you so that you can't see much outside it. At 1.5 miles *2.4 km* you will reach a place where a side trail goes uphill to the right. This goes up to a viewpoint and is the place to quit.

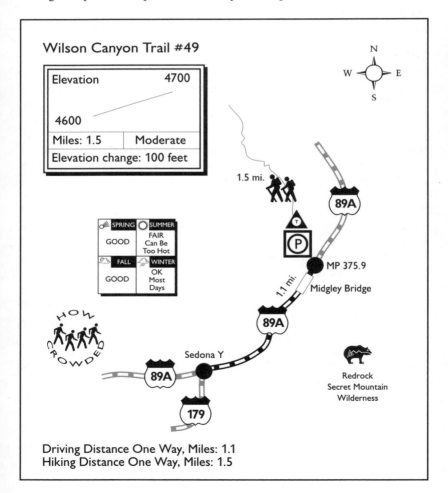

Wilson Canyon Trail #49

Elevation	4700
4600	
Miles: 1.5	Moderate
Elevation change: 100 feet	

1.5 mi.

89A

MP 375.9

Midgley Bridge

1.1 mi.

89A

SPRING	SUMMER
GOOD	FAIR Can Be Too Hot
FALL	WINTER
GOOD	OK Most Days

HOW CROWDED

Sedona Y

89A

179

Redrock Secret Mountain Wilderness

Driving Distance One Way, Miles: 1.1
Hiking Distance One Way, Miles: 1.5

Wilson Mountain North Trail #123

General Information
Location Map C5
Munds Park and Wilson Mt. USGS Maps
Coconino Forest Service Map

Driving Distance One Way: 5.3 miles *8.5 km* (Time 10 minutes)
Access Road: All cars, All paved
Hiking Distance One Way: 4.3 miles *6.9 km* (Time 4.0 hours)
How Strenuous: Hard
Features: Views

NUTSHELL: Located just north of Sedona, Wilson is the highest mountain in the area. This trail climbs Wilson's north face.

DIRECTIONS:
From the Sedona Y Go:
　　North on Highway 89A (toward Flagstaff) for a distance of 5.3 miles *8.5 km* (MP 379.5), where you will see the Encinoso Picnic Area to your left. Park in the Encinoso parking lot.

TRAILHEAD: From the parking lot, walk up the canyon on the shoulder of the road about 100 yards. There you will see a trail sign reading, "Wilson Mt. #123" with the trail heading uphill.

DESCRIPTION: The trail climbs to the top of a small ridge at about 0.25 miles *0.4 km*, where you have a good vantage point to look across the canyon at the cliffs of the east wall. During spring runoff and after hard rains, the Encinoso Waterfall appears there and this is one of the best places from which to see it.
　　From this ridge the trail climbs gently for another 0.75 miles *1.2 km* along a refreshing, wooded side canyon through a lovely mixed forest of pine, fir, spruce, oak and maple. The streambed here seldom carries any water, but when it does, it is delightful.
　　At 1.0 miles *1.6 km* the serious work begins. Here the canyon pinches in and the trail begins a steep climb up the north face of Wilson. If you want an easy hike, the 1.0 mile point is the place to stop. The ascent beyond the 1.0 mile point is treacherous if the trail is slick with mud or snow. When dry, it is only strenuous. You will climb 1,300 feet in 0.5 miles *0.8 km*.
　　After this hard haul, you top out on a flat flank of Wilson called First Bench. You will have great views to the north from here. Across Oak Creek Canyon you will see a major tributary, Munds Canyon, which empties into

Oak Creek at Indian Gardens.

Keep walking south along First Bench. At the 1.8 mile *2.9 km* point, at the edge of First Bench, you will intersect the Wilson Mt. South Trail coming up from Midgley Bridge. The junction is well marked with cairns. Take a look off the rim; it's great! You may want to quit here.

From this trail junction, you can go to the top of the mountain. See **Wilson Mountain South** for details. You have to hike 1.0 miles *1.6 km* to the Tool Shed, at the top of the mountain, 800 feet, then hike a level trail 1.5 miles *2.4 km* to the North Rim viewpoint, a total of 4.3 miles *6.9 km* from Encinoso.

One way to do this hike is with 2 cars, parking one car at Midgley Bridge and the other at Encinoso. Go up from Midgley Bridge on the South Trail and then come back on the North Trail, doing both on one long hard day.

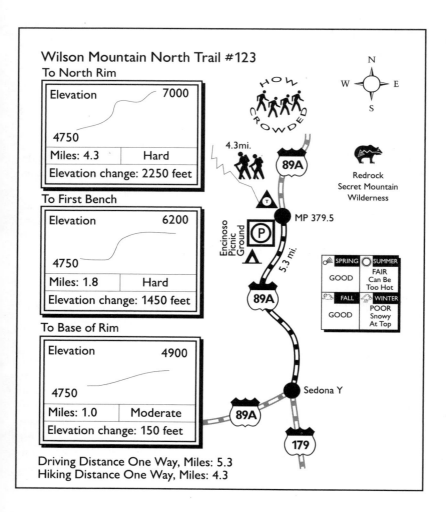

Wilson Mountain South Trail #10

General Information
Location Map D5
Munds Park and Wilson Mt. USGS Maps
Coconino Forest Service Map

Driving Distance One Way: 1.1 miles *1.8 km* (Time 5 minutes)
Access Road: All cars, All paved
Hiking Distance One Way: 5.3 miles *8.5 km* (Time 4.5 hours)
How Strenuous: Hard
Features: Views

NUTSHELL: This popular hike starts at Midgley Bridge, north of Sedona, and goes up Wilson Mountain to the highest point in the area, then crosses the mountain top to a fabulous lookout point.

DIRECTIONS:
From the Sedona Y Go:
   North on Highway 89A (toward Flagstaff) for a distance of 1.1 miles *1.8 km* (MP 375.9). Just across Midgley Bridge is the parking area.

TRAILHEAD: You will see a rusty sign at the parking lot. It reads, "Wilson Mt. #10."

DESCRIPTION: The trailhead is easy to locate. Just walk toward the picnic tables. There you will find a bronze plaque set in stone, and two trail signs. The sign to the left is **Wilson Canyon #49.** The other, uphill, is Wilson Mountain #10, which we call **Wilson Mountain South** in this book, and is the trail you want to take.

   This hike is divided into three phases, each with a different feel:
   Midgley Bridge to First Bench, 2.8 miles *4.5 km*, a 1,600' climb;
   First Bench to Tool Shed, 1.0 miles *1.6 km*, an 800' climb;
   Tool Shed to North Rim, 1.5 miles *2.4 km*, fairly level.

   Midgley Bridge to First Bench: This is a steep climb from the start. Ahead of you on the skyline you will see the saddle that is your destination. Along the way you have constantly enjoyable views of the formations of Wilson Mountain. You are in a high desert landscape, with juniper, manzanita and cactus. As you rise higher, you get into an area with little shade where you switchback to the top. This stretch would be murder on a hot sunny day. Finally you break over the top of First Bench, a long plateau running the length of the east side of the mountain. The views from here are

very fine, though the bench itself is pretty drab and featureless.

First Bench to the Tool Shed: Take the path going left, toward the high cliffs. You will soon climb above First Bench and get into a heavy forest of pine and oak. This has a decidedly alpine feeling compared to the desert you have just been through. After a 500 foot climb you will come onto the top, where the land is pretty level, then make a modest 300 foot climb to the Tool Shed, where fire fighting tools are stored. The main trail goes ahead here, with a side trail to the left.

Tool Shed to North Rim: This is a delightful walk through a cool forest on nearly level ground, very easy compared to the first two phases of the hike. You will be walking out to the mountain's north edge. When you come to a pond on the east side of the trail, you are almost at the end. Keep walking from here and you will soon come out onto a cliff face where you will find a soul-stirring view.

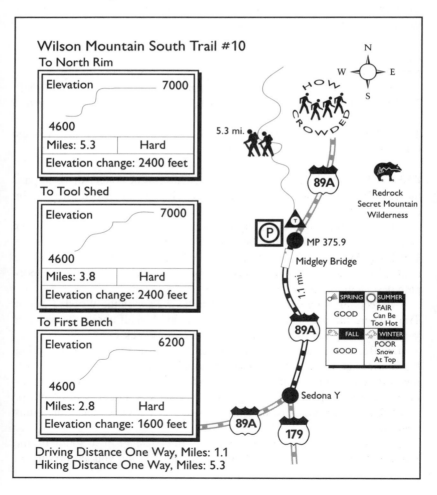

Wilson Mountain South Trail #10

To North Rim

Elevation	7000
4600	
Miles: 5.3	Hard
Elevation change: 2400 feet	

To Tool Shed

Elevation	7000
4600	
Miles: 3.8	Hard
Elevation change: 2400 feet	

To First Bench

Elevation	6200
4600	
Miles: 2.8	Hard
Elevation change: 1600 feet	

Driving Distance One Way, Miles: 1.1
Hiking Distance One Way, Miles: 5.3

HOW CROWDED

5.3 mi.

89A

Redrock
Secret Mountain
Wilderness

P   T   MP 375.9

Midgley Bridge

1.1 mi.

89A

	SPRING	SUMMER
		FAIR Can Be Too Hot
	GOOD	
	FALL	WINTER
	GOOD	POOR Snow At Top

Sedona Y

89A

179

Woods Canyon Trail #93

General Information
Location Map G5
Munds Mt. and Sedona USGS Maps
Coconino Forest Service Map

Driving Distance One Way: 8.6 miles *13.8 km* (Time 15 minutes)
Access Road*:* All cars, All paved
Hiking Distance One Way*:* 3.25 miles *5.2 km* (Time 90 minutes)
How Strenuous*:* Moderate
Features*:* Views

NUTSHELL: South of the Sedona Y 8.6 miles *13.8 km*, this trail follows Woods Canyon, through which Dry Beaver Creek flows.

DIRECTIONS:
From the Sedona Y Go:
South on Highway 179 (toward Phoenix) for 8.6 miles *13.8 km* (MP 304.8) to an unmarked dirt road to your left. Turn left and park at the gate.

TRAILHEAD: At the gate where you will see a rusty sign reading, "Woods Canyon #93."

DESCRIPTION: Walk through the gate. One can no longer drive in past the gate for some distance as was possible when we described this hike in earlier editions.

To follow the trail walk along the main jeep road. At 2.0 miles *3.2 km* you will come to a fence. Just beyond the fence you will find a sign for the **Hot Loop Trail**, which branches off to the left, going uphill. It looks like a road. The Woods Canyon trail forks to the right here and turns into a footpath descending to the bottom of the canyon.

We recommend going to about 3.25 miles *5.2 km* on the Woods Canyon Trail, where the path goes onto a sloping redrock shelf above the water, a very attractive place to sit and enjoy Dry Beaver Creek.

Dry Beaver Creek usually is dry, living up to its name. During the spring thaw, however, it can carry a lot of water and we have seen it at times when it was flowing bank to bank. This hike is more interesting when water is running. Your best chance of hiking it when water is running is in March or April. There is another stream nearby called Wet Beaver Creek, which runs year around.

Woods Canyon goes all the way to Interstate-17 just south of the Pinewood Country Club in the Munds Park area. When you are driving on

Interstate-17 you will see a sign for an exit marked "Fox Ranch" where the highway bridges Woods Canyon. Woods Canyon and Munds Canyon, which is located to the north, are major lateral canyons that cut into Oak Creek Canyon. You can see why Interstate-17 is located where it is: it crosses these canyons at their heads, where they are narrow. Even so, the highway department built high bridges at both places. These canyons were major obstacles between Sedona and Flagstaff in the old days and detouring around them added miles to the trip.

The developed part of the trail ends at the 4.0 mile *6.4 km* point, but we think the best stopping place is at 3.25 miles *5.2 km*. To hike the entire length of the canyon would mean going a rough 12.0 miles *19.2 km*. It can be done, but only by very strong and very well prepared hikers with someone ready to "catch" them at the far end.

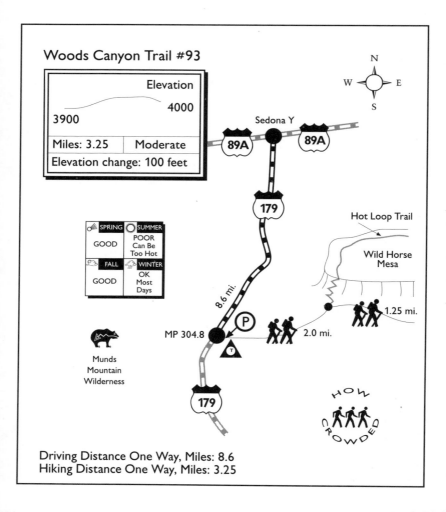

Woods Canyon Trail #93

Elevation

4000

3900

| Miles: 3.25 | Moderate |
| Elevation change: 100 feet | |

Sedona Y

89A 89A

179

Hot Loop Trail

Wild Horse Mesa

SPRING	SUMMER
GOOD	POOR Can Be Too Hot
FALL	WINTER
GOOD	OK Most Days

8.6 mi.

1.25 mi.

MP 304.8

P

T

2.0 mi.

Munds Mountain Wilderness

179

HOW CROWDED

N
W E
S

Driving Distance One Way, Miles: 8.6
Hiking Distance One Way, Miles: 3.25

INDEX

254

Yesterday

Flagstaff visitors entering Oak Creek Canyon on the Thomas Point Trail

Vortexes

Many persons claiming to be authorities have spoken about the Sedona Vortexes. Some of these people make very specific claims: that a particular Vortex is male, female, electric, magnetic, Yin, Yang, etc. These authorities don't always agree with each other.

We think it is a mistake to go to a Vortex expecting to find a certain anticipated experience. If you do, you may set up a self-fulfillment trap, where you deceive yourself into thinking that you have found what you were *told* you would find, rather than having your own authentic experience. We recommend that you approach a Vortex openly, seeking no pre-determined result.

The Vortexes are not hard to reach. You could easily visit all of them in a single day if you wish. Approach each one as a reverent seeker, open to what is there for you. Be quiet and unobtrusive so that you do not disturb others who are at the sites.

Experiences at the Vortexes range from negative, to neutral to cosmic. Each site is a place of beauty, worth visiting for aesthetic reasons; so your time will not be wasted even if you do not have a life-altering reaction. See the Index, page 253, for Vortexes that we recommend.

Scenic Drives

• **Airport Hill:** This is a very easy, short drive. The road is paved all the way. It takes you past one of the Sedona Vortex spots to the top of the hill where the Sedona Airport is located, an excellent viewpoint from which to see Sedona and some of its famous landmarks. When you get to the top, turn left and go toward the cross. You will find a fine lookout point there. See Overlook Point Trails, page 162.

• **Boynton Canyon:** If your time is limited and you want to see some of the redrock back country, this is a nice, short drive over paved roads. See Boynton Canyon, page 44.

• **Honanki Ruins:** You will drive 8.5 miles of good unpaved roads through some unspoiled country, allowing you to get away from town and see some great redrocks. At the end of the trip you will be within an easy walk from the best Indian ruin in the area. See Honanki Ruins, page 112.

• **Oak Creek Vista:** By taking this drive you will travel the length of Oak Creek Canyon, a beautiful scenic area. At the end of the drive you will be at a high point from which you can see the canyon, take a nature walk and learn about the area. See Oak Creek Canyon Recreation Map, page 14.

• **Schnebly Hill Road:** This is a favorite six mile drive that takes you through some beautiful redrock country to the top of a hill from where you can enjoy sweeping views. The road is paved the first 1.0 mile. The unpaved portion is rough, a real tire eater, suitable only for jeeps. See Schnebly Hill Trail, page 194.

Leave No Trace Outdoor Ethics

Plan Ahead And Prepare
• Know the regulations and special concerns for the area you'll visit.
• Prepare for extreme weather, hazards, and emergencies.
• Schedule your trip to avoid times of high use.
• Visit in small groups. Split larger parties into groups of 4-6.
• Repackage food to minimize waste.
• Use a map and compass instead of rock cairns, flagging or marking paint.

Travel And Camp On Durable Surfaces
• Durable surfaces include established trails and campsites, rock, gravel, dry grasses or snow.
• Protect riparian areas by camping at least 200 feet from lakes and streams.
• Good campsites are found, not made. Altering a site is not necessary.
In popular areas:
• Concentrate use on existing trails and campsites.
• Walk single file in the middle of the trail, even when wet or muddy.
• Keep campsites small. Focus activity in areas where vegetation is absent.
In pristine areas:
• Disperse use to prevent the creation of campsites and trails.
• Avoid places where impacts are just beginning.

Dispose Of Waste Properly
• Pack it in, pack it out. Inspect your campsite and rest areas for trash or spilled foods. Pack out all trash, leftover food, and litter.
• Deposit solid human waste in catholes dug 6 to 8 inches deep at least 200 feet from water, camp, and trails. Cover and disguise the cathole when finished.
• Pack out toilet paper and hygiene products.
• To wash yourself or your dishes, carry water 200 feet away from streams or lakes and use small amounts of biodegradable soap. Scatter strained dishwater.

Leave What You Find
• Preserve the past: examine, but do not touch, cultural or historic structures and artifacts.
• Leave rocks, plants and other natural objects as you find them.
• Avoid introducing or transporting non-native species.
• Do not build structures, furniture, or dig trenches.

Minimize Campfire Impacts
• Campfires can cause lasting impacts to the backcountry. Use a lightweight stove for cooking and enjoy a candle lantern for light.
• Where fires are permitted, use established fire rings, fire pans, or mound fires.
• Keep fires small. Only use sticks from the ground that can be broken by hand.
• Burn all wood and coals to ash, put out campfires completely, scatter cool ashes.

Respect Wildlife
• Observe wildlife from a distance. Do not follow or approach them.
• Never feed animals. Feeding wildlife damages their health, alters natural behaviors, and exposes them to predators and other dangers.
• Protect wildlife and your food by storing rations and trash securely.
• Control pets at all times, or leave them at home.
• Avoid wildlife during sensitive times: mating, nesting, raising young, or winter.

Be Considerate Of Other Visitors
• Respect other visitors and protect the quality of their experience.
• Be courteous. Yield to other users on the trail.
• Step to the downhill side of the trail when encountering pack stock.
• Take breaks and camp away from trails and other visitors.
• Let nature's sounds prevail. Avoid loud voices and noises.